Best Wishes
John Jarrett
Sept. 1992

Byker to Broadway

The Fighting Life and Times of Seaman Tommy Watson

by
John Jarrett

Copyright © John Jarrett
Published by Bewick Press, 132 Claremont Rd. Whitley Bay
Tyne and Wear NE26 3 TX

ISBN 1 898880 06 9

This book is lovingly dedicated to my wife Mary, and to my good friend Bob Graham, a real champion.

Printed by TUPS Ltd.,
30 Lime St.
Newcastle upon Tyne, NE1 2PQ.
Tel: 0191 2330990

ACKNOWLEDGEMENTS

I am most grateful to the family of Seaman Tommy Watson...his sister Frances, son Tom, and daughter Kath, who have breathed life into my words with their memories, and with the photographs which illustrate this book, to my dear friend Bob Graham for his unyielding support and encouragement, to my pal Archie Potts of Bewick Press for keeping a promise, and to Frankie Hutchinson for being in my corner. My thanks also to the staff of Newcastle upon Tyne Central Library for allowing me to consult their files of newspapers and periodicals, and to Vic Hardwicke for his fine job of compiling Seaman Watson's boxing record.

As most writers will tell you, writing the book is the easy part. Getting the book published is the hard bit! To this end I am most grateful for the financial assistance of the following without whose support this baby would never have been born...Tommy Conroy, Norman Fawcett, Jack Forbes, Tommy Gilmour, Paul Gooding, Bob Graham B.E.M., Dave Gregory, Albert Hemmer, Richard Jacques, Derek & Susan Jarrett, Diane Jarrett, Jeffrey Jarrett, Albert Kelleher, David Ogilvie, Fred Potter, John Spensley, Alan Trotter, Glenda & John Wadsworth, Gerald Watson, Tom Watson Jnr.

John Jarrett
July 1997

CONTENTS

INTRODUCTION

The subject of this biography could wish for no finer introduction than the following word picture painted by Norman Hurst, the star boxing writer for the old Kemsley Press, which appeared in the *Sunday Graphic* on 30 April 1933 on the eve of Seaman Watson's world featherweight title challenge against Kid Chocolate in New York.

"His Majesty's Navy has always supplied the ring with one-hundred-percent fighting men. The calls of the Senior Service however are such that some of the best of the navy's ringsters have been unable to attain titular honours for the simple reason that they could not always get the time nor the right class of sparring partners to bring out the best in them. But in their rough and ready way, training between decks on their sea-going homes, the sailor lads have managed to present the fighting game with some red hot members.

"Here are a couple to start with, Jack Ripper and that tough, hard-slugging reckless heavyweight Petty Officer (Nutty) Curran, who were the big noises in Plymouth some twenty years ago. Seaman Parsons, who was once regarded as a heavyweight hope, that great lightweight Seaman Wilkinson of Liverpool, and last but by no means least, Seaman Hayes of Hoxton, whose deadly punch to the body ruined many aspiring titleholders and earned him the title of wrecker of champions.

"And now we come to the little fellow from Newcastle upon Tyne who has topped them all, Tommy Watson. Although these days he tacks an ex before the Seaman, he is still hailed by the lads in blue as one of their own when they speak of Britain's featherweight champion.

"There has been through the years a similarity in all sailor fighters, there is no fancy stuff about any of them, they are just plain straight forward fighters with a job to do who go straight to their job as soon as the first bell rings for action. That is Tommy Watson in a nutshell. See him seated in his corner before the bell goes for the first round of an important contest and you can imagine him saying to himself, 'Let's clear the decks and get going.' Sturdily built and deep-chested, square-shouldered, a fighting head well set on a good strong neck, a face that tells you plainly business only meant! Get that photo set in your mind and you have the little fellow from Newcastle upon Tyne who twelve days from today steps into the ring in New York against that formidable customer Kid Chocolate to try to bring a world title to this country.

"I have seen Britain's champion on many occasions and he never alters, quiet, modest in his speech, and ready to draw in his shell at a moment's notice should too many leading questions be shot at him as to his future, his ability, or his opinion of a rival boxer.

"I think this gallant tar led all the critics a dance when he took the featherweight title away from Nel Tarleton. While it was admitted that Watson was dour and determined enough to fight to the last gasp, they instanced against all this the speedy footwork, the subtle ringcraft, and the snappy punching of the Merseyside battler who had also the greater advantage in height and reach. Frankly, I went along there to see the sailor go down fighting with his flag nailed to the mast, and like many others was given a rare surprise.

"Tarleton, tall, slim, nicely-muscled, with hair slicked well back, looking confidence personified, and nodding smilingly at the many friends who greeted him from ringside. In the opposite corner, the sailor was listening seriously to the advice given by his trainer and manager Alec Lambert, who a quarter-of-a-century ago was one of the cleverest boxers in the business.

"A few words from Mr Jack Smith, the referee, a last shuffle of feet in the resin, the bell rang and the sailor moved from his corner flat-footed with the stance that told of many hours boxing with the roll of a ship's deck beneath him instead of a solid ring, to face in Nel Tarleton the last word in easy grace and speed. For all the world like a sturdily-built steamer ploughing his way through the sea, Watson went to work.

"Tarleton had style, he had speed, and he had poise, but while the champion was staging little tricks like leaning well back over the ropes to make his challenger's attack look cheap, the seaman was boring in and punching at every possible opportunity. As round after round went by with the champion promising to do things

2

while the sailor was actually doing them, it became apparent that unless Tarleton wakened up the title was going to change hands.

"In the last round Tarleton fought like a man possessed to retain his crown but in spite of taking hefty punches to body and jaw Watson kept on under a full sail to receive the referee's verdict and so win for Tyneside the British title and the much-coveted Lord Lonsdale Challenge Belt.

"I saw the new champion the next day in the Lord Nelson Hotel, and had one been searching it would have been hard from his demeanour to find the new champion. There he was in a corner, talking to some friends in a low voice, a cap was tossed any old how on his head, and pulled up high around his neck was his old blue navy jersey, for all to see that champion or no champion he was still the same Tommy Watson of His Majesty's Navy."

I saw Tommy Watson in action many times at the New St James's Hall in Newcastle but it was in the role of referee, not as the fighting man many still consider the greatest ever to come out of the North-East. I remember asking him to sign my programme one night in 1952 as he stepped down from the ring after British lightweight champion Frankie Johnson had knocked out Jim Findlay of Scotland and I swear he was more embarrassed than I was. "You don't want to bother with me, man," he said softly, and nodding towards Johnson, added, "He's the champion!"

Seaman Tommy Watson was a champion, too. He was applauded and admired from Newcastle to New York, from Torquay to Toronto, from Liverpool to London. From Byker to Broadway and back again! However it would appear he was not too well known in Colwyn Bay. For in December, 1932, Cornelius Marsden, a thirty-year-old Bolton man, arrived in the Welsh seaside resort, made his way to the local YMCA, and announced himself as ex-Seaman Tommy Watson, featherweight champion of England and Lonsdale Belt holder. "I have just won a fight against an Italian in Newcastle," he said.

"I have come here because it is quiet. I like the town and am thinking of training here for my forthcoming fight with Kid Chocolate in America."

During the following week, Cornelius was feted everywhere he went, courted a local girl and arranged to marry her, signed hundreds of autographs, telephoned bogus messages to himself, and promised the YMCA a donation of £300. He was attended, massaged, and entertained by a small army of admirers, and every time he went out, crowds followed him around the town. One message purporting to be from his manager, ordered he be given a special room for training, also that he be kept on a diet of eggs, vinegar, and porridge.

Some ten days elapsed before Cornelius Marsden was exposed for the imposter he was. He was arrested and charged with obtaining food and lodgings worth three pounds by false pretences and given three months in prison to ponder the error of his ways.

That was how the good citizens of Colwyn Bay learned what the rest of the world already knew. There was only one Seaman Tommy Watson! This is his story.

John Jarrett

Newcastle upon Tyne 1996

1

A BOY GROWS IN BYKER

Jane Eleanor Laws ran away from home as a young girl because she had a dream. She wanted to be an actress, to speak and dress like a lady, to have people point her out as she passed by in her carriage, to see her name splashed across the bills posted up outside the finest theatres in the land. "Miss Jane Eleanor Laws appearing in..."

Sadly for Jane Eleanor, the dream remained just that. Life in the Newcastle of the 1890's had already cast its role for her, that of a wife, of a mother, and it was in that role that her dream finally manifested itself as she gave birth to a champion in the person of her third son, the sixth of the nine children she would bear. Through him, Jane Eleanor finally reached centre stage, finally stood in the spotlight as the cheering of the crowds washed over her. Through him, the boy she named Thomas Samuel Watson, after his father.

Watson was the second of Jane Eleanor's husbands. The first, a building labourer called May, died as the result of an accident at work, leaving Jane Eleanor a widow with four children to raise, Betty, Donald, Osborne, and Bella. There was no welfare state in those days and there was little help from her family. Her brother Tom, a publican in the city's West End, thought she was wrong to leave home the way she did and hadn't approved the marriage to May, thinking his sister could have done better for herself.

But there was a streak of independence as wide as the River Tyne in the widow May and she soon found herself another husband, a colliery stone man named Thomas Samuel Watson. She bore him a daughter, Annie, in 1906, and two years later, on 2 June, 1908, a son was born at 55 Cannon Street, a narrow thoroughfare off Glue House Lane, just behind Scotswood Road.

The boy was named after his father but grew up barely knowing him. The marriage was not a happy one and within a few years Jane Eleanor would divorce Watson and take her six children to

5

Byker, in the East End of Newcastle. There she moved into a downstairs flat at 26 Fuller Road, a pleasant little street of terraced houses that ran down from Wolseley Road to Dunn Terrace.

Jane Eleanor was home. Here she found happiness. She found love again, too. She found Luke Hunter, a ship rigger who came from Seaham Harbour and who lived with his sister Frances when he was home from the sea. And it was during one of Luke's shore leaves that Frances began wondering what her brother was doing staying out until eleven o'clock at night. So she waited up one night and asked him. With a shy grin Luke confessed to his sister that he had been seeing a nice widow who lived in Byker with her six children.

Early the next morning, Frances dressed in her Sunday best and rode the bus to Byker, making her way to 26 Fuller Road. "I was determined to see who this Jane was," she would recall. "Well, I was invited in, and you know, you could eat your meat off her floors! On the way back home I decided our Luke would take no harm with Jane."

Nor did he. Jane Eleanor married Luke Hunter and bore him three children. Margaret Jane, who was called Peggy, was born in 1912; Frances, named after Luke's sister, was born in November, 1914; and Luke, named after his father, came along in 1916. Frances, a widow whose appearance and demeanour belie her eighty-two years, still lives in the Walker district of Newcastle, and there is a sparkle in her eyes as she recalls those early days.

"They were wonderful, wonderful memories," she says. "There were four boys and I was the youngest of five girls. We lived in the downstairs flat, the people upstairs were called Nixon and they were hawkers, they sold fruit and vegetables off a horse and cart all over Byker.

"They were terraced houses, all very nice people. We only had one bedroom, a living room, and a scullery, but we thought we were so posh because we had our own backyard, and we would brag to the kids on the bottom row, 'We don't have to go in the yard to get washed,' because their tap was in the backyard.

"In the bedroom there was a little dressing table with a marble top where the washstand used to go, the big desk bed, and two other beds. The lads slept in the desk bed which would be let down

6

at night and our Peggy and me slept in our own bed. Sometimes our Lukey, he was only a little lad then, would climb into the bottom of our bed to sleep because he said it was warmer.

"Although my mother had had three husbands, three families, I knew nothing about any of that until I was married and had children of my own. There was never any talk of half-brothers or half-sisters, such a thing was never talked about in the home because we were so close and so much love was shown to us because we were the three little ones, our Peggy, our Lukey, and me.

"My Dad, Luke, was just a wonderful man, and when my older sisters talked about him they cried because of the love and kindness they received from him. They would say to me, 'If your Dad didn't have a sweet for us, there wouldn't be a sweet for you.' Our Tommy was six years older than me and he always let me know it, but I was his little lass. He would have given me the moon and the stars if I'd needed them, because of the love he had for my Dad, and that he told me many times. He was the only Dad our Tommy wished to remember, ever did."

Little Tommy Watson started selling newspapers when he was eight-years-old, from his pitch at the top of Byker Bank. Keen and alert, he quickly learned the ropes in the paper-selling business...only the fittest and the strongest survive!

"I have vivid recollections of turning out early every Sunday morning, collecting my *Sunday Suns*, and setting off on my round," he would recall many years later. "And I found out early in my career as a newsboy that it was a hard school and if you weren't able to take care of yourself the other lads would soon get you down. There were plenty of arguments, usually ending with a walk up a quiet lane, sleeves rolled up, papers put on the ground, and then a stand-up fight. Many were the back lane fights I had and my subsequent experiences in the boxing ring showed that a few years among the Newcastle newsboys is the finest way of hardening one."

Two of the newsboys were brothers, one the same age as Tommy, the other much older, and they started throwing their weight around and bullying the other paper lads. One day, as they gathered outside the *Sunday Sun* offices on Westgate Road, young Watson's sense of fair play surfaced and he told the brothers to knock it on the head or he would do the same to them. In the fight that followed,

7

Tommy flattened the younger lad then belted the bigger one to become king of the newsboys!

Tom Watson Jnr. related a story of those early days in the life of the boy who became a champion. "My father was very small when he was young and I think that's why he started fighting. Whenever he was in the queue to collect his papers, he was always being pushed to the back because he was so small. Then one day this big lad shoved him and my father had a go at him and gave him a good hiding. From then on my father was always allowed to go to the front of the queue! I think it was just the kind of world where you had to take care of yourself and his early days were spent just fighting in the streets of Byker with all the other hard lads there.

"He always smoked, from being a small boy, and even when he was boxing. When he was at school he would tie his cigarettes inside his rope belt that kept his pants up. And talking about his pants, another story I heard often was that he had gone to the swimming baths one day and when he got out of the water he discovered that someone had pinched his trousers. So he found a pair hanging on a nearby hook, put them on, and happily went off home. When his mother saw what he was wearing, she gave him a good hiding for losing his trousers and promptly marched him straight back to the baths. When they got there, they saw this other lad running around with no trousers on because my father had taken them. So he got another good hiding from his mother."

Selling newspapers proved to be a profitable sideline for young Tommy Watson and on a Saturday afternoon he would be up at St James's Park selling programmes for Newcastle United matches. He was earning around three pounds a week of which he would give his mother two and keep one for himself. He would hide his money in the lavatory cistern or in a disused drainpipe and was most upset one week when he found his pound had disappeared. Afraid to tell his mother in case he got into trouble for keeping the money for himself, he planted another pound note and let out a yell when he spotted one of his sisters raiding his secret place. She never did it again but Tommy had to find a new hiding place after that.

Like most young lads in those days, Tommy liked to run around in his bare feet, although with a lot of kids it was not a question of choice because they didn't have any boots or shoes to wear. One Sunday morning, Tommy was on New Bridge Street selling his papers, and he had taken his boots off, knotted the laces together, and slung them around his neck, as was his habit.

Luke Hunter was out walking that morning, and when he spotted his stepson, he crossed the road and took him by the shoulders. "Now Tommy, sit down there and get those boots on," he said, "because as long as you're a son of mine, you'll never go barefoot."

Jane Eleanor's idyllic marriage to Luke barely survived ten years. He had come home on shore leave to spend some time with his family in Fuller Road and Frances had gone up to the shops to buy some new clothes for her Dad to take back to the ship. By the time she got back home, it was all over. Luke had suffered a massive heart attack. "I can still hear the screams of my mother to this day," says Frances. Jane Eleanor, now a mother of nine, was alone again.

"Shortly after my Dad died," remembers Frances, "the teacher told us at school that we could get free boots because we had no father, and I was bubbling over to tell my mother when I got home. I can see her standing there in the scullery, with the towel over her arm and the look on her face. 'Charity!' she said defiantly, 'there's no damn charity coming in this house. When you need boots or shoes, I'll work for them.' And, mind you, she did. She took in three washings a week. My brother and I would go and fetch them and we took them back all ready to put in the drawer and there was five shillings put in our hand to give to our Mam."

Like his brothers and sisters, Tommy attended the Ouseburn School until his fourteenth birthday, in June, 1922, and like most of his mates, he preferred soccer to sums. "He was a harum, scarum kid," remembers Frances. "We all were, I suppose. We loved to take our shoes off and go plodging in the Ouseburn, and on summer days, me and our Tommy would go to the ice factory down the burn and get great lumps of ice, wrapped in paper, to suck on the way home. The summers always seemed warmer in those days and even the tar on the roads would melt. And didn't our Tommy have his boots off as usual, get his feet covered in tar, couldn't get it off, and got a good hiding when he got home."

Young Tommy did receive one hiding from his mother which he didn't deserve. He was thirteen at the time, not long after Luke's death, and with a few shillings saved from his paper round, Jane Eleanor put the rest and bought him his first pair of long trousers.

He was only allowed to wear them on Sundays but after a few weeks of pestering, Jane relented and let him wear them for school. That first Monday however, Tommy didn't come home from school for his usual bite to eat before starting his paper round, in fact it was very much later in the evening when he did get home.

"Where have you been 'til this time?" stormed his mother. "What have you been up to? No good, I'll be bound. Off to bed with you!" Without a word, young Tom went off to bed.

Later that night Jane Eleanor was tidying up around the house when she found Tommy's new trousers lying in a corner of the room, along with his boots, socks, and jersey. They were all soaking wet! Tommy was promptly hauled from his bed and given a good hiding for playing down by the burn near the Ouseburn Kipper House.

Some weeks later the postman brought a letter to 26 Fuller Road, addressed to Mrs Jane Eleanor Hunter and signed by the Lord Mayor of Newcastle, Alderman Richard Henry Millican. It was an invitation for Jane to be at the Ouseburn School where her son Thomas Samuel Watson was to be presented with the Royal Humane Society's Certificate for Bravery.

"This was in front of the whole school," Margaret Jane (Peggy) would later recall in a letter to the Sunday Sun. "What a day it was and I was so proud to be his sister. That first day at school with his long pants on, wor Tommy had rescued a boy from the Tyne. I think his name was Jimmy McCartney and he lived at the bottom of Byker Bank or Cut Bank. Anyhow it was opposite Mrs Melton's lodging house and she was the lady who partly dried our Tommy before he went on his paper round. She and her family were very good friends of my brother for many years. I very much doubt if my Mam ever said she was sorry for that hiding she gave our Tommy!"

Frances recalls that her mother and Tommy were invited to tea at the Mansion House. "He was presented with a big penknife with all the gadgets on, as well as the parchment certificate. My mother was so proud of him and so sorry that he hadn't told her the full story of why he had come home with his clothes wet through."

Jane Eleanor had related the anecdote to the Lord Mayor and some months later, when Tommy was due to leave school having attained the age of fourteen, she received a letter from Alderman

Millican stating that there was a job for Tommy as errand boy with his family firm, Reed Millicans, the Newcastle glass works on Market Street.

At fifteen, Tommy left the glass works to start work in the Tyneside shipyard of Swan, Hunter as a heater for the riveters, but the job didn't last long. An older lad took a dislike to young Watson and kept prodding his backside with a steel bar. When he failed to see reason, Tommy took him behind one of the workshops "and belted him good and proper!"

Oddly enough, Tommy's sister Frances has no recollection of her brother working in the shipyard, which he would later relate in a newspaper article. "I can't remember ever seeing our Tommy with a dirty face," she says. "I could never imagine our mother ever wanting him to go in the shipyard. His older brother Osborne became a master cobbler, Donald was a butcher in the Grainger Market, Tommy went in the Navy, and our Luke served in the Royal Marines. Every one of us five girls had to go into service, my mother didn't believe in any factory work for us and I don't know of any of my brothers ever working in a shipyard."

In 1924 Tommy Watson reached the age of sixteen. He also reached a decision. Sailing the seven seas in one of these big ships that grew in the steel and concrete forests along the banks of the river had to be better than working amid the deafening clangour that had become his daily life. He would join the Royal Navy!

2

CHARLEY KNOCKER!

"I can remember when he was just a youngster," says Frances, "and my brothers used to go to Jimmy Britt's underneath Byker Bridge to spar. It was just a wooden hut in those days but it was a place where they all congregated, and they all had the gloves on, you know, my brothers all sparred with Tommy.

"They used to call him Charley Knocker! That was his nickname as a lad and he never lost it, not even when he grew up. My older brothers would always ask, where's Charley Knocker? I think he got it from the gym, from knocking the punchball, you know. Charley Knocker!"

Young Tommy Watson was barely fifteen when he wandered into Jimmy Britt's gym, a makeshift wooden structure along Stephen Street, just off Byker Bank and in the shadow of Byker Bridge which carried the road into the city and was a toll-bridge as late as 1895.

"I want to be a boxer," he said to the man in gym togs who was showing some young lads how to hold their hands up. The man was Jim Falcus, well known professional boxer who was an inspiration to every potential pug in the district. And rightly so.

Jim Falcus sold newspapers on the streets of Newcastle before enlisting in the Northumberland Fusiliers at the age of sixteen. The army taught him to fight with rifle and bayonet. It also taught him to fight with his fists and over the eleven years he spent in uniform Jim won battalion titles from featherweight to middleweight while collecting a glistening array of ten gold medals and nineteen cups. He never forgot "those fine army instructors who first showed me the meaning and usefulness of a straight left."

It was at Ambala in India just before World War I broke out that Jim fought a tremendous, albeit losing, battle with Sergeant Christian of the Lancashire Fusiliers for the Army championship of India, a battle that was remembered for years afterwards by the local natives who spoke in awe of "Falcus sahib, the lal pugari adam" meaning "the man with the red band round his topi," the distinctive red pugari worn by all ranks of the Northumberland Fusiliers in India.

In 1915, a German bullet and a touch of frostbite sent Jim home from France to a hospital in England and when he recovered he managed to spend a few days at home in Newcastle. Short of a few bob he went along to the St James's Hall and asked Tommy Murphy if there was any chance of a fight. Murphy matched him with Sergeant Wright of the West Yorks Regiment over fifteen rounds, his purse seven pounds ten shillings! Sadly out of condition, Falcus was hammered from pillar to post and decked an amazing twenty-one times inside ten rounds.

Even more amazing was the fact that he was able to get off the canvas twenty-one times and in round eleven, after hearing local bookie Tom Moore shouting at ringside, "I will lay 100 to 1 against Falcus," Jim smashed a wicked left into Wright's body, threw a right to the jaw, and Wright crashed to the floor. Even if he had been able to hear the count above the roar of the crowd he could not have gotten up. Falcus reeled to his corner and collapsed on to his stool, winner of a fight he would never forget.

"I returned to my regiment in France shortly afterwards," he would recall many years later, "but nothing the Germans sent over could do the damage to me that Sergeant Wright had done and to this day I still carry the scars."

In 1919, with the war over, Jim returned home and decided to become a professional boxer. At this time Nicol Brady was a big favourite of the boxing crowd and Tommy Murphy was looking for someone to fight him at St James's Hall. Jimmy Britt reminded him of Jim Falcus, the fighting soldier.

"There's a lad named Falcus who has done some fighting in India," he said. "I have seen him perform. He's your man."

Jim was training at St James's Park with Frank Ray, the Irish heavyweight champion, and Sergeant Lonz Webster, a favourite in the Newcastle ring, when Brady rolled up with two taxi-cabs full of his pals who had come to see him spar with Falcus. Jim allowed Nicol to show off his skills so it was no surprise that

Brady entered the ring a big betting favourite when they met at the Gallowgate arena shortly afterwards.

Brady had an excellent left hand and after landing the jab he would hook with the same hand and these tactics gave him a comfortable lead going into round fourteen. Then Falcus hit him on the chin with a left and right and when Brady recovered he had to be sent home in a taxi.

Jim met Brady twice after that and racked up a hat-trick, knocking his local rival out in four, then three rounds. There was a wild night at St James's Hall when Jim met Andy Brack, a miner from Ashington known as the Pitman Apollo, in a match for £25-a-side. In the second round a terrific body smash decked Brack for the full count but when his corner created a disturbance, claiming the punch was low, Falcus pleaded with the referee to let the fight go on. Jim knocked Brack out in the fifth with a punch on the jaw and this time there were no arguments!

"I want to be a boxer," the boy said that night in the old wooden gymnasium. Jim Falcus studied the lad for a few minutes then threw him a battered pair of boxing gloves. "Come on then, young'un, let's see what you can do," he said, waving one of the other lads into the ring to spar with little Tom Watson from across Byker Bank.

Falcus called time and the lads went at it hammer and tongs, throwing leather as though their very lives depended on the outcome. Young Tom's nose bled as his opponent's left fist beat a tattoo on his face but it couldn't wipe the grim look of determination from that face and after three hectic rounds Falcus had seen enough.

"H'm, you'll do all right," he said to Tom, pulling the gloves off and handing him a towel. "Now go and wash your face before your mother sees you like that."

"Out of my meagre wage as a boy worker at the shipyard of Messrs Swan Hunter," Watson would relate, "I paid one shilling-and-sixpence a week to train at the Byker gymnasium. Jim certainly knew how to teach the boxing game, but although he saw promise in me I failed to get a fight and I came to the conclusion there was nothing for me in the North-East.

"I decided to join the Royal Navy, a hard school but at least one where I would be given a chance. My possibilities of becoming a boxer were quickly detected soon after joining the boys' school at Devonport where there were plenty of opportunities of proving what I could do with the gloves. I trained conscientiously and was rewarded by winning the boys' championship three times within a year. I was a proud little Bluejacket in those days."

It was on a Monday night, 28 September, 1925, that seventeen-year-old Seaman Tommy Watson had his first taste of professional boxing. Back in Newcastle on a spot of home leave, he could have gone along to the Theatre Royal to see The Sport Of Kings, Ian Hay's three-act comedy featuring Mr Lester Matthews, Mr Paul Blackwell, and Miss Dorothy Freshwater...the Palace Theatre advertised a bright and breezy bill featuring the clever and amusing dancing of Lauri Howard, the burlesque of Arthur Haynes, and Cliff Berzac's comedy pony circus...the Stoll Picture House was showing The Wizard Of Oz, a Larry Semon comedy.

Instead, young Watson headed straight for St James's Hall to see if he could get a fight. There was a good house in to see Tommy Murphy's second bill of the new season, topped by a fifteen-rounds contest between Con O'Kelly of Hull, one of the most promising young heavyweights, and that popular Bishop Auckland boxer George Hetherington. Another fifteen-rounder featured Harry Crossley of Rotherham and George Williams from Felling, while the six-rounders paired Peter Kelly and Charlie Edie, Billy Page and Young Dryden, and Alf Paolozzi against Jack Jones. Watson's luck was in for when the Paolozzi-Jones fight fell through, Murphy offered him a pound to box six rounds with Tom Pinkney, a useful boy from Annfield Plain.

Next morning Tommy was out bright and early to get a copy of the *North Mail & Newcastle Daily Chronicle*. Quickly turning to the sports pages he read how O'Kelly had beaten Hetherington in ten rounds, the Bishop Auckland man being disqualified for holding by Referee Willie Curley Jnr...Crossley had knocked out Williams in five rounds...Peter Kelly beat Charlie Edie on points in a fast six rounds bout...Newcastle flyweight rivals Young Dryden and Billy Page fought a draw...and last but by no means least, he read that "T. Pinkney (West Stanley) was beaten on points by Seaman Watson (Newcastle). It was a good exhibition."

For a little fellow, Seaman Tommy Watson felt ten feet tall! Tommy Murphy had been suitably impressed by his showing and when he learned that the lad was not due back in Devonport for another week, offered him a pound for another six-rounder the following Monday night against Alf Paolozzi.

Born of Italian immigrant parents at Bill Pit, Longbenton, then a small mining community just outside Newcastle, Paolozzi was another protege of Jim Falcus and had turned pro earlier in the year. Alf was a couple of years older than Watson but the young sailor ploughed forward full steam ahead from the opening bell and in round four Paolozzi's seconds threw the towel in.

Losing the contest was bad enough for Alf Paolozzi. He was upset again when he read the report in the *North Mail* next morning for the anonymous boxing writer who had covered the show at St James's Hall had mis-spelled his name as Prolozzi. But that was something he would get used to in a career that would span three decades for, as Ron Olver noted when featuring Paolozzi in his excellent *Boxing News* series The Professionals, Alf's surname would be spelled an incredible seventeen different ways on fight bills!

With those two winning fights under his belt, young Watson packed his kit bag, said goodbye to the family, and made the long train journey back to Devonport. The sailor boy was off to sea, his boxing limited to sparring on deck with his mates when duties permitted. His son Tom Jnr recalls one duty his father didn't particularly relish.

"Whenever they were in port, the ship would be open to the public at certain times and it was one of my father's duties to show visitors around when they came on board. One day, this French couple came aboard with their young daughter and my father was giving them the Cook's tour. But every time they nodded approval and said, "Oui, oui," my father would take them to the toilets! Just being an unsophisticated Geordie lad he didn't know that "oui" was French for "yes!"

"The best days I remember of our Tommy," says Frances, "were when he was in the Navy, because he was so handsome in his uniform and, you know, he never lost his Navy swagger. I was so proud of him and I loved to be with him. Each time he was away it would be two years, eighteen months, but as long as my mother got the letters from him she was quite happy. I used to watch for the postman coming down the street and look for the postmark on the letters, it would usually be Malta, or Gibraltar, because he spent a lot of time with the Mediterranean Fleet.

"Tommy would sometimes bring one of his shipmates home with him when he came on leave and he would stay with us in Byker. I would get little notes shoved into my hand by girls wanting a date with Tommy. 'Your Tommy's coming home on leave isn't he, Frances?' they would say to me, and when I said he was, it would be, 'Will you give him this little note from me, please.' Remember the old song, 'All the nice girls love a sailor,' well, you know, some of them were like painted dolls!"

Early in 1927, Ordinary Seaman Watson returned to Blighty from a tour of the Mediterranean and was transferred from Devonport to Chatham. By this time he was having to make room in his kit bag for the boxing trophies he was winning at any and every opportunity, notably the lightweight championship of the Mediterranean Fleet.

"As champion, I came home to fight in the championships of the Royal Navy," he would recall. "I fought my way into the final where I was beaten by A B Pledger of Portsmouth, but the following year I made amends by defeating Pledger in the Navy final and two weeks later I beat him again in the final of the Imperial Services Championships."

It was in March, 1927, that Seaman Watson resumed his professional boxing career which had been on hold for seventeen months. At Plymouth, poor Jim Pemberton took a hammering for five rounds before the referee rescued him. A few days later, Tommy was in Devonport to beat Seaman Cartlidge over six rounds in the final of the Port lightweight championship. A trip to Torquay saw him whip local lad Billy Jones in a six rounder.

A spot of leave saw him back home in Byker for a couple of weeks and back in the ring at the St James's Hall for a couple of fights. Tommy Murphy gave him a return six-rounder with Tom Pinkney and at the final bell Sailor Tom had confirmed his previous victory. *The North Mail* noted, "The West Durham man put up a splendid show against a stronger opponent."

A week later Watson was back in the Gallowgate ring for his first ten-rounds bout, against a tough local lad, Billy Graham of Walker. Billy had to be tough for Watson punched much the harder of the two in taking the decision, but the *North Mail* thought, "he relied on his right hand too much." Tommy's purse was two pounds, ten shillings!

Happy as he was to be home for some time with the family in Fuller Road, Tommy couldn't wait to get back to Chatham and the long train journey from Newcastle seemed to take forever. For the Senior Service now had a rival for the love of Ordinary Seaman Thomas Samuel Watson. Her name was Kitty and she served behind the bar at a hotel in the town.

Shortly after transferring to Chatham, Tommy got to know a local hotel proprietor named Darran who was an enthusiastic follower of the Noble Art. There was a well-equipped gymnasium at the hotel and Mr Darran gave the young sailor the use of the place whenever he was ashore.

"On my first visit to the hotel," Tommy would relate many years later, "I saw a very attractive barmaid. Sailors always have an eye for a winsome girl you know, and it was not long before I was taking her for a walk. However, a peculiar incident almost marred our courting days. It might easily have led to our romance being broken off and certainly caused my girl a very unpleasant hour.

"It happened the first time Kitty saw me fight, which was at the Rochester Casino against George Swinbourne of Maidstone. Being from Newcastle, I was always known as Geordie, or George. As luck would have it, Kitty was sitting next to the sister-in-law of my opponent, and half way through the fight this lady suddenly pointed to the other side of the ring and remarked to her companion, 'Look, there is George's wife sitting over there.'

"Of course Kitty assumed it was MY wife who was being pointed out and started thinking to herself well, you know what sailors are, or are supposed to be! I won the fight on points but I had a harder job convincing Kitty that the lady in question was indeed the wife of my opponent George Swinbourne and not of 'Geordie' Watson!"

By this time Watson's prowess in the professional ring was beginning to draw favourable comment from the boxing writers of the day. In October, 1927, the sailors outpunched the marines in a services tournament held at the Globe Theatre, Royal Marine Barracks, Chatham, with Seaman Tom knocking out Lance-Corporal Davis in round two with a heavy right swing to the jaw. One reporter wrote, "Watson certainly accomplished his task in workmanlike style and more will be heard of this promising young boxer."

Tommy managed to get a few days leave to celebrate the dawn of 1928 with the family and took the opportunity to get another fight under his belt in the Newcastle ring. George Willis was boxing Frank Lane at St James's Hall and Watson was matched with Bobby Lees of London in one of two 10-rounders. When Lees failed to put in an appearance, Watson stepped in with Billy Graham again and improved on his previous points win by forcing the Walker man to retire after six punishing rounds.

A week later he was back in barracks at Chatham and taking a fight with Tommy Hall from Lambeth, twelve rounds at the Rochester Casino. Next day the local paper reported "one of the fiercest fights yet seen in the Casino ring...Watson won and won well but he was given a rare battle by the ex-sapper. The winner, despite the torrid nature of the battle, did not neglect to employ a left lead and varied his attack with commendable judgement, his hitting being most punishing...right to the final bell the pair battled all over the ring with the sailor the more accurate in his execution and a few points to spare at the close." Tommy beat Hall a month later in the same ring and won two fights in London at the National Sporting Club, beating Fred Fox of Sheffield and Chesterfield's Ernie Beresford to take his pro record to 19 fights without defeat. He was on his way!

3

THE MAN WITH THE GOGGLES

It was just after his victory over Beresford in February, 1928, that Seaman Tommy Watson became acquainted with Alec Lambert, the man who would guide him to the top of the boxing tree, the man he affectionately called "the man with the goggles."

Alec Lambert came from the St James's district of London and broke into boxing as an amateur in 1909 when he entered and won a nine-stone novice competition. A few weeks later he caused a sensation by boxing his way to the ABA featherweight championship. From there it was a short step into the paid ranks. He once fought twice in the same evening at the famous Ring, Blackfriars, beating Bill Lewis of Liverpool over 15 rounds, then taking the measure of former amateur champion Charlie Morris of Kilburn, this time over 20 rounds! By 1913, Lambert was one of the leading contenders for Jim Driscoll's British featherweight title.

When Driscoll retired, the National Sporting Club decided on a set of eliminators with the winner to meet Lambert for the vacant title and the new belt. Ted Kid Lewis, a tough battler from St Georges in the East End of London, won through the series and was matched with Lambert for £100-a-side at the NSC, 9 October, 1913.

Fancied to win, Lambert was a sound boxer whereas Lewis liked a fight. Yet the trade paper *Boxing* reported, "Lewis won well and skilfully by the best display of boxing and sheer generalship which he has ever put on in our recollection."

There was nothing between them for thirteen rounds, but Lambert seemed to be feeling the pace more. The Kid sensed this and stepped up a gear, flooring his man with a right to the jaw as the bell ended round fifteen. Lambert never recovered and when he was floored twice in the seventeenth the referee waved Lewis away, the winner and new champion.

Alec Lambert was proud to have fought for the British title and he took umbrage with people who were led to believe he was knocked out by Lewis, destined to become one of Britain's greatest ever fighters. "I was knocked down, but not out, and the referee stopped the fight," he would take pains to point out.

Lambert found his niche in the fight game when he started lacing gloves on the fists of other men rather than his own, when he stopped fighting champions and started training them. His name became linked with men like Benny Lynch, Phil Scott, Alf Mancini, Jack Bloomfield, Harry Corbett, Hamilton Johnny Brown, Johnny Brown (St George's), Nel Tarleton, Jack Hood, and Harry Mason. The biggest names in the business worked out at Lambert's Bell Street gym in Marylebone, where any fighter heading for the shower would probably trip over the impeccable Alec who used to bathe four times a day!

"By a coincidence, it was the sister-in-law of George Swinbourne, who had given Kitty such a shock that night at the Rochester Casino, who introduced me to Alec Lambert," recalled Watson some years later. "Being entirely ignorant of many of the wiles the hooks in the boxing game were wont to practice, I travelled up to London from Chatham to see Mr Lambert and he was good enough to take me under his wing.

"Soon afterwards I was given a good chance to make an impression when I was fixed up to fight Don Jeal at the Ring, Blackfriars, eight rounds for a purse of three pounds. The money did not seem a lot, I know, but I did not forget that I was an unknown quantity and that I wanted the chance to show my paces in London."

That March night in 1928, Seaman Watson stormed into his opponent from the opening bell and the man from Plumstead was hammered from pillar to post before being rescued by the referee in round two. The spectators at the famous London venue knew a good fighter when they saw one and they liked what they saw of Seaman Watson. Mr Lambert was also pleased and he had Tommy back there three weeks later against Billy Handley, his first fifteen-rounder, for a purse of seven pounds, ten shillings.

Tommy warmed up for the match when he topped the bill at the Rochester Casino with Joe Batten, the Notting Hill welterweight. An excellent defensive boxer, Batten didn't do enough fighting and Watson forced the action all the way, winning eight of the twelve rounds. Ten days later he was at Blackfriars to meet

Handley, the Hackney veteran who numbered Len Harvey among his opponents. "The sailor fought well," reported one paper, "his work a tribute to Lambert's training. Tommy was too fast with his hands and his feet and although Handley staged a fine rally through the last three rounds Watson was a worthy winner."

It is one of the oldest cliches in boxing that hungry fighters make the best fighters, but in the late 'twenties and early 'thirties there was another side to this coin. Fighters who were hungry because they hadn't eaten a decent meal in days..men desperate to fight for a few pounds, often just a few shillings, so as to keep a roof over their families, to put food in their bellies..fighters not physically fit enough to go a few rounds with a half-decent opponent.

Seaman Tommy Watson met such a fighter in his first top-of-the-bill fight at the Blackfriars Ring, on 10 May 1928. Matched over fifteen rounds with Billy Brown of Barnsley, it was soon apparent that Brown should never have left Yorkshire. The weight for both men was announced as 9st 3½lbs but that was the only thing they had in common.

Brown came out swinging his punches and was soon struggling against Watson. In round two Watson was on top, scoring with straight lefts and heavy rights to the jaw. In the third, Brown was hurt by a smashing right to the jaw and a similar punch in round four sent him sprawling on the canvas. No sooner was he on his feet than another right sent him down for a six count and after a further knockdown, Referee Jim Kenrick stepped in to halt the one-way traffic.

Tommy had quickly realised Brown's condition and it was not a fight he enjoyed. "I knew if I hit him very hard," he said later, "I might maim him for life. So I started pulling my punches and was only just tapping him. The referee must have been off his head, he should have stopped the fight. My opponent was up against the ropes, all in. The referee didn't want to but when he looked more closely he realised I wasn't having him on. The fight was stopped and that poor bloke was taken to hospital. He was on the danger list for nearly a week. I was sick with worry!"

Billy Brown had collapsed in the dressing room after leaving the ring and his handlers frantically summoned a doctor. The stricken fighter appeared to come round briefly, but when he collapsed again he was taken to Guy's Hospital where he remained for a few days before being allowed to travel home.

Whatever the merits of the match, the performance of the Geordie in the sailor suit drew favourable notices from the London boxing writers. "We want to see more of Watson, he's a real find," was a typical comment in next morning's papers. A month later Seaman Watson was back in the Blackfriars Ring, matched with George Rose of Bristol, fifteen rounds or less.

The same age as Watson, Rose was much more experienced, having packed in sixty-three contests against men like Arnold Kid Sheppard, Sam Steward, Harry Brooks, and Saverio Turiello of Italy, appearing regularly at venues such as Blackfriars, Premierland, the Royal Albert Hall, and the National Sporting Club. He figured to be Watson's toughest test, and he was.

As usual, the Geordie went for his man from the first bell, worrying away like a terrier with a bone, but he found Rose a difficult customer, a clever boxer with a sound left jab that gave him a slight points lead after twelve rounds. But Tommy refused to be discouraged and kept plugging away, forcing Rose around the ring through the last three rounds. In the fourteenth he shook George with a terrific right hand smash to the head but the boy from Bristol weathered the storm and at the final bell was awarded the decision.

Watson was bitterly disappointed, but received some consolation when leaving the ring as the crowd saved their biggest cheer for him. There was a wry smile on his face as he followed Mr Lambert to the dressing room but his heart was heavy. He had lost for the first time in 29 fights!

Tommy's defeat at the talented fists of George Rose did not trouble Alec Lambert unduly. The Bristol boy was vastly experienced with twice the number of contests under his belt as had Watson, and even then the decision had been close enough for argument with the Blackfriars crowd split as to its merits. There was also the disturbing sequel to the Billy Brown fight which had brought the grim reality of life as a professional boxer home to the young Geordie with the impact of a Dempsey knockout wallop.

So it was just as well Tommy had something good to look forward to as he travelled back to his Chatham barracks with the memory of his first defeat still gnawing at his insides. He was going home to marry Kitty.

4

MARRIAGE OF NORTH AND SOUTH

It must have been something of a culture shock for Miss Kitty Vines when she left her home in Gillingham in Kent, and arrived in Byker in the East End of Newcastle to marry her sailor sweetheart in that summer of 1928. There were the ham bones for a start.

"I must tell you," says Frances. "My mother, when she made broth, everything went in the pan, the sheep's head, the ham bones, all went in the pan. Kitty was watching her one day in the kitchen and when she saw Jane Eleanor lifting the ham bones out of the pan with the big wooden tongs, she said, 'Oh, they look nice.' So my mother says, 'You can have one, hinny. Plenty of meat to suck off that one.' With that my mother puts the ham bone on a separate plate besides Kitty's dinner and she thought that was wonderful. She'd never tasted a ham bone before. Of course it became a standing joke in our house after that.

"Every time Jane Eleanor made broth, she would put the biggest ham bone on a separate plate beside Kitty's dinner, saying, 'There y'are bonny lass, get stuck into that!' For years afterwards, Kitty and I had many a good laugh over that. 'Your mother and her bloomin' ham bones,' she would say in her south country twang."

Jane Eleanor's kitchen held many mysteries for the petite young brunette from the Garden of England. "Usually on a Monday night," recalls Frances, "my mother would put a sheep's head in the pan to steep through the night. She would take a spoon and scoop the brains out, wrap them in muslin, and they would be dropped into the broth when it went on the stove. Then when it was ready, she would lift the brains out, unwrap them, and put them on the side of her plate to have with her dinner."

Kitty would smile in wonder as Frances and her sisters prepared for their night out at a local dance..a burnt matchstick became an eyebrow pencil, red dye off the wallpaper put rouge on their cheeks,

24

then down to Mrs Shepherd's rag shop on Byker Bank with some jam jars which would fetch a few coppers for their dance money.

"It was my job to do all the darning on a Wednesday night," remembers Frances. "But when Kitty stayed with us she would say to me, 'Don't you worry, Frances, you go out with your friends and I'll do the darning for you.' Well, I loved her for that of course, but she was such a kind, loving lass, a lovely person."

In the days before she married Tommy Watson, Kitty had a furnished room on Albion Row, just around the corner from Fuller Road and a few doors from where Mrs Goldwater lived, the mother of Benny Sharkey, who would become the scourge of champions and Seaman Watson's arch rival in three memorable battles.

With the wedding all set for Monday 6 August, Tommy went along to St James's Hall to see Tom Murphy about getting a fight to help with the expenses. Murphy matched him with Harry Pitt, the dour Hazlerigg pitman, on the Saturday night, fifteen rounds for twelve pounds.

Sunderland's Fred Charlton, referee, matchmaker, and boxing writer, used to tell a nice yarn about Pitt, whose real name was Henry Poppitt. Tommy Burns, former heavyweight champion of the world, came to Newcastle in 1924 and was licensee of the Forth Hotel in Newcastle's Pink Lane for several years. Retaining his fondness for the fight game, Burns looked after a few promising boxers and Harry Pitt was one of them.

Jim Ruck was around Newcastle in those days, famed as a civil engineer with Dorman Long and often referred to as "the man who built the Tyne Bridge." A former middleweight boxer and a long-standing friend of Burns, Ruck was a man who would go to the ends of the earth to see a good fight. He was managing Jim Carney at the time, a tough Middlesbrough fighter who was working as a barman in the town.

Jim was relaxing in the Royal Station Hotel in Newcastle one night when in walked Tommy Burns with some friends. The former champ promptly announced that he was willing to back Pitt against Carney for £200-a-side and the Northern lightweight championship. Ruck agreed immediately but further negotiations reduced the stakes to £50-a-side, the money to be lodged at the offices of the *Newcastle Journal*.

Promoter at the St James's Hall at the time was the great Will

Curley with Tom Murphy as his matchmaker. Curley fancied the fight but his purse offer did not suit either Burns or Ruck, so the latter came up with the idea of hiring the Hippodrome in Northumberland Road.

"You can give an exhibition as an added attraction and with your name as promoter we'll clean up!" enthused Jim. Burns liked the idea so the old theatre was booked for Saturday afternoon, 11 December, 1926, with Arthur Clarance, an experienced showman, acting as publicity man and general factotum, and famed referee Eugene Corri as third man in the ring.

Crowds rolled up on the big day and with prices ranging from five- shillings-and-ninepence to thirty bob ringside, the place was sold out. Burns duly appeared in a three-rounds exhibition with Sheffield heavyweight Don Shortland before Pitt and Carney entered the ring for their 20-rounds contest. Carney had a reach advantage but failed to use it until late in the bout which suited the Hazlerigg pitman with his short arms and Harry revelled in the close quarter exchanges, building up an early lead. Then Carney finally got his left working and picked up enough points to earn a draw from Mr Corri.

Six months later, on 10 June, 1927, Pitt met Carney again, this time at the Middlesbrough Theatre Royal with backing by George Elliott, the former 'Boro footballer. Again matched over twenty rounds, the boys staged a terrific battle with Carney emerging a clear winner on the card of the referee, Mr Fred Charlton.

Just over a year later, Harry Pitt climbed into the St James's Hall ring to meet Seaman Watson and the *Journal* predicted "a battle royal as Watson, like Pitt, is possessed of unusual toughness." As it turned out, the mariner was tougher than the miner. "Judged on his display against Harry Pitt on Saturday night," reported the *Journal*, "Seaman Watson is one of the most improved boxers seen at the hall for some time. Against an opponent possessed of tremendous power, Watson gave a polished performance, particularly in the last five rounds.

"For a time the rugged methods of his rival troubled the Seaman and at the end of the ninth round there was little between them. Then came the turning point of the contest. Boxing with supreme confidence, Watson gave one of the best exhibitions of his career and he punished his opponent in a scientific and approved manner.

Pitt was the essence of gameness but the end must have come as a great relief to him for it is doubtful if he has ever taken such a beating before."

As dawn broke over Newcastle that August Bank Holiday Monday, the weather prospects were anything but promising. Skies were gray and there was a heavy mist, the outlook dull. But by nine o'clock the sun was shining out of a clear blue sky and the mass exodus had begun. "Never has there been such traffic," reported the *Evening Chronicle*, "and the main roads from the city were literally black with the streams of cars, 'buses, motor-cycles, bicycles, carts, and even old-fashioned carriages and perambulators. The scenes at Newcastle Central Station were extraordinary, the bulk of the traffic concentrated on the electrified lines to the coast, and from nine o'clock onwards the queues waiting for trains increased, by noon the queue was waiting outside the station as well as in."

There was something for everyone, whatever their taste. The golden sands at Whitley Bay gradually disappeared beneath a seething mass of people and those who couldn't find a spot on the beach could enjoy the annual flower show...at Tynemouth there was a big carnival...the Tynedale Agricultural Show drew thousands to Hexham, as did the Durham County Show at Houghton-le-Spring...Morpeth staged its own Olympic Games, while near Seaton Sluice, big open-air meetings had been arranged by Socialist and Communist propagandists.

Byker had its own big event that sunny Monday morning, the wedding of local boxing star Seaman Tommy Watson and his sweetheart from the South, Miss Kitty Vines. Family and friends gathered in the little Parish Church just up the road on the corner of Clifford Street and Burton Street for the service conducted by the Vicar of Byker, Mr F Baker.

Jane Eleanor was dressed in her finery and looked a picture, as indeed did the brown-haired bride standing there with her groom who was wearing his best uniform. So did Thomas Samuel Watson, twenty-year-old Able Seaman of the Royal Navy Barracks, Chatham, take unto himself a wife, Miss Kathleen Blanche Vines, twenty-three-year-old spinster of the Parish, late of Gillingham, Kent.

Early in the afternoon, they were all back in church for the wedding of Tommy's sister Annie Watson to Thomas Charles Cartwright. Tom Cartwright had been Seaman's best man in the morning and Tommy returned the favour as his older sister walked to the altar.

"I can tell you it was a right old do in Byker that day," recalled Frances. "My mother had been baking for days, I think she made everything but the wedding cake. The furniture was moved into the bedroom, the oil cloth was rolled back and we had an accordionist there so we could have a bit dance. There was a little barrel of beer in the scullery and the house was full of people right through the day. A wonderful day!"

There would be no honeymoon for Tommy and his bride. The short leave flew by and a few days later he was on the train as it snaked its way out of the Central Station and across the River Tyne on the long journey south. He was due back in Chatham and in a few weeks time he would be back on the high seas on HMS Calliope as she sailed to take up duty with the Mediterranean Fleet.

In those few weeks however, Seaman Watson managed to cram in three fights. He needed the money for one thing. The twenty-four shilling Navy Allowance for Mrs Watson meant he had only four bob left for pocket money! So he was back in the Newcastle ring on Monday 3 September, fighting Billy Jones for a purse of twelve pounds. Jones was a popular performer at St James's Hall where he had made a big impression beating Harry Pitt on his last appearance.

He could bang a bit and he forced the fight, trying to land his big punch at close quarters. Near the end of round six a fierce right uppercut shook Watson to his toenails but Tommy kept a solid left jab in Billy's face all night and finished the stronger to take the decision after fifteen hard rounds.

Three weeks later Tommy was again in action at St James's earning another twelve quid for fifteen two-minute rounds with Harry Best. The Sunderland man had been in with the top lightweights in the country and he made Watson step lively. Seaman relied on his speed, toughness, and fast left hand, but he could never relax against a dangerous opponent. In the seventh Best staged a tremendous attack and in round ten dropped Watson with a savage right hook. Tommy took a count of six then rallied well enough to take the verdict after a cracking fight.

28

A few days before embarking on HMS Calliope, Watson climbed into the ring at the Gillingham Pavilion and steamed to victory over Aldgate's Johnny Gordon. Matched at 9st 9lbs for twelve rounds, they went at it hammer and tongs the whole way much to the delight of the big crowd. Gordon had a wicked right and continually tried to set Tommy up for the knockout, but Watson was too clever and too tough and the decision in his favour was greeted with loud applause.

In the fight with Gordon, his second win over the Aldgate boxer within seven months, Watson was billed as the Imperial Services lightweight champion. He was also champion of the Royal Navy and the Royal Marines and helping him keep in fighting trim on board HMS Calliope was Mark Spiller, Imperial Services heavyweight titleholder.

Tommy continued to dominate the opposition in service bouts in 1929, winning his lightweight bout in the Mediterranean v. Atlantic Fleet tournament at Gibraltar, even moving up to welterweight to come out tops in the Mediterranean Fleet Open Championship.

Seaman loved the hot weather and enjoyed his tour of duty, Algiers being his favourite port of call. But by this time he had another reason to feel homesick for Byker...in Jane Eleanor's bed at 26 Fuller Road, Kitty had given birth to a bonny baby girl, to be named Kathleen after her mother.

5

FAMILY MAN

Naval duties kept Tommy in Malta for a year and by the time he was able to get back to Byker with a boat-load of presents for Kitty and the new baby, it was September, 1929, and Kathleen was almost a year old. Seaman enjoyed being home again, being back with the family and all his old pals, but after a few days he was restless for action. He was a fighter, he wanted to fight. Fred Charlton was promoting at the Holmeside Stadium in Sunderland at the time and a chance meeting with Joe Henderson, one-time clerk of the scales at St James's Hall, brought Watson to his attention.

"There's a young Navy man named Watson who is looking for fights," said Henderson, "and believe me, he can fight! Could you fix him up?" Fred knew Henderson to be a good judge of a fighting man so he matched Watson with Horace Barber, a good class featherweight from Leicester, over fifteen rounds on 12 October.

"I liked Watson's mein," recalled Charlton. "Poker-faced, dour, and inarticulate, the Byker boy looked a battler from tip to toe. It had been my experience that the less a fighter had to say for himself the better he could fight.

"Pallid and bespectacled, Barber looked anything but a prizefighter when he entered the Stadium dressing room. His appearance belied his ring prowess however. Horace could fight all right, as Watson would agree. He gave as good as he got against Watson for twelve rounds, but subsequently Watson's continuous body attacks began to slow up the Leicester lad, and Referee Jimmy Britt declared Tommy the winner at the end of fifteen rounds."

Then it was back to Chatham where one of his gym pals was Bill Cope. Many years later, Bill wrote to *Boxing News* from his home at St Ives to say, "I was in Chatham Barracks the same time as Tommy. He was in MM Mess. We used to train at Shortt's Aeroplane factory in Rochester in 1929-30. He boxed George Rose

30

of Bristol at Rochester Casino and I boxed on the same bill. Alf Craig, trainer at Shortt's, was matchmaker and M.C. at the Casino, and that's how I started as a pro.

"In 1929, Tommy boxed in the annual boxing event, Med. Fleet v. Atlantic Fleet Destroyers. He represented the Med. Fleet and I boxed for the Atlantic."

Now that Able Seaman Watson was back on shore duties, manager Alec Lambert was able to arrange a busy schedule of fights for him around southern rings. Lambert was well connected with the National Sporting Club in London where his father, Jimmy, had been matchmaker for Peggy Bettinson before becoming the first Chief Inspector for the newly-formed British Boxing Board of Control.

Tommy whipped Harry White at the NSC, then hammered tough Welshman Charlie Chew twice in eleven days. At Paddington Baths, the man from Aberdare sustained a heavy body bombardment for fifteen rounds and no sooner had Watson's glove been held aloft in victory than Charlie asked for a return match.

They met on a Sunday afternoon at Kilburn's Vale Hall and this one was even harder. Charlie had the strength of an ox and the heart of a lion and he needed both to survive the punishment handed out by Watson. Tommy bounced right hands off Chew's chin but he was there at the finish, beaten but unbowed.

Three days later, 20 November, 1929, Lambert had another one of his proteges, Tommy Little from Notting Hill, engaged to box the former British lightweight champion Ernie Izzard fifteen rounds at Paddington's Central Baths. But a few days before the fight, Izzard pulled out with 'flu and Little, who would go on to become one of Britain's Star referees, was left without an opponent.

Lambert promptly offered the services of Seaman Watson. Little had a reach advantage and his left hand gave Watson problems, but the Geordie forced his way inside and banged a hard right to the ear in round two. Little moved up a gear in the fifth and five left hooks thudded against Watson's chin.

In the seventh, Watson forced his man to the ropes but a savage right floored him for a count of eight. He was down again in the next round as a left put him on one knee and as the ninth was ending another right to the jaw sent him toppling to the canvas.

31

But the Seaman weathered the storm and fought hard enough through the final rounds to grab a well-earned decision after fifteen tremendous rounds.

When Watson met Billy Reynolds of Ealing at Rochester, he was described on the posters outside the Casino as, "one of the Navy's big guns!" Next morning's paper reported, "The Seaman is among the best at his weight in England and clearly demonstrated his superiority over Reynolds but had to be content with a points decision...The sailor's right hand was not as sound as he could have wished and he consequently used that member very sparingly, otherwise the referee might not have been called upon to make any arithmetical calculations."

Going into 1930, Watson had only the sole defeat to George Rose to mar an excellent record of forty wins as a money fighter, yet his first bout of the new year saw him forced to share the points for the only time in his professional career. Matched with Joe Cadman of Sheffield at Lime Grove Baths, Shepherds Bush, Seaman used his superior boxing to keep the heavy punching Yorkshireman at a safe distance and he looked a good winner after fifteen rounds. But the referee scored it a draw, much to Tommy's disgust.

Next stop was Fulham Baths where Watson stepped in with clever Johnny Quill of Stepney. Johnny made a good start, shooting lefts to the face, but after being shaken by a hard right from Watson, made the mistake of mixing it with the sailor and found himself outpunched over the fifteen rounds. A month later they were back in the Fulham ring with the Geordie confirming his previous victory.

Johnny Quill couldn't beat Seaman Watson in two fights, but he did beat such men as Fred Webster, Stoker Reynolds, and Dave McCleave, and in 1934 he stopped Pat Butler six months before Butler became the British welterweight champion. A year later, on 29 June, 1935, the boxing world was stunned by the news that Johnny had died in St George's Hospital, London, following an operation for pleurisy.

In those first few months of 1930, Tommy was able to confirm his superiority over Quill, George Swinbourne, and Horace Barber in return fights, but his luck ran out when he tangled with George Rose again, this time at the Rochester Casino. Since beating Watson narrowly in June, 1928, the Bristol boxer had lost only two of 36 bouts, one of them to Fred Webster who went on to become British lightweight champion.

A few weeks before meeting Seaman in their rematch, Rose journeyed to Manchester where he whipped Webster over fifteen rounds, but the champion had insisted on an overweight bout so his title was not on the line. Rose proved himself to be Watson's bogeyman when he again emerged a close winner after twelve absorbing rounds that delighted the Casino crowd.

A few days leave spent back in Newcastle helped Seaman get over his disappointment at suffering his second professional defeat. Kitty was expecting again and it was good to see her looking so well, while Kathleen was toddling all over the place and being spoiled by Jane Eleanor, enjoying her role as doting grandmother.

"Our Tommy was home on leave," recalls Frances, "and he and Tom Cartwright, our Annie's husband, went down to the Quayside market and they brought loads of stuff back home. Now, my mother loved her gramophone, and the lads were always buying her lovely records. Jane Eleanor was putting the Sunday dinner out when they came in and our Tommy went straight to her little gramophone which she always had by the scullery door when she was busy in the kitchen. He put this record on, it was 'Me And Jane In A Plane, Flying High In The Sky.' When my mother heard it, she looked at our Tommy, then at Tom Cartwright, and she said, 'Why, you pair of cheeky buggers!' And of course, those two were just doubled up with laughter, because they knew how my mother would react when she heard the record."

Back to Chatham and back to business. Boxing business. Alec Lambert had Tommy matched with Nipper Pat Daly for 20 April, at the Vale Hall, Kilburn, fifteen rounds or less, the Marylebone wonder boy against the navy lightweight champion, tickets going like hot cakes for this Sunday afternoon attraction.

The story of Nipper Pat Daly is one of the most incredible in the annals of British boxing. Born at Abercrave in South Wales, he was still a toddler when his family emigrated to Canada where his father worked as a miner. Within the space of five years they moved to Australia and New Zealand before returning to London to settle in Marylebone.

Young Pat was just nine-years-old when his father took him

along to the gymnasium run by Professor Andrew Newton who was looking after middleweight champion Roland Todd. Newton was impressed by the boy who looked like an angel and fought like a devil and agreed to take him in hand.

"I made my pro debut at Letchworth," Daly recalled for *Boxing News* writer Ron Olver in 1987. "Top of the bill was Joe Bowker and my opponent was George Brown. I was just ten-years-old! It was a scheduled three-rounder but the fans enjoyed it so much that we boxed an extra two rounds. I had never been happier."

Young Daly was truly a fistic phenomenon, boxing regularly over ten, twelve, and fifteen rounds at venues such as Premierland, the National Sporting Club, and the Blackfriars Ring. He was still only fifteen when he whipped Bert Kirby, leading contender for the British flyweight title, in his own Birmingham backyard. A few months later he defeated Petit Biquet over ten rounds at the Royal Albert Hall, before the Frenchman went on to win the European bantamweight title.

Bethnal Green bantamweight Dick Corbett was leading contender for the British championship when Nipper outboxed him at the Albert Hall and ten days later he hammered Kid Socks at Premierland. His services were sought by promoters all over the country and he was the darling of the fans in places like Leeds, Liverpool, Plymouth, Preston, Nottingham, and Blackburn. He won five fights in the Sunderland ring before agreeing to make weight for Douglas Parker. It was a grave mistake. The Sunderland-based Scot could hit like a mule and it took him just three punches and ninety seconds to convince Nipper he should have stayed home that night.

Now it was April, 1930, and Nipper was meeting Seaman Tommy Watson over fifteen rounds in a bout made at 9st 6lbs. Still a growing boy at seventeen, Daly was overweight on the morning of the fight but he made it with barely an ounce to spare. He had been sparring with Al Foreman who was training to challenge Fred Webster for the British lightweight title and had sparkled in gym workouts.

However, Professor Newton had seen Watson in action around the London rings and he advised caution as Nipper answered the bell. But Daly took the fight to Watson and was feeling confident as he shaped up for the second round. Then the Seaman landed a

34

cracking right to the jaw to send Daly reeling to the canvas. He was up at eight only to be felled again, this time for nine. Round three and Nipper was out on his feet as Watson pounded him with thudding punches from either hand, yet he staged a remarkable comeback to have the place in an uproar. Daly fought like a tiger through rounds six and seven but the pace told on him and Watson had him in serious trouble in the tenth with vicious left and right hooks. The kid came out for the eleventh but he had nothing left and the referee waved him back to his corner, leaving Watson a worthy winner.

The victory over Nipper Pat Daly set the ring pundits ruminating over the championship prospects of Seaman Tommy Watson and manager Lambert had a serious talk with the Geordie sailor about his future in the fight game. By this time Tommy had served six years in the Royal Navy, been halfway round the world, and enjoyed every minute of it. But he loved this fighting game and Mr Lambert was convinced he had the makings of a champion.

Tommy's mother was not too happy at the thought of him leaving the navy, but by now she had realised that he had a special talent for boxing and that this was what he really wanted to do with his life. Jane Eleanor also realised that one of her sons had the chance to become the star she always wanted to be. She couldn't stand in his way.

Besides, Tommy's family responsibilities were growing. He had just become a father again, a bouncing baby boy who weighed in at just over fourteen pounds and would be named Thomas James.

6

COMING HOME

On 13 September, 1930, the following item appeared in the sports pages of the *Newcastle Evening Chronicle*. "Seaman Watson, the erstwhile Newcastle boxer now domiciled in Chatham, has bought his discharge from the Navy so as to be able to devote the whole of his time to the Noble Art."

"Towards the end of 1930," said Tommy, "I realised that I had made enough progress to start making some money out of the boxing game, and after giving the thought much consideration I put down thirty pounds when paying off from HMS Royal Oak at Portsmouth and purchased my discharge from the Navy."

"I remember my mother being a little bit annoyed because he was coming out of the Navy," recalled Frances, "but he had people advising him what his qualities were as a boxer and it was worth him coming out of the Navy to get where he wanted."

Once free of his naval duties, Watson buckled down to serious training under the expert tuition of Alec Lambert, yet he never forgot one important tenet of naval lore. Lord Fisher had laid down a rule to be obeyed in all naval combats, viz., to hit first, to hit hard, and to hit often. Ex-Seaman Watson followed that rule to the letter as he steamed into combat in the rings of Kilburn, Paddington, Shoreditch, and Shepherds Bush.

Irishman Jack Garland landed in London with a great flourish but he was well beaten by Watson over fifteen rounds, and when he asked for more, the Geordie hammered him from pillar to post for a seventh round stoppage. Sheffield's Joe Cadman, who had held Seaman to a draw earlier in the year, thought he could do better in a rematch. He was wrong!

They met at Lime Grove Baths, fifteen rounds at 9 stone 4 lbs, with Tommy scaling 9 st 3 1/2 lbs. But Cadman missed the weigh-in and when he stepped on the scales that night the bar settled at 9 st 9 lbs. Watson calmly waived the forfeit, climbed into the ring, and forced the fight all the way, scoring with left hooks to the jaw and punishing body blows. Joe fought back desperately and had his best round in the tenth when he landed crisp punches under the heart. Watson turned the pressure up over the last five rounds however to finish a good winner.

Saturday night, 13 December 1930, saw Tommy back in the Newcastle ring for the first time since his victory over Harry Best just over two years earlier. There had been a few changes on the local scene since then and the ring in which Watson would face Nash Shakespeare of Wakefield was in the New St James's Hall. The old arena had been rebuilt and re-opened just seven months previously by Mr John Jacob Paget, a successful builder and contractor from Washington in County Durham where he had a reputation as a fine sportsman.

As a young man, J J Paget was no mean performer on the athletic tracks around the North East, beating Billy Reed after Reed had beaten the great Downer. Another fine sprinter to get a good view of Paget's heels was Billy Hogg, the Sunderland footballer who started a 5 to 2 on favourite when they clashed at the Penshaw Hill sports. Paget also starred at football and cricket as well as being a great boxing fan.

Ironically it was a nationwide campaign against boxing in Great Britain that gave birth to the original St James's Hall in Newcastle, one of the finest purpose-built boxing arenas in the country. In 1908, the fight game was thriving in Newcastle where the Monday and Saturday night bills drew capacity crowds to Ginnett's Circus, an old amphitheatre next to the Olympia Theatre in Northumberland Road, where the promoters were Will Curley, the great Newcastle boxer who fought George Dixon for the world featherweight title in 1899, and the Baker brothers, Dick, Tom, and Billy, along with Tom Murphy.

Ginnett's Circus formed part of the Magdalene Estate which was administered by the Schools and Charities Committee with the income being devoted to various charities. However, when the anti-boxing campaign gained ground, spearheaded by certain religious zealots, the administrators of the estate became so anxious that they felt it would not be right for them to allow boxing to be staged at the hall.

The promoters were informed accordingly and started looking around the city for alternative premises, determined that boxing would survive in Newcastle. Eventually they found what seemed an ideal place, an engineering shop in Gallowgate owned by Mr George Donkin. Negotiations were soon completed and work began to build a first class boxing hall.

On 6 September 1909, St James's Hall opened for boxing, with all the very latest facilities and seating for almost 3,000. With prices from one shilling to ten shillings (5p to 50p) the crowds rolled up to see a fine bill topped by Spennymoor middleweight Tom Lancaster, still Curley's greatest attraction. Tom Murphy had gone to London where he secured the services of Young Johnson, an American fighter with a reputation as a knockout specialist who had just beaten Gunner Moir. Lancaster beat him at every phase of the game to run out an easy winner.

Like Young Johnson, the anti-boxing lobby lost their fight, and the city's brand new boxing hall was on its way to becoming the Mecca for the sport on Tyneside, indeed in the North-East. Some twenty years later, after a benefit show in June 1929 for Tom Murphy, manager and leading referee at the hall, Will Curley disposed of the property to Mr J J Paget, the Washington contractor, who immediately set about demolishing the old place.

Within a year the New St James's Hall was ready to open, with every one of its 4,000 seats giving a clear view of the ring and standing room for a further thousand patrons. On opening night, 12 May 1930, the crowds were so great that the turnstiles failed to operate and the police had to be called. Local fighter George Willis, who had actually been employed in the construction of the hall, had the honour of winning the first fight to be staged there when he beat Farmer Jackson of Doncaster. Top of the bill was a fifteen rounds heavyweight contest with Frank Fowler of York giving a boxing lesson to Maurice Griselle, the French champion.

Griselle, the first champion to be beaten at the Gallowgate hall, was by no means the last, for Mr Paget not only kept his promise to bring the best to the Newcastle ring, he managed to find men to beat them with such regularity that the hall became known as the Graveyard of Champions.

Patrons at the Gallowgate arena on a cold December night in 1930 saw a champion in the making when Seaman Watson returned to his local ring with a vengeance. Nash Shakespeare had a weight advantage over the Byker lad but he trailed in every other department. The Yorkshireman was sent reeling to the canvas four times in the third round, the bell saving him on the last knockdown, and when he failed to come off his stool for round four the referee awarded the fight to Watson.

"North's New Belt Hope! Seaman Watson Out For Honours!" headlined the following story in the *Newcastle Evening Chronicle* a few days later. "Mr Alec Lambert, the well-known London boxers' trainer, who for many years has been associated with the National Sporting Club, has long cherished the hope that he would some day train the winner of a Lonsdale belt. His wish came very near to being fulfilled when he trained and nursed Mick Hill of Tooting for the bantamweight belt. Hill removed every obstacle except Johnny Brown. That the Tooting man ought to have won that memorable belt match leaves no room for doubt, for after establishing a big points lead, Hill foolishly chose to have a fight and was knocked out in the twelfth round. Hope springs eternal however, and Mr Lambert has a new belt hope in the person of Seaman Watson of Newcastle. True, Watson may have a few stiff hurdles to negotiate 'ere he can qualify for a title match, but those who are best fitted to judge do not hesitate to tell us that Watson will get there sooner or later."

Watson cleared another hurdle at New St James's Hall when he disposed of Oldham's Jim Travis. The Geordie boxed well but some of his hooks and swings were delivered with the open glove and Travis survived until the twelfth round. Then Tommy closed his right glove and slammed it against the Lancashire lad's jaw for the knockout.

If Watson's ring work lacked its usual sparkle that Monday night it was hardly surprising. On Sunday night he was in London boxing fifteen rounds against Francois Machtens at Shoreditch, surviving a late rally by the tough Belgian to win a gruelling contest on points. Then he caught the night train to Newcastle, arriving home early on Monday morning for a few hours sleep before the weigh-in with Travis.

In January 1931, the age-old sporting rivalry between Newcastle and Sunderland once again manifested itself, this time in the boxing

39

ring, when Tommy was matched with Douglas Parker. Unfortunately for the fans of both boxers, the bout took place in London, on a Sunday afternoon at Kilburn's Vale Hall. The reason? Fred Charlton would later venture the opinion that it was possibly because both boys had London-based managers, Watson under Lambert and Parker under Nick Cavalli. Whatever the reason, north-east fans missed a cracking contest!

When Duggie Parker collapsed and died a few weeks before Christmas 1965, aged just fifty-seven, veteran Newcastle matchmaker Joe Shepherd told me, "Parker was undoubtedly one of the finest fighters never to win a title. He fought three minutes of every round and gave it everything he had. And he was never more dangerous than when he was hurt. A truly grand ring warrior."

Joe's words were echoed by Fred Charlton. "Parker was aggressive, he punched hard with either hand, and altogether possessed such a variety of dashing ring moves that the customers always left the halls fascinated. The great Len Johnson matched Duggie with Young Dusty and immediately recognised Parker's scrapping sagacity. When Duggie was declared the winner, Johnson said to me, 'This boy could be a sensation.'"

Duggie Parker was a sensation, never more so than the night he faced Nipper Pat Daly at Sunderland's Holmeside Stadium in June 1929. Charlton, who made the match over fifteen rounds at 8 st 9 lbs, recalled what happened that night.

"Duggie leapt towards Daly, and downed him for nine with the first punch of the encounter, a left hook to the jaw. Pat rose unsteadily, instinctively sticking out his long left to Parker's face. Crash! A right to Daly's chin and Pat is taking another count, this time for eight. Pat is now a sitting duck, and a right uppercut puts him down for the limit. A three-punch fight! What punches, though. No man could have lived with Parker on that memorable evening."

Newcastle fans will never forget the night Parker faced Johnny Cuthbert in the ring at New St James's Hall. Cuthbert was British featherweight champion that September night in 1931 and if he hadn't insisted on the match being made at two pounds over the class limit he would have left the ring an ex-champion.

Cuthbert was sent to the canvas in round two for a six count and he was down again in the fifth from a sizzling right to the body. Round ten and a crashing right to the jaw decked the Yorkshireman for eight and Parker finished it in the next round with another right to the jaw. The Graveyard of Champions had claimed another victim!

Johnny Cuthbert was also the target for Seaman Watson when he tangled with Parker that Sunday afternoon in London and he wasn't about to be side-tracked by his north-east rival. Tommy cut out the pace in a fast opening round, working to head and body, but he was soon alerted to the danger in Parker's punches when a sizzling right just scraped his chin.

Watson was not so lucky in the second round when a terrific swing to the body dropped him to one knee. He was quickly back on his feet however and back in the fight, taking the action to the Scot from Sunderland. The speed and ringcraft of Watson was putting points on his side of the scorecard and in the sixth, a thudding left-right to the head floored Parker for eight.

Duggie fought back on regaining his feet, hammering hooks to the mid-section, but another vicious right hook to the jaw staggered him before the bell. Watson was in the driving seat now and his superior boxing and hitting ability with both hands brought him to the finish line a worthy winner. But Duggie Parker had proved himself a tough, game rival who battled stubbornly every inch of the way. They would meet again.

7

UNCLE JOHN

"Our Tommy had a wonderful manager and promoter," remembers Frances, "I knew them very well, Alec Lambert and Mr Mortimer. They used to come to my mother's home after the fights at New St James's Hall. She would have had her oven on all day, making rabbit pie, stottie cakes, everything you could think of, and the table would be laid with a beautiful white linen tablecloth. They were lovely people and they thought the world of my mother. After one of Tommy's big fights, I remember, they brought her champagne. Jane Eleanor thought that was lovely. I can picture Mr Mortimer even now, with his horn-rimmed glasses and his lily white hair."

Born in Southampton, John Edwin Mortimer settled in Portsmouth shortly after the Great War where he soon became known for his boxing and wrestling shows at the Connaught Drill Hall. He was a tireless worker for charity and supported the Abbey House Orphanage School at Romsey for many years.

"I had my eye on a good boy in Nobby Baker who I thought would make a world beater," he would recall some years later. "He fought for me often at the Drill Hall where he was known as the Rhondda's Toy Bulldog. A colourful little fellow, always going in for a fight, he beat some good men. He went to Premierland as a substitute for Selwyn Davies and stopped Nipper Pat Daly, in Nipper's next fight after losing to Seaman Watson.

"By January 1931, Watson was making a good name for himself, being under manager Alec Lambert. My matchmaker Jim Croucher arranged a fight between Watson and Baker at nine stones and they met at the Connaught Hall. To my utter astonishment, Tommy well defeated the game little Welsh boy over twelve rounds. After the fight, I asked Lambert what he intended doing with Watson, then got to know Tommy and found him to be a likeable boy, a great character, and the soul of honour."

From then on, Mortimer, or Uncle John as he was affectionately known in the fight game, worked ceaselessly on Watson's behalf to help the tough little ex-sailor from Newcastle make the transition from battleship to championship, something Watson never forgot.

"I know that but for the persistence of Mr Alec Lambert, my manager, and Mr John Mortimer, my claims for a crack at the featherweight title would never have been recognised by the Board of Control and I would have been forced to remain in the background."

A couple of weeks after beating Baker, Tommy improved on his previous win over Jim Travis, this time stopping the Oldham man in eight rounds at the Rochester Casino. He licked Victor Cohen of Egypt in five rounds at The Ring, Blackfriars, but came out of the fight with sore hands and pulled out of a bout with Evan Lane of Wales. He wanted to be fighting fit for his meeting back in Newcastle with Teddy Brown.

From Forest Hall, Brown was called the pitman's champion and he had considerable local backing for the contest with Watson which was to be staged at the city's Festival Hall, in Prudhoe Street. A week before the fight, Tommy was working in the gym when he was approached with an offer of £100 to lose the fight against Brown.

"I told the bloke, who I knew was linked with a local bookie, to get lost!" he recalled grimly. "I was keen on hitting the championship jackpot, more than a measly hundred quid."

The fight took place on 13 March 1931, Friday the 13th, which proved unlucky for Teddy Brown. Still troubled by a mouth injury from his last fight at Liverpool, Brown nevertheless pronounced himself fit for the fray, and the *Newcastle Journal* reported, "A large audience manifested a warm interest in these two local aspirants for honours in the featherweight class."

Brown tried infighting from the first bell and they stood head to head, both punching to the body, but whenever they broke clear it was Watson who showed himself superior in direct hitting and aggression. Again and again Watson broke through Brown's guard with a straight left and landed right hooks to the head. The Forest Hall fighter took his punishment gamely and was almost knocked out in round thirteen, but he was still there when the final bell rang with Watson a worthy points winner.

Lambert and Mortimer had agreed a return match between Watson and Nobby Baker at Rochester, but the little Welshman pulled out of the contest and Tommy found himself in the Casino ring with Bert Swaddle. After ten punishing rounds Bert had had enough and retired, leaving Watson the winner of a fight he would rather not have had. He would much rather have been in Newcastle that Monday night in March.

Appearing at the New St James's Hall was the great Panama Al Brown, bantamweight champion of the world, matched over fifteen rounds with Sunderland favourite Douglas Parker, Tommy's recent victim with whom he was scheduled to fight a return in the Newcastle ring a week later. The Byker lad would have jumped at the chance of fighting Brown but all he could do was read about it next morning when he arrived back on Tyneside.

The Panamanian was a truly remarkable fighter, standing five-eleven in his socks yet he could make the bantamweight limit of 8st 6lbs with ease. In the words of *Ring Magazine* publisher Nat Fleischer, Brown "possessed a reach that recalled the boast of Rob Roy MacGregor, famed Scottish swordsman and outlaw, who, history says, 'could garter his hose without stooping!'"

Fabled American journalist A J Liebling, in one of his celebrated boxing essays, described Panama Al thus after watching him knock out a Frenchman in Paris. "He was black, skinny, and had a long, pointed head. Two thirds of his length was legs, and he had long arms swinging from shoulders like a crossbeam. His torso was so narrow that his heart had standing room only."

On the morning of the Parker fight, the world champion and his American manager Dave Lumiansky were given a conducted tour of the *Newcastle Evening Chronicle* offices by works manager Frank Parsons and boxing writer George J Ogilvie. Under his GJO byline, Ogilvie had covered sports for the *Chronicle* for forty-odd years, but he got little more than an enigmatic smile from Panama Al during his visit.

"What does it feel like to be a world's champion?" he asked.

"Oh, it is all right, you know," Brown replied quietly. "I do like to drive a high power motor."

Panama Al Brown preferred to let his fists do the talking for him, and that night in the Gallowgate ring they spoke eloquently. Duggie Parker got their message but he did manage to prolong the conversation until round eleven before he succumbed.

"The KO seemed to me," wrote GJO in next day's *Chronicle*, "to be a pull in with the right and a short cross with the left to the jaw. The punch did not travel a great distance but it stung on the point and beat the timekeeper."

Parker had waged his usual sterling battle, making a good start against the world champion, but Brown's phenomenal reach controlled the action and his class told as the rounds ticked by. Duggie was on the canvas several times before the knockout.

Yet a few days later, GJO observed in the *Chronicle*, "Considering the punishment he took from Al Brown, I must say that Douglas Parker appears to be in fine trim for his fight with Seaman Watson at the New St James's Hall on Monday. Parker has clamoured for a return ever since the ex-seaman outpointed him in London, and though Duggie is confident that he will prove Watson's master, his chances of success would have been much brighter had not this bout followed so soon after the Al Brown fight."

But Parker seemed untroubled at the weigh-in, where he scaled 9st 0½lb against 9st 2lbs for Watson. "It is silly to say that I should not fight Watson so soon after my contest with Al Brown," he said. "As a matter of fact I have done more thinking than real work during the past week for this fight. I have aimed at keeping myself fit mentally, as well as physically."

"Don't you worry about me," said Watson, "I look upon this as the biggest fight in my life so far, and know exactly what Duggie is capable of. But he will not beat me!"

Nor did he. The *Journal* reported next morning, "Possessing the more muscular physique as well as the more direct style in attack, Watson took the first six rounds with brilliant left hand work and solid right hooks. Parker was effective with his counters, especially with the left hand, and he forced the action in rounds eight and nine.

"Again in the eleventh he roused the hopes of his supporters when in a series of fierce exchanges, hard rights to the head and body dropped Watson for a count of nine. He survived to the bell and came up strong for the twelfth, hitting Parker with powerful counters as Douglas tried to cash in on his success of the previous round. In the final three rounds Watson took command to come out a good winner."

That second victory over Duggie Parker brought Watson's professional record to 75 fights with only two defeats, both at the hands of Bristol lightweight George Rose, and it took a virus to stop his incredible run of success. A virus and a guy named Volante.

Dominico Volante was born of Italian parents in Gerrard Street in Liverpool, one of eight children. He started fighting at school and soon became known as one of the toughest kids in the neighbourhood, but every time he came home after a street fight, he got a belting from his father. He was determined to be a fighter however and upon hearing of a novice flyweight tournament being held at Manchester, young Dominic set out to walk the forty miles, along with two of his pals.

It took them three days and nights and they earned a few shillings along the way, Dominic playing his mouth organ and his pals begging for pennies. Young Volante won the competition and sold his medal to buy food for their return home, where he received such a beating from his father he couldn't sit down for a week!

But the boxing bug had well and truly bitten young Dominic and he became a professional boxer, having his first contest at the famed Liverpool Stadium. A two-fisted crowd pleaser, Volante soon became a favourite of the Stadium crowd and in a long career lost only 22 of some 223 fights, beating sixteen champions along the way at various stages of their careers, among them Nel Tarleton, Harry Corbett, Johnny Cuthbert, and Johnny Curley. But when he got a crack at the British featherweight title in May 1930, champion Cuthbert beat him on points. Liverpool promoter Johnny Best Jnr called Dom, "one of the greatest fighters this city has produced."

"I was fixed to fight for what I consider to be my first big purse," recalled Watson years later. "That was £50 for eight three-minute rounds at the Royal Albert Hall against that great little battler Dom Volante from Liverpool. That fight was secured for me by Mr Lambert who was approached by Ted Broadribb."

The Albert Hall tournament that Wednesday night in April 1931 was in aid of the Greater London Fund for the Blind and was to be topped by Jack Hood against Alex Morin. In the event, Hood was indisposed and his place was taken by George Brown.

"When Watson got his first big break, a match at the Albert Hall, it seemed that he was really on the championship trail," wrote

46

Gilbert Odd some time later. "It was unfortunate for Watson that he suffered an attack of tonsillitis a week before the fight, in fact his doctor told him that he would be well advised to ask for a postponement.

"But so keen was Tommy to get into the big time that he would not hear of crying off, even though the opposition was to be provided by the redoubtable Dom Volante, well known on Merseyside for his dynamic punching powers.

"Before the fight was a minute old, the Liverpool lad had landed a vicious right to the chin that bowled over Watson like a shot rabbit. He was up at six and from then on fought an uphill battle against a man who was determined to put his rival away for keeps. Tommy was on the canvas seven more times before his seconds retired him midway through the sixth round. While he was on his feet he outboxed Volante without difficulty, but Dom would not be denied and his swiping rights kept coming over and connecting. The crowd rose to the gallant sailor as he kept getting up and he received a storm of cheering as he went disappointedly to his dressing room."

Some time later, Norman Hurst wrote in the *Sunday Graphic*, "My introduction to Seaman Tommy Watson was rather an unusual one. He was sent head-long through the ropes at the Royal Albert Hall by a punch from Dom Volante of Liverpool and only my upflung arms prevented him from landing like a sack of coals on my head. I remember thinking then, and I probably wrote, that there wasn't a lot to this sailor fellow.

"I did know however that the spirit had been stronger than the flesh, that it was sheer will power that sent Watson into the ring while still suffering from the flu and against all doctor's orders when really he should have been in bed."

"I should never have entered the ring," Watson later admitted. "I was suffering from tonsillitis, flu, and an abcess in the ear, with a temperature of 103! I remember standing in the ring facing an opponent who, to me, was a blurred object just hitting me how and when he liked. But I made up my mind to fight because the tournament was in aid of a very deserving charity." Charity never had a braver champion.

8

THE GEORDIE CHAMPION

"When leaving the navy," said Watson, "I had made Gillingham, my wife's hometown, my temporary headquarters. But to me there is no place to compare with Newcastle and I always looked forward to the time when I would be able to return north and settle down. My chance came when I was offered the managership of the New Hawk Inn which stood at the bottom of Byker Bank. I agreed to take the post and lost no time moving my home from Gillingham to Newcastle."

The man who put Tommy behind the bar was Mr Ned Wilkinson, the one-time cycling champion. In fact the New Hawk Inn had quite a sporting background. Built in the early 1880s as a free house, the pub was at one time run by Mr Bob Gray, former champion sculler on the River Tyne and in his later years a popular referee for the river races which took place from Hawthorn Leslies yard up to Scotswood.

Manager Alec Lambert kept Watson out of the ring for seven weeks after that disastrous meeting with Dom Volante and it was 10 June 1931 before Seaman climbed through the ropes again in serious combat, beating Frenchman Julian Verbist over twelve rounds at Oxford. Then it was back to Newcastle for a local derby match with Byker rival Benny Sharkey.

"Make no bones about it," Sharkey once told me, "I liked boxing. But if there had been easier ways of making good money in my younger days, I might never have stepped in the ring."

Like Tommy Watson, Benny was one of nine children. His father, Leon Goldwater, was the eldest son of an immigrant Jewish bootmaker who settled in Leeds. They were hard times and to ease the burden on his family Leon enlisted in the army at seventeen. It was while in service that he started boxing and upon his release became a professional, taking the name of the old American heavyweight Tom Sharkey.

He fought all over England and Scotland, working on the markets and rearing a family as he went. They were in Glasgow when

48

Benjamin was born and he was still a child when the family moved to Newcastle, settling in Byker. Benny's brothers Freddy and Willie had eagerly followed their father into the boxing ring but young Benny had other ideas. Determined to have a trade at his fingertips, he declared he would be a bricklayer and began his apprenticeship upon leaving school at fourteen.

But destiny had already decreed that the dark-eyed young Jewish boy would become the greatest of the fighting Sharkeys from Byker. Benny was lying on the couch one night after a hard spell on a local building site when one of his brothers burst into the room, shouting, "Come on Benny, father says you have got to box tonight!"

"What!" cried Benny. "Box! Why, I don't know anything about it." But he did know that father had to be obeyed and off he went to the Byker Stadium where a novice competition was being held. One of the entrants had failed to turn up so old Tom had entered Benny, and much to everyone's surprise, most of all Benny's, he won the tournament!

"What will you have as a prize, young Sharkey!" asked the promoter, "a silver medal or half-a-crown!" Benny took the money and so began a professional career that saw him cross gloves with the biggest names in the business, including eleven men who held world, European, or British championships. He beat six of them!

He was only nineteen when he whipped British bantamweight champion Teddy Baldock over fifteen rounds at New St James's Hall in Newcastle. When Bradford referee Harry Jennings held up Sharkey's glove that September night in 1930, the champion stood in his corner seemingly amazed, while Benny, elated at his success, raised his arms to the cheering crowd before rushing over to shake hands with Baldock.

Although two pounds the lighter man, Baldock had decided advantages in height and reach and was a firm favourite when the gong summoned them for round one. But it was Sharkey who made the running, forcing the champion back with a vicious left swing to the head. Again in the second Benny punched Baldock into the ropes and it was not until the fifth that Teddy got into the fight.

In the seventh Baldock hammered Sharkey across the ring and he was again on top in the eighth when a heavy left from Benny bloodied his mouth. But the Byker lad was feeling the pace and Baldock fought like the champion he was in rounds eleven and twelve. He couldn't keep it going however and Sharkey turned in a sizzling final round to snatch the verdict.

Many years later, Benny recalled for me that glorious night when he beat the champion. "The deafening cheers of the crowd, the scrambling to shake my hand, the enthusiastic scenes that lasted for almost half-an-hour, will always remain among the happiest memories of my experiences in the world of boxing."

News of Sharkey's sensational victory over the British champion set the wires buzzing and promoter Jeff Dickson booked him for his Royal Albert Hall bill which would be topped by Len Harvey and the American Dave Shade. Benny was to meet veteran Kid Socks of Bethnal Green over eight rounds.

"When you enter the Albert Hall for the first time," he remembered, "you feel absolutely lost!" Benny found his way to the ring however and survived a few bad moments to come out a worthy points winner. Mr Dickson liked the young Geordie and signed him to fight Dick Corbett a month later.

"The dressing room I was allotted seemed miles away from the ring," recalled Benny, "and, as I sat there waiting to be called to meet Corbett, I felt as if I was in a dungeon. I was feeling as cold as an iceberg when I was eventually called to enter the ring and to that I attribute my points defeat. I know I did not, could not, give of my best under the strange and rather awe-inspiring conditions."

Benny was back to his brilliant best in April, 1931, when he went back into the Albert Hall ring to fight former world flyweight champion Emile Spider Pladner of France. It was the night Tommy Watson defied the doctors and came a cropper against Dom Volante. Benny evened the score for Byker when he beat the Frenchman over eight rounds, his accurate left hand hitting and superior strength the deciding factors. But what the young Jewish lad remembered most about that night was being invited to dine with Lord Tweedmouth at the Savoy Hotel after the fight.

Back home in Newcastle a newspaper war was raging between the *Evening Chronicle* and the *Evening World,* and on the sports pages a fight was being steamed up between Sharkey and Billy Farrell of Winlaton. The *Chronicle* was backing Farrell while Sharkey had the *World* in his corner, so to speak.

"What those papers said Farrell and I were going to do to each other was nobody's business," remembered Benny. "We didn't actually say anything but it was good for the box office. Some fifteen thousand people turned up at Brough Park to see the fight."

The Farrell supporters in the crowd didn't have much to cheer about as their man sustained a tremendous beating from Sharkey. Benny virtually won the fight in the second minute of the first round when a terrific uppercut sent Farrell crashing to the canvas. Clambering to his feet at eight, Billy was hammered to the deck twice more before the bell saved him. Floored again in round two, the Winlaton warrior fought on gamely but it was an uphill battle.

It ended in round seven when Billy rushed in to close quarters only to be to poleaxed from a tremendous right to the jaw. As the count reached five he got to his knees but couldn't make it any further, rolling over to lie under the bottom rope, whereupon his seconds threw the towel into the ring. His surrender was accepted by referee Jimmy Wilde, the former world flyweight champion, and Benny Sharkey had won another fight.

The Battle of Byker, Seaman Watson versus Benny Sharkey, would take place just down the road at Brough Park Stadium on Tuesday 23 June 1931, over fifteen three-minute rounds at nine stones. It was Race Week in Newcastle and a big crowd was expected to attend the fight after the Gosforth Park meeting.

In his preview of the fight in the *Chronicle*, GJO wrote, "Seaman Watson visited the promoter's office yesterday, and was upset at the rumours which had gained ground that the match was squared. He should not let this trouble him, for the wicked Dame is always busy. Both men are fit and I am convinced that it will be a great clash."

The weigh-in was held at Avery's in the city at two o'clock on the afternoon of the fight with Watson a couple of ounces under nine stones and Sharkey scaling 8st 12lbs 1oz. The *Chronicle's* final summing up said Sharkey would lead quicker and Watson hit harder. Seconds out!

Everything was fine but the weather. Grey, leaden skies hung low over Brough Park and by seven o'clock the rain had started along with the boxing. It became so bad that it was decided to cancel two of the fights in case the main event should be washed out. As it was Watson and Sharkey answered the opening bell in a veritable downpour and both had trouble keeping their feet on the soaking wet canvas.

At the start of the fifth round, Referee Owen Moran, the old-time battler from Birmingham, ordered sawdust to be thrown across the canvas. This improved matters and the pace picked up afterwards. Watson had scored well in the first round with left hands but he was shaken by a hard left hook to the jaw from Sharkey.

From the fifth Benny never let Watson settle down, rushing in to land both hands to the body, and Watson was disturbed by these attacks. During round ten heavy rain sent many spectators running for cover but those who stood their ground enjoyed the best rounds of the fight. Both men hammered away to the body with Sharkey doing well and he almost dropped Tommy in the final round with a heavy right, but the Seaman was seldom in danger of defeat and finished a good points winner.

"It was atrocious weather at Brough Park last Tuesday night," wrote GJO in the *Chronicle*, "but really the great fight between Seaman Watson and Benny Sharkey was a sufficient reward for any inconvenience caused. The result was as I had anticipated, brought about in the way I thought it would. Watson's heavier, and more direct punch, was the telling factor in his victory on points.

"There was little in what he sent over that failed to find the mark, and his right hand digs to Benny's body must have hurt the lad very badly. I had previously expressed the opinion that Sharkey would have the quicker left lead. He had, but his direction was bad, many of his leads went astray, and Watson's heavy counters to the body after every miss, made the verdict, to me, a certainty a long time before Owen Moran, the referee, declared it.

"After such a fight, of course, the men must meet again, and the handicap may be evened if Seaman will come down to about 8st 12lbs. Benny made a great fight of it last Tuesday, especially in the last rounds, but he was beaten by a stronger man with a heavier punch, and, I think, a more calculating brain.

"Mr Paget has already secured Watson's signature, and the suggested date for a return fight is 10 August. I would like to see the men meet again, and it would now appear to rest with Sharkey.

The other night the Seaman told me he is ready for Sharkey again at any time."

After a short holiday in London, Benny and his father sat down with promoter John Paget to iron out the details. The return fight was announced for Monday 17 August, fifteen-threes at nine stone, in the ring at the New St James's Hall. Wisely, Mr Paget had decided against an open air promotion after the Brough Park deluge.

Both men prepared at the Bridge End Gym in Byker, Watson doing his work in the mornings and evenings while Sharkey trained in the afternoon. On the day of the fight both looked the picture of health as they stripped for the scales in front of a big crowd at the Gallowgate arena. Watson was exactly the same weight as he had been for the first bout, just a couple of ounces inside the stipulated weight of nine stones.

When Mr Paget announced Sharkey's weight as 8st 13½lbs, Benny said loud enough to be heard by those gathered around the scales, "Yes, with my singlet and slips on."

"Well, put him on the scales stripped," snapped Watson.

"In those trifling observations," wrote GJO in the *Chronicle*, "I noticed the needle in the match. Two fitter men I have not seen go to the scales, and not for a long time have I known so much money loose for gambling purposes. Watson, this afternoon, was favourite at 5 to 4 on, but after fifty pounds to forty had been taken, I was told that there was another £300 for Sharkey at the same odds. These, however, appear to be difficult to get.

"Sharkey will spend the interim in a game of billiards, a reasonable meal, and a rest. Watson told me that he was only going to have a quiet time and live his normal life. 'I'm fit, and I think I will win again,' he observed in that solemn monotone that is one of his characteristics."

It was not common knowledge but Seaman Tommy had an added incentive to win this fight...his mother was going to be there. She had made up her mind on the night of their first meeting when Tommy's brothers arrived home from Brough Park to tell her how Mrs Goldwater had sat through the downpour and kept up a barrage of voluble support for her Benny as he battled the elements and his Byker rival.

"Strange as it may seem," Benny would recall, long after he

retired, "my most enthusiastic supporter was my mother, yet on the first occasion she saw me fight, she ran out of the hall during the first round!"

Jane Eleanor had never seen Tommy fight, but when her sons told her about Mrs Goldwater, who lived just a couple of streets away, she decided to be there for the return fight and support her son.

"That night," recalled Frances, "she dressed in her finest, as she did when going anywhere special, and off she went to New St James's Hall to see our Tommy fight Sharkey. Well, once the fight got started, both the mothers were shouting encouragement to their sons, and everybody around them was highly amused by it all. But my mother became so excited she had to go to the toilet, and she stayed there until it was all over. So she missed most of the fight but she had the last laugh on Mrs Goldwater because our Tommy won! And that was the first and last time that Jane Eleanor went to one of Tommy's fights."

New St James's Hall was packed to the rafters that night and they gave a big hand to Douglas Parker when he climbed into the ring before the fight to issue a challenge to the winner. It was also announced that similar challenges had been received from Welshman Phineas John and British featherweight champion Johnny Cuthbert of Sheffield, who wanted a match at 9st 2lbs in order to protect his title.

The fight had been advertised as for the North of England feather-weight championship and Sharkey was hoping for victory this time as he was booked for a fighting trip to South Africa, leaving on the 28 August. But his hopes were dashed along with those of his supporters as Watson came through with a fine win, although it must be said that Benny would never fight harder and still come out on the losing end.

Watson held a slight advantage in all physical aspects and early on it was apparent that Sharkey was up against one of the toughest opponents of his career. Benny's strong points had always been aggressiveness and heavy punching at close quarters, but tonight he met his master in both respects. It was soon evident that Watson would only be beaten by a knock-out and in round after round he added to his points total.

Sharkey raised the hopes of his supporters in round eight when he crossed a vicious right that was just off the target and followed with a left hook that unbalanced Watson. Tommy's ring generalship stood him in good stead however and the bell found him holding his own in a heavy punching spell on the ropes.

Benny made a great effort in the last two rounds and landed several damaging shots to the body but Watson was always coming back with his own punches and the final bell found them locked together in the centre of the ring. Watson was a popular and deserving winner, and as he made his way to the dressing room, thunderous cheers reverberated around John Paget's palace of punch as the crowd hailed their champion...Seaman Tommy Watson, The Geordie Champion!

9

THE COCK OF THE NORTH

Alec Lambert was adamant. When British featherweight champion Johnny Cuthbert said he was quite willing to fight Seaman Watson so long as the match was made at 9st 2lbs to protect his title and Lonsdale Belt, Lambert announced to the press that he would only allow his man to meet the champion if the fight was made at the featherweight limit of nine stones and the title was on the line.

Enter Douglas Parker. Since his second defeat by Watson earlier in the year, the Scot from Sunderland had been boxing well and had just knocked out Dom Volante, the tough Liverpool man who had beaten Watson in London. Parker jumped at the chance of meeting Cuthbert in an overweight match and Newcastle promoter John Paget announced that the fight would take place at the New St James's Hall on Monday 14 September 1931, fifteen three-minute rounds at 9st 2lbs.

Still only twenty-six, Johnny Cuthbert was in his second reign as British featherweight champion and had already won a Lonsdale Belt outright. As a lad of thirteen in Sheffield, he started boxing at Sunday school where the Rev. Harold Ewbank taught boxing after class. Johnny's father, the landlord of The Old Brown Cow in Radford Street, set up a gym at the back of the pub and young Johnny was on his way.

A professional at seventeen, Cuthbert was British champion at twenty-one, beating Johnny Curley on a narrow decision over 20 rounds. A year later, in March 1928, Johnny lost the title to Harry Corbett. The return two months later was noteworthy as being the first British title match over fifteen rounds and the draw decision the first in a Lonsdale Belt contest.

Johnny regained the championship in May 1929 and made the belt his own when beating Dom Volante in London. Lured to Liverpool for a defence against Nel Tarleton, Cuthbert hung on to his title when the referee gave them a draw. The Liverpool man's clever boxing at long range was cancelled out by the champion's work at close quarters.

When the National Sporting Club offered Johnny a shot at Al Foreman's British and Empire lightweight titles, the Sheffield man jumped at the chance and, although conceding half-a-stone, he climbed off the floor three times to hold the hard-punching Foreman to a draw. Incidentally, that was Cuthbert's third draw in a British title bout.

Something of a globetrotter, Johnny was a big favourite in Paris where he boxed a draw against the great Panama Al Brown and scored a sensational fifth round knockout over Gustave Humery. This was the man Duggie Parker faced in the Newcastle ring that September night in 1931. If the Sunderland man could beat the champion, he would put himself right back in the running for a title bout.

Sitting quietly in a ringside seat, smoking one of his favourite cigarettes, was Seaman Tommy Watson, his challenge to the winner for a match at nine stones already announced to the big crowd.

The fireworks started in round one. Parker banged over a hard left to the jaw and Cuthbert staggered off balance. He fought back but was rocked by another thudding left just before the bell. Round two and Parker came out fast, left jabs making the champion blink, a solid left hook then a lovely right to the jaw and Cuthbert was down!

Up at eight, Johnny fought back like a tiger and he kept out of trouble through rounds three and four. But in the fifth Parker slammed a terrific left into the body and Cuthbert was down again, for six this time. In the seventh a tremendous uppercut almost took Cuthbert's head off. He rallied well, but this night belonged to Duggie Parker.

In the tenth round, the bell saved Cuthbert after a savage right to the jaw sent him crashing to the canvas. Johnny came out for round eleven but he was boxing on borrowed time. A thudding right dropped him in a heap and it looked like the end. But Sheffield steel is tough and Cuthbert was on his feet at eight, gloves up, ready for his tormentor.

He didn't have to go looking for Duggie Parker. With the crowd screaming his name, Duggie exploded a sledgehammer right to the heart and Cuthbert fell like a tree before the axe. This time he didn't get up and the Graveyard of Champions had claimed another victim. At ringside Tommy Watson stubbed out another cigarette, and as he made his way to the exit he knew he would have to fight Duggie Parker again, the man who had just knocked out the British champion. Three days later Mr Paget announced that the third meeting between Watson and Parker would take place in the Newcastle ring on Monday 5 October in a match made at nine stone.

"I don't think I am exaggerating when I say that this is the most important local contest that we have had in the North for some years," wrote GJO in the *Chronicle*. "Here we have two men who are as near the featherweight championship as makes no matter and they are fighting at the championship weight. Mr Paget tells me that the bookings already are better than they have been for any fight that he has promoted."

Both men buckled down to serious training, Parker at Jack Casey's gym in Sunderland where he was ably assisted by Casey and Billy Smith as chief sparmate, and Watson at Teddy Brown's well-equipped gym at the Newcastle end of the New Tyne Bridge. Sparring with the Byker lad were Brown and Jim Falcus, who must have wondered at the wisdom of his instructions to Tommy that he should under no circumstances pull his punches.

"I've never known Watson hit harder!" old Jim told a reporter.

"It is not the fighting that worries," confided the Seaman. "It is the training for it."

A few days before the fight, the sports pages carried two interesting items of news. From Liverpool came a report of Nel Tarleton's great points victory over Johnny Cuthbert to win the British featherweight championship, and from Paris came a Reuters bulletin stating that Gustave Humery of France had knocked out Douglas Parker in four rounds at the Salle Wagram!

As promoter Paget reached for the aspirin bottle, the *Newcastle Journal* printed a follow-up to the Paris story headed, "BARKER, NOT PARKER! Owing to an unfortunate error in Reuters Agency, Douglas Parker was reported to have been knocked out by Gustave Humery in Paris. It was not Parker, but Albert Barker who was beaten by the Frenchman. The report had caused some consternation in North East boxing circles as Parker was contracted to meet Watson in the Newcastle ring on Monday."

Two slices of toast, a poached egg, and two cups of tea. That was the breakfast prepared by Kitty Watson at the New Hawk Inn for husband Tommy on the morning of his big fight, and it also transpired that Douglas Parker enjoyed the same breakfast at his Sunderland home. By another quirk of coincidence, both men scaled exactly the same weight at two o'clock that afternoon when they met at the New St James's Hall, 8st 12 lbs. Stepping down from the scales, Parker sank his teeth into a juicy pear as Watson had his weight checked. The ritual completed, Tommy slipped back into his dressing gown and drank half-a-pint of egg mixture.

"I was rather surprised to see that both men were a pound-and-a-quarter inside the featherweight limit," observed GJO in that night's *Chronicle*, "and hope that their preparatory work has not been overdone in their anxiety to keep within nine stones."

It was Standing Room Only that night at the Gallowgate arena with the crowd estimated at some 5,000 by the time Watson and Parker entered the ring at nine o'clock. Referee Tom Murphy lost no time getting them started and they went to work straight away with punches to the body. Parker was very aggressive and a short right to the head unbalanced Watson. Tommy fought back and a series of punishing straight lefts steadied Parker, but Duggie ripped home a terrific right that almost floored Watson and Tommy was on the defensive at the bell.

Coming out for the second he got behind his left jab and steadied Parker time after time as he tried to mount another big attack. The man from Sunderland was too eager and his timing was off but he did score with heavy punches to the body. Round three was a good one for Watson as he boxed cleverly, his defence sound against Parker's powerful blows and his counter punches finding the mark.

The first big thrill came in the fifth round. Fighting ferociously, Parker absorbed heavy punches to the head to force his way through Watson's guard and a tremendous right to the jaw smashed Seaman to the boards. Tom Murphy's count reached nine before the Byker lad was back on his feet and the bell rang before Parker could do any further damage. Tommy appeared to have recovered when he came up for round six and he kept out of trouble, good left hand work winning him the round.

By the seventh he was back on top, solid lefts and countering rights pulling Parker up in his tracks, and it was Watson's round as was the eighth. But Douglas Parker was a volcano waiting to erupt and a minute into round nine it happened. A wicked left to the body crumpled Watson to the canvas. The punch looked low and although Tommy beat the count he was badly shaken and Parker took the round.

He roared out for the tenth and a savage right to the jaw dropped Watson for a count of seven and he was floored again as the Sunderland man tried desperately to finish it. Then Watson staged a fantastic rally that brought the fans to their feet and almost took Parker off his. A veritable avalanche of leather engulfed Duggie and he was a happy man when the sound of the bell penetrated his befogged brain.

Round eleven and it was obvious that Seaman was lasting the furious pace the better of the two men, Parker looking the worse for wear as he returned to his stool. He still looked groggy coming up for the twelfth and Watson, sensing the kill, tore in with both fists working overtime. Parker reeled around the ring before falling to the canvas. Gamely he hauled himself up but he was an easy mark for Watson's finishing punches. As Duggie crashed to the deck again, the towel fluttered in from his corner and Tom Murphy raised Watson's glove with six seconds left in the round.

"I suppose I have seen thousands of fights during the last forty years," wrote GJO in the *Chronicle* next day, "and I am sure that I cannot recall one that I anticipated with greater interest or witnessed with greater pleasure...Parker was up against a steady, brainy boxer who refused to allow himself to be rattled...We have got used to the idea that Watson's main asset is his straight left lead, but we were taught last night that he has more behind him than this, and I think there was not a bigger factor in his latest victory than his left hooks, either as leads or counters. How often Parker was more or less unbalanced by this blow. Watson won by his calmness, his steadiness, and his ability to make attack a real means of defence. The way he made the fighting when he was evidently in trouble was the work of a great boxer."

Some years later, with the gloves put away for good, Watson had time to reflect upon his career and some of his fights. "One, at least, will live in my memory forever," he recalled. "It was my third clash with Douglas Parker, and I can pay Duggie the compliment of having made me see more stars than I had ever seen before the fight, or since!

"Phew! How he could hit. I shall never forget the first piledriver that stretched me on the canvas and made the stars dance before my eyes like a fireworks display. If I am asked who was the hardest puncher I ever met, I shall answer unhesitatingly, Duggie Parker. That fight was over fifteen rounds and my end of the purse was £100. I beat Duggie in twelve rounds but believe me there had been many occasions before the end when I thought I had been put down for keeps. Believe me Duggie has a terrific wallop and nobody realised it more than I did when he put me down several times during our fight. I can assure you that when Duggie gets one there, down you go!"

In July 1933, Parker recalled his three fights with Seaman Watson in an article in the *Sunday Sun*. "Though, personally, I have no complaint, I may say that the result of our first meeting at the Kilburn Hall, London, met with some opposition from the spectators. The second and third contests were at the St James's Hall and were among the hardest I have had in the whole of my career. One he won on points and in the other he knocked me out in the twelfth round.

"I don't think I ever fought such a fight as on the last occasion. Previously we had boxed pretty much on the same style, straight left leading with the right for a guard and occasional use. This time, however, I decided to go in, take all Tommy cared to give me, apart from a knockout, so long as I could get in and finish him. I think I was on top, and I know I hurt him when I got him down in the fifth round. Nine out of ten would have been my victim after that punch.

"Watson is a strong man however, and more than strong. He knows all the secrets of generalship. After he had been down he kept on sending out his left. On the other hand, I could not get the idea of a knockout out of my mind. I might have varied my attack, but didn't. I can see the clever Watson tactics now that I look back on the fight. He kept measuring his distance with his straight left without carrying much of a punch. Then he sent over his right from really short range and away I went for the full count.

"It is possible that if I had eased him off a bit instead of plugging away, the result might have been different. My fault was over-

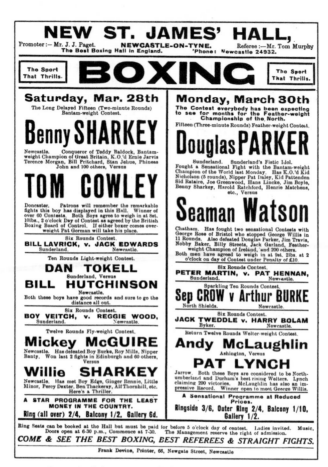

eagerness, and probably not quick enough thinking. His special virtue was coolness and generalship. As near as he was mine, at least as near as I had him, he was never rattled."

"Watson, with Parker's punch, would be a world beater!" That was the view of Tommy Steckles, the dapper local sportsman who was ever ready to back a good man, whether on the running track, the river, or in the ring. A member of the National Sporting Club for many years, Tommy, along with Bill Chambers, thought he had a champion in Jimmy Berry of Dinnington who fought Joe Fox at the Club for the Lonsdale Belt and bantamweight championship of Great Britain. That was in 1915. Now it was 1931 and Tommy Steckles was backing Seaman Tommy Watson to become a champion.

10

THE CONTENDER

The immediate aftermath of the Watson-Parker fight saw North-East pundits and patrons clamouring for another helping, but this dish was not on the menu at the New Hawk Inn down Byker Bank where landlord Seaman Tommy Watson told an *Evening Chronicle* reporter, "I think Duggie is one of the best fellows in the world, but please don't couple my name with his for any future fight. You can tell your readers that I will never fight Parker again, either before or after I meet Nel Tarleton."

Parker's manager, a Mr Eckberg, had already offered to put up a £200 sidestake for another contest under the same conditions, but Alec Lambert was aiming Tommy at the British crown, now sitting on the sleek head of Liverpool's favourite son Nel Tarleton. Besides, Watson had beaten Parker three times in three fights and Duggie, ordered to rest by his doctor, had gone back to Aberdeen to spend some time with his parents.

Wednesday 28 October 1931 found Seaman back in London to meet the tough Belgian featherweight champion Francois Machtens over twelve rounds at Paddington Baths. Tommy had beaten the stocky continental ten months previously in a gruelling fight at Shoreditch and he beat him again even if he failed to sparkle.

"I cannot but record the opinions of one or two Tynesiders who saw the fight," wrote GJO in the *Chronicle*. "According to some of the accounts, Watson won easily; according to his own pals he was just a winner. That is the kind of criticism I like. It is no good playing the game of the ostrich, let us face the facts. From what I have heard I can imagine that the Seaman was playing his own game, pushing out his left against a rugged fighter who wanted to mix matters. I don't blame him. He has a big objective to achieve, and that is the featherweight championship."

Tommy had something else on his mind. Kitty was expecting again, and on 13 November customers at the New Hawk Inn raised their glasses to toast the arrival of a daughter who would be named Joan.

A month later, Watson was in action again at one of his old stamping grounds, the Rochester Casino, where he tangled with Doncaster's Ernie Bicknell in the top-of-the-bill contest. At the weigh-in, Tommy was half-a-pound inside the stipulated 9st 4lbs, but when Bicknell scaled a stone heavier, manager Lambert insisted on claiming the £5 forfeit before allowing his man to enter the ring.

Tommy forced the action from the opening bell, scoring well with his left, and in the second round a thudding right to the jaw dumped Ernie on the canvas for an eight count. The Yorkshireman improved as the fight wore on but Watson was always one step ahead of his man and finished a good winner after twelve rounds.

In his eagerness to prove his worth as a challenger for Tarleton's title, Watson announced that he was ready and willing to meet the featherweight champions of Scotland, Wales, and Ireland. He had already beaten Irish titleholder Jack Garland inside seven rounds, and on 21 December 1931 he faced Peter Cuthbertson, champion of Scotland, in the ring at New St James's Hall.

Although he emerged a clear winner after fifteen rounds, it was generally agreed that Watson had given better displays. He often misjudged punches and sometimes seemed to lack confidence, even if the Scot was a wily customer who demanded respect. The first round, fought at close quarters, was pretty even, and in round two the Scot made Watson miss cleverly and scored with good lefts to the face. Tommy was finding Cuthbertson a difficult target and in the third the Scot worked Watson into a corner where he banged both hands to the body, then slammed a short right to the head.

It was the fourth round before Tommy gave his fans something to shout about, hammering away with both hands to steady the Scot, and in the fifth he found an opening for a crashing right to the jaw. Round six and Watson landed two left hooks but he was hurt by a left to the body and Cuthbertson failed to follow up after knocking his man off balance. Seaman edged the seventh and the eighth was a thriller as he rocked Cuthbertson with heavy rights to the jaw.

The Scot survived as Watson became wild in his efforts to land

64

a finishing punch and Peter was still battling away in the thirteenth after taking two hard rights. He fought well through the last two rounds but at the final bell Watson had managed to hang on to his points lead and was declared the winner.

"One of the brainiest boxers in the game." That was the considered opinion of a veteran ringsider at the Blackfriars Ring after watching Watson take the measure of Battling Sandjack of Egypt in a tremendous battle over fifteen rounds. It was Tommy's first fight of 1932 and a couple of weeks later he was at Lime Grove Baths tangling with Boyo Rees. The man from Aberdare was a fighter of the never-say-die school and he was still coming forward in the last round, but Watson was a good winner.

For his London fights, Seaman always trained at Lambert's Bell Street gym in Marylebone, and it was there he was observed by one of the leading boxing writers of the day, who wrote, "Tommy is a wonderful gym worker and when he is in training for a fight he talks even less than ever. He is very quick in making up his mind and often changes it. He always makes his mind up as to what he will do the next day, doesn't tell anybody, and only trainer Lambert can read his mind. He will come to London to prepare for a fight, but after a couple of days in the metropolis, he will say, 'Alec, I'm going back home to complete my training.' The next day he will arrive at the gym as usual!"

For his next contest, against Welsh champion Ginger Jones at New St James's Hall on 2 May, Watson buckled down to serious training at North Shields, a few miles down the road from his Byker home. However he did break training two weeks before the fight to take a ringside seat at the Gallowgate hall. Topping the bill that Monday night in April was a boxer in whom Tommy had more than a passing interest...Nel Tarleton, featherweight champion of Great Britain. Facing Tarleton over fifteen rounds was Benny Sharkey and Mr Paget had a full house on hand to cheer the Byker lad against the champion. Watson, of course, had twice beaten Sharkey and he watched intently as Tarleton answered the bell against his neighbour.

Promoter Paget was fortunate indeed that night, for he had originally matched Sharkey with Dick Corbett, bantamweight champion of Great Britain, in a non-title fight. Both Corbett and Tarleton were managed at that time by Ted Broadribb.

"I had Corbett matched with Sharkey at 8st 10lbs," recalled Broadribb, "and I was getting 35 percent of a gate I knew would be a good one, for Sharkey was a great attraction on Tyneside. Corbett came to me a week before the fight was scheduled and told me he would not fight at eight-stone-ten. 'Sharkey's got to do eight-eight, or I don't fight,' he told me. At once I pointed out to him, 'There's a £25 weight forfeit and appearance money. If you don't want to go through with it, pay the £25 and I'll give you back your contract.'

"That is exactly what happened, and I wired the promoter and said that Corbett could not box, and asked if Sharkey would take Tarleton, whom I took to Newcastle. Sharkey had beaten Teddy Baldock but he could do nothing with the Liverpudlian, who got £170 for his night's work, an appreciable figure for a substitute in those days."

"Do they like good boxing up here, or real fighting?" Tarleton asked a *Chronicle* reporter when he arrived in Newcastle on the Sunday evening. He had his answer twenty-four hours later when his hand was raised as a clear winner over Sharkey, part of the capacity crowd booing him for failing to score a knockout. The headline in next day's paper told the story of the fight. BENNY SHARKEY IS OUTCLASSED...Magnificent Defence of Nel Tarleton!

Two weeks later Seaman Watson was back at New St James's Hall for the fight with Jones. That afternoon, when Tommy was 1¼ pounds over the stipulated 9st 2lbs, he removed the surplus within an hour, saying that the scales he had been using at North Shields must have been inaccurate.

In the Gallowgate ring that night, the Seaman was in deep water on more than one occasion before he triumphed over the man from Ammanford who was forced to retire after ten rounds with a badly cut left eye. Maybe it was the hiccup at the weigh-in that upset him, maybe it was the three months inactivity.

"Watson fought well below his best form," reported *The Journal* next day, "and if Jones had carried a heavy punch Watson might have been decisively beaten."

In the *Chronicle*, GJO reported, "I am in as much doubt as most of the spectators as to what would have happened if it had come to a points decision. Without keeping a score card, I thought it was very even, but I am told that at times the betting was 2 to 1 on Jones."

Lambert quickly arranged another fight for Tommy and two weeks later he whipped another Welshman in Selwyn Davies at Oxford. At long last the Board of Control were coming to recognise the ability of the man from Newcastle, and a few days after the Davies fight they announced that the managers of Tarleton and Watson had until 9 June to make arrangements for a championship contest.

Broadribb immediately protested at this deadline, claiming that the champion already had commitments that would keep him busy until the end of July. In any case said the manager, he himself was no longer a member of the Board of Control, and Tarleton would not be renewing his licence when it expired. There was no way the fight was going to be arranged within the Board's deadline under these circumstances, so the Stewards invited purse bids to be submitted from interested promoters. Mr Paget made an offer but it was not enough and it was announced that the fight would take place in Liverpool on 18 August.

"While I am naturally delighted at the opportunity to place a second notch on my Lonsdale Belt," Tarleton told a Liverpool reporter, "I do not regard my task as being by any means a cakewalk. I have not seen Watson in action, but I know sufficient about his style, and more particularly his record, to realise that I am in for a hard fight."

At the time of the interview, Tarleton was busy studying a copy of Watson's record, which he showed to the reporter. The name of Julian Verbist of Belgium was underlined.

"The man who can beat Julian Verbist," added the champion, "is somebody to be treated with respect. I know Verbist to be an extremely clever boxer. I know because I could only get a draw when I fought him."

Within a couple of weeks however, the hopes and dreams of Seaman Watson along with those of his supporters were dashed when Broadribb announced that Nel Tarleton was not prepared to defend his title for what was reportedly a £500 purse!

The Board of Control acted immediately and the following announcement was made to the press. "Featherweight

67

championship of Great Britain. Nel Tarleton, having refused to comply with Regulation 31 Para 5 Sub-clauses D and F, declare the above championship title vacant." It meant that Tarleton had, "refused to conform to the regulation which demands that a champion should accept the purse offer which, after invitation had been sent out to all promoters, is received from the highest bidder."

Manager Lambert, anxious to keep Watson ticking over, arranged with Paget for Tommy to box Francois Machtens at New St James's Hall on Monday 19 September. Seaman had beaten the Belgian twice already but Machtens was a popular performer in British rings and he had just beaten Benny Sharkey in Newcastle two weeks previously.

"It was doubtful if he won one round against Watson," reported the *Journal*. "Watson had height and reach advantages over his stocky rival but looked frail by comparison. Watson was on top of the Belgian all the way and was his equal when he forced his way inside...In the eighth round Watson cut loose and several times shook Machtens with rights to the head. Over the last two rounds Watson boxed with caution, and the Belgian's final round effort came to nought."

Nel Tarleton had been inactive since his drawn fight with Panama Al Brown in June, due to a ruptured muscle, but was now back in training and anxious to have his title restored. The Board agreed that Nella would be re-instated as British champion provided terms were agreed for the Watson fight within a month. But Ted Broadribb was still playing his cards close to his chest. The title fight with Tarleton was pencilled in for Liverpool in early November, provided Watson could beat Phineas John in their contest at New St James's Hall on Monday 10 October. Taking a calculated gamble, Lambert and Watson signed for the fight.

Phineas John was a stablemate and frequent sparring partner to Nel Tarleton and a damn good fighter in his own right. From Pentre in the Rhondda, Phineas was a schoolboy boxing champion before going into the mines. At seventeen he joined brothers Eddie and Tommy as a professional fighter, receiving full backing from Mama John who was a great boxing supporter. Phineas proved the star of the family and after winning the Welsh fly and bantamweight titles he moved to London where there were more opportunities for fights. A two-fisted fighter who liked to get close and punch away, he beat men like Cuthbert Taylor, Jackie Brown who would become world flyweight champion, Bert Kirby who became British titleholder, Kid Socks, and British bantamweight champion Kid Pattenden.

The Watson-John fight was scheduled for twelve rounds at 9st 2lbs and at the afternoon weigh-in, the Welshman scaled 9st ³/₄lbs. Watson was within the stipulated weight but Alec Lambert refused to have his actual weight disclosed. When a *Chronicle* reporter asked Ted Broadribb if his fighter could be regarded as Tarleton's "trial man" the manager merely smiled and said, "Take care he does not upset all arrangements."

That night in the Gallowgate ring, John certainly gave the local hero a run for his money. "I am not sure that even Tarleton will give him more trouble than Phineas John gave him last night," wrote GJO in the *Chronicle*. "At times it was well on the carpet that the Welshman would win. This was only after the fifth round when the Seaman was careless in a breakaway and took a nasty left jab to the jaw. The hard fighting that Watson did after this in this round appeared to me a fight of desperation. He knew that he had been caught, and he took the right way out of it.

"He gave punch for punch, haphazard probably, but it had the effect of frustrating John's efforts to carry his advantage to full fruition. I don't want to call Seaman an old war horse, but he did prove what a really good general he is. He calmed down for some rounds after this without giving away any or many points, and, finishing with some wonderful two-handed work, made Referee Murphy's task easier than at one time appeared probable."

"Tommy had to fight harder than ever to get the verdict over Nel Tarleton's sparring partner," reported the *Journal*. "John based his attack on the body with heavy punches but found Watson his equal while at long range Tommy was the better man. In round five Watson left his chin unguarded and John switched a left to the jaw to shake the local man. Watson came back to send the Welshman into the ropes with two left hooks to the head.

"The eighth was a bad round for Watson as John's heavy punches forced him to the ropes but Watson came back in the ninth scoring well with right uppercuts and sharp lefts and Phineas was glad to hear the bell. The final round was a ding-dong affair but Watson's left jabs kept him on top and he took the decision at the bell."

"When they were still quibbling over my claims to a fight with

Tarleton," Tommy recalled a few months later, "they fixed up a fight with John, he's from the same stable. That wise old crow Ted Broadribb was in charge of both. John was sent as a tryout. From his corner Ted Broadribb commanded operations. John was merely there to find my strength. He employed every style known in boxing under the instructions of Broadribb, tried every move, he boxed, he fought, he tried infighting, he tried long range, he ran the whole hog out.

"At that time, my fight with Tarleton for the championship was in abeyance. There was the ever present danger that if I lost to John, bang went my chance of the fight. There were some who said I was foolish to jeopardise my chance of a championship fight by meeting John, but I wanted a fight badly. Did I make elaborate plans, did I nothing! I took him on and blast the consequences. A jolly good job I didn't make plans. He changed his style so frequently during the fight that I had to take him just as he came. Fortunately I have always done that. It is time enough to start making plans when they shout Seconds out!"

"In three months this lad will beat the lot of them," said Broadribb as he said goodnight to Mr Paget, adding that it was practically certain that Watson and Tarleton would fight for the British championship at Liverpool sometime in November. A week later came confirmation that the contest would take place at Liverpool Stadium on Thursday 10 November 1932.

The boy from Byker was overjoyed at the news that at long last he was to get his chance. He had earned it. In 89 pro fights only two men had beaten him, George Rose and Dom Volante, and he was a sick man when he fought the latter. Phineas John had been the final test and he had passed with flying colours. Now all he had to do was beat the champion!

11

THE CHAMPION

In the world of professional boxing, Nel Tarleton was that rare phenomenon, a legend in his own lifetime. Gilbert Odd, Britain's leading historian on the fight game, described the Liverpool idol thus, "Built on slender lines, very tall for his weight and without an ounce of spare flesh on his bones, it is a tribute to his boxing skill and ringcraft that he was able to meet the roughest and toughest without being belted into oblivion.

"Much of his success he owed to his long reach which proved an effective barrier to unrushing opponents. Like Driscoll, he quickly realised the value and worth of the straight left and he exploited this weapon to the full. That long arm would flash out to check an aggressive rival in his stride and of course he piled up the points with its use. A hard trainer, a clean liver, and a real craftsman, Tarleton deserved all the success that came his way and was a credit to the game he made his life business."

"I doubt if we shall see a featherweight of Tarleton's class for many years," said Liverpool promoter Johnny Best Jnr in 1950. "He had a wonderful boxing brain and his ring artistry was superb. It may be said that he enjoyed physical advantages over the majority of his opponents. True he was extremely tall (5' 6½") for a featherweight and possessed a good reach, but it must not be forgotten that he had only one sound lung and often fought on sheer will power.

"His greatest asset was that he never had weight worries. He always fought on the gate and he was one of Liverpool's greatest drawing cards, equalled only by Peter Kane in that respect. He drew two gates of over 30,000 to Anfield against Panama Al Brown and Freddie Miller."

"I called him the prince of make-believe," said Ted Broadribb who managed Tarleton for a five year period. "He was amongst the best 'foxers' and 'kidders' of an opponent I ever saw."

Born in 1906, Nelson Tarleton was the eldest boy in a large

family from a Liverpool back street. Surviving tuberculosis at the age of two, he was left with only one sound lung, and he was a pale-faced, skinny youngster when starting school. There was nothing wrong with his heart however and when an older boy took a grudge against his kid brother, Nelson challenged him to a fight.

"If you want a fight," replied the bully, "come along to our club any time. I'm not taking any chances being caught scrapping by the headmaster." Young Tarleton, who didn't play football because it was too rough, went along to the Everton Red Triangle Club after school prepared to defend the family honour. He didn't get inside the door! A bunch of kids saw him coming in on his own, promptly set upon him, gave him a beating, and threw him out.

Nelson eventually went back to the club and became fascinated by the boxing. But the club leader wouldn't let him put the gloves on, telling him, "No son, not until you get a few more dinners inside you." At the age of twelve he was entered for three different weights in the Liverpool Boys' Championships and won his way to all three finals. He took the 6st 5lbs title and the 7st 5lbs title, but refused to box in the 7st 12lbs final because it would have meant fighting his best pal.

The club members carried him shoulder high from the Liverpool Stadium to his home where his mother was waiting, bursting with pride. Nelson gave his mother one medal and kept the other one for himself. "That was the greatest thrill of my whole life," he would say many years later.

He was nineteen before becoming a professional boxer. Walking the streets one night after a row with his father, he met Charlie Mitchell, a local fight trainer. "If you want to earn yourself a few pounds," said Charlie, "I can get you a fight at Birmingham." Tarleton was working as a plasterer at the time and readily agreed, asking only that he be introduced as Young Nat Nelson as his parents were opposed to him becoming a pro and he didn't want them to find out.

Tarleton walked out at the first bell and dropped his opponent with a left hook. But the other lad got up and handed him a boxing lesson for the rest of the ten rounds. Nelson collected his six pounds purse and went home, thinking his secret was safe. But next day the local paper carried the story, headed, "Nel Tarleton turns pro under another name!" There was a row at home but he sat down with his parents and told them he was going to make some money out of boxing. The next day he went round to the Stadium to see the promoter, Pa Taylor. The old man was somewhat dubious, saying, "One thing, if you stand edge on, no opponent will see you!"

Taylor shortened his name from Nelson Tarleton to Nel Tarleton so that it would fit on the posters and the lad celebrated his twentieth birthday on 14 January 1926 with a ten rounds decision over George Sankey. Against Les Tarrant, who had beaten him five times in the amateurs, Nel learned a trick for which he would become famous. In the seventh round, Tarleton was rushed into the ropes where Tarrant came in with a right hook. Nel swayed back into the ropes to make Les miss, then catapulted himself off the hemp to land a right flush on the jaw, knocking his man cold.

After local rival Dom Volante beat Nel in the Stadium ring, they became great pals, sparring together in the gym and earning money for charity with Tarleton tap-dancing while Dom accompanied him on the harmonica. But inside the ropes it was all business and Volante never did beat Nel again in a further three fights, one of them for the Northern Area featherweight title.

Tarleton figured a trip to America would toughen him up and in October 1929 he sailed for New York with Volante and Bobby Carvill of Scarborough. Removing his dressing gown for his debut against tough Archie Bell, the Liverpudlian's slender white-skinned frame drew derisory laughter from the hard-bitten fans and Nel was almost reduced to tears. He had the last laugh however as he settled down and gave Bell a fancy boxing lesson.

When he walked into the New York gym where he was to train, wearing three sweaters as he did at home, eyebrows were raised. Whitey Bimstein eventually got him into trunks and tights for his workout. Tarleton amazed the Americans by the ease with which he could make the weight for a lad so tall. "I'm a natural nine-stoner," he told them. "I never have weight troubles." But he did have trouble with Allie Ridgeway who beat him and sent him back home nursing an aching jawbone.

Five months later, Nel was back on the boat to New York, along with Kid Berg who was a tremendous favourite with American fans. Joey Scalfaro tested his jaw with a thumping right hand shot and although Nel was up at nine and managed to keep out of further trouble he lost the decision. His fight against Jimmy Slavin in September 1930 was actually the first bout under the new No Foul rule. A boxer hitting low would not be disqualified but would lose all the points for that round. However, if his opponent was unable to carry on, the transgressor would emerge triumphant!

Tarleton became the first victim of the new rule. Smashed to the canvas by a savage body punch, he was in agony as the referee pleaded with him to get up. Nel somehow hauled himself erect only to be dropped again by another low punch. Five more times he would be dumped on the canvas with the crowd by this time howling for Slavin's blood. When the gutsy Liverpool lad was given a draw the fans invaded the ring to shake his hand.

Top New York sports columnist Paul Gallico wrote, "The gameness of Tarleton, who was fouled, was commendable, but the spectacle of a boy dragging himself along on his stomach by his elbows, his legs paralysed like a shot animal, was hideous, and to see him rise again in great pain and stand off the onslaught of a fresh and unweakened opponent was pitiable."

With his American record a respectable five wins and a draw in eight fights, Nel returned home to find himself nominated to box Johnny Cuthbert for his British featherweight title. Johnny Best secured the fight for Liverpool Stadium 6 November 1930 and Nel went into strict training. But a sparring session with his pal Volante brought trouble. "Your left hand is too low," yelled Dom, and promptly illustrated his point by smacking Nel with a solid right to the chin.

The punch cracked Tarleton's jawbone but he kept quiet about the injury, and on the big night he climbed through the ropes ready to do or die. It was the first Lonsdale Belt match to be held in Liverpool and only the second to be staged outside London, and the city was fight crazy with fans lining up from ten in the morning outside the hall. With Lord Lonsdale looking on, Tarleton boxed on the defensive through most of the fifteen rounds, keeping the terrier-like champion at bay with that rapier of a left hand. Confident that he had won, he was sorely disappointed when Referee Charlie Thomas voted a draw, Cuthbert thus retaining his title. Nel won his next 11 fights to keep his name in the frame and Johnny Best signed the return contest for 1 October 1931.

In March of that year, the old Liverpool Stadium in Pudsey

Street had closed its doors for the last time. Formerly a roller-skating rink, the hall was taken over in 1911 by Mr Arnold Wilson who brought the biggest names in the business to Merseyside. Featuring such men as Jimmy Wilde, Tancy Lee, Freddie Welsh, Johnny Basham, Ted Kid Lewis, Digger Stanley, Johnny Summers, and Jack Hood, the Stadium rapidly acquired a reputation second only to the National Sporting Club in London.

With Wilson serving in World War I, Pa Taylor took over the boxing at the Stadium until forced to close down in 1928. That was when Johnny Best took over. Against the advice of his friends he rented the hall and staged his first show on 10 January 1929, showing a profit of exactly £39. In just over two years Best promoted 113 shows before shutting up shop, the stadium having been purchased by a film company who wanted to erect a new cinema on the site. Johnny kept the pot boiling, running boxing at the Lyric Theatre in Liverpool, New Brighton, and Southport, losing money, and all the time searching for a site for his new Stadium.

He eventually found what he was looking for, an old graveyard in St Paul's Square adjoining Exchange Station, but his plans for a boxing stadium on the old burial ground horrified the clergy and a local minister organised a petition that was circulated around the city. One businessman, who happened to be a keen boxing fan, scribbled a rude word across the petition before passing it on. It was defeated and Johnny Best proceeded with his plans to bring a new Liverpool Stadium to the city. In July 1932 the foundation stone was laid by Lord Lonsdale with the Lord Mayor of Liverpool, Mr Jimmy Cross, looking on, and three months later the hall was ready for the first show.

By that time, Nel Tarleton had become featherweight champion of Great Britain. Realising he had a first rate attraction on his hands, Johnny Best hit on the idea of staging the championship contest in the open air and set his sights on Anfield, home of Liverpool Football Club. However, the club's directors were not at all keen on the idea, fearing their beloved turf would be damaged should the spectators, in their excitement, invade the pitch. Best got his way, helped by Mr Ernest Edwards, a sportswriter on the *Liverpool Echo*, who in his column pleaded with the fans not to encroach upon the hallowed turf. To their credit they never did.

So on that October night in 1931, with 15,000 fans sitting out there in the darkness, Nel Tarleton moved out of his corner to meet champion Johnny Cuthbert from Sheffield. In the opening round, the referee accidently stepped on Tarleton's foot to send him hopping around the ring in pain with Cuthbert in hot pursuit as he tried to cash in. But Nella, as he was affectionately called by his Mersey fans, settled down to give a brilliant exhibition of boxing, dropped the champion for two long counts, and at the final bell was acclaimed the winner, and new champion.

"My mother was so pleased that she made me take my breakfast in bed," smiled Nel the next day. "My father and brother were at the fight but mother waited at home, and didn't she greet me when I told her I had won. It was a great fight, Cuthbert is a fine boxer and I think we both enjoyed it immensely. My shoulders and hands are sore with so many congratulations. I think sometimes it is harder to ward off congratulations than to keep off one's opponent's punches."

A master boxer, Nel Tarleton could never be considered a puncher with only a dozen clean knockouts to his credit, although he did stop a further 29 opponents. Two of those knockouts came against Tommy Watson's north-east rival Douglas Parker and Tarleton always called the first of those two fights, "the best knockout victory of my whole career."

It took place at Belle Vue, Manchester, on a February night in 1932. Early in the fight Tarleton caught his man with a terrific left uppercut and Duggie reeled across the ring. It was round seven before Nel got the punch home again, and as Parker staggered, the champion opened up with both hands and a short right hook dropped Parker in a heap. He was on his feet at seven but, still dazed, couldn't see the following right that sent him down and out.

On top of the world, Nella fancied a crack at Al Foreman's British lightweight championship, but Foreman would only agree to a non-title bout. On St Patrick's Day, 1932, a crowd of some 20,000 gathered on the Anfield ground to see their hero go up against the hard-punching Foreman. The fight was nearly called off at the weigh-in when Tarleton stepped on the scales and his manager announced him as 9st 3lbs. Foreman's brother Maurice shouted that the fight was off. He hadn't wanted the weights made public in case Tarleton should win and claim the title.

Johnny Best spent the afternoon arguing, pleading, threatening, and it was five o'clock before the Foreman brothers agreed to go ahead with the fight, and only then on condition that Al be allowed to use his own special gloves. Tarleton and manager Ted Broadribb nodded their acceptance and the fight was on. That night Nella was at his brilliant best, boxing superbly as Foreman tried to take his head off with every punch, and at the finish there was only one winner. The Anfield crowd roared their appreciation as Nel's glove was held aloft and even Foreman had to concede, "Nel is a great fighter."

Liverpool would see another great fighter when Panama Al Brown signed to fight Tarleton at Anfield in June. A fistic freak who stood five-ten in his socks yet easily made 8st 6lbs, Brown towered over his subjects as king of the world's bantamweights. His title would not be on the line against the British featherweight champion but his reputation would.

"For this fight, Nel," Broadribb instructed, "you must forget your usual style. Change tactics. Don't lead. Forget those left leads. Let Brown come to you, let him come, slip the leads, duck under his arms and bang away to the body with both hands."

A huge crowd cheered Nella as he waited for Brown to lead then came in underneath to score with both hands before escaping. Panama Al was a very frustrated warrior when the sound of the final bell cut through the still night air, the signal for Tarleton to leap for joy, thinking he had won. But Referee Gus Platts held both their hands up to announce a draw, much to Nel's disgust. It was later revealed that he had fought with a ruptured spine muscle and had defied medical advice to go through with the fight. It was four months before he boxed again, scoring a kayo in round ten over Douglas Parker at the Blackfriars Ring.

Tarleton was glad to get back in the ring, but most upset when he learned that the Board had stripped him of his British title for refusing to accept the purse offer submitted by Johnny Best for his title defence against Seaman Watson. Nella had good reason to be upset, for he had now been accepted by the American ruling bodies as a genuine contender for the world championship.

Broadribb moved quickly, announcing to the press, "I have applied to the Board to have Tarleton re-instated. We have agreed to meet Watson for the British title and when that is over we will immediately negotiate for a match with Kid Chocolate for the world title."

On 3 November 1932, a week before his championship defence against Watson, Tarleton received a cable from American fight manager Sol Goldie stating that articles had been signed for Tarleton to meet the Californian champion Baby Arizmendi in Los Angeles on 6 December. The man from Liverpool was already recognised as a world title contender by the National Boxing Association of America, and passage was booked on the Berengaria, sailing from Southampton to New York.

Tarleton told a reporter, "At the moment I am training for my fight with Seaman Watson next week, but I hope to sail two or three days after that contest in order to have time in which to become acclimatised before my Los Angeles fight. I realise that I must first beat Watson for it is essential for me to go to America as a champion if I am to have a chance of winning another world championship for Great Britain."

12

"WINNER, AND NEW CHAMPION!"

When he arrived on Tyneside some ten days before the big fight, manager Alec Lambert was delighted to find his pride and joy bursting with fitness and ready to fight for his life.

"I trained as I had never trained before for that fight," remembered Tommy some years later. "Had I been in London or a provincial centre other than Newcastle, I would have had decent gymnasium facilities, but in the North East these were nil. My training was done in a small room above the New Hawk Inn at Byker Bank, which I had converted into a crude gymnasium. I was fortunate, I suppose, to have even that at my disposal."

Seaman trained for his big chance with one good punchbag and lots of exercise and roadwork to build wind and stamina for the fifteen rounds journey against the champion, although he himself was quietly confident of beating Tarleton inside the distance.

In his days as an active boxer, Alec Lambert had fought in Newcastle, at the old St James's Hall. The date was 12 October 1912 and his opponent was Johnny Robinson of South Shields. A tremendous battle over twenty rounds ended in a draw and they drew again in January 1913, this time over fifteen rounds and this time at the National Sporting Club in London. A few months later came his defeat by the great Ted Kid Lewis when contesting the British featherweight title vacated by Jim Driscoll. Now Lambert was going after the title again, telling the Chronicle's boxing writer, "What I failed to do myself, I hope my pal Seaman will do on Thursday."

Newcastle was fight crazy and to cater for those anxious to see the fight in person, the London & North Eastern Railway announced that they would run a special excursion to Liverpool on the day of the fight, leaving Newcastle Central Station at twelve noon, the cost of a return ticket being eleven shillings (55p). But there was a warning from promoter Johnny Best in a letter sent to the Sports Editor of the Chronicle stating that the Stadium was practically sold out and anyone making the journey without a ticket would have little chance of gaining admission.

A large crowd gathered at the Central Station to give Seaman a rousing send-off as he left Newcastle the day before the fight, accompanied by manager Lambert and his backer Mr Steckles. Kitty would travel to Liverpool by car on Thursday morning, her ringside seat already booked. Before boarding the train, Tommy told reporters, "You know that I seldom have much to say about any fight I am engaged in. All I can say now is that I am glad that I have got my chance to fight for the championship. I want to win it for my own sake, for my family's sake, and for the honour of Tyneside. You have heard the boys wish me good luck, and say, 'Do your best, Tommy.' I always do my best, but, if possible, I will do a bit more tomorrow night."

Thursday 10 November 1932 began like any other day in the life of Thomas Samuel Watson of Newcastle. It would end like no other, in the seething cauldron of the Liverpool Stadium as a capacity crowd of some 9,000 spectators threatened to lift the roof off the brand new arena when they realised that their beloved Nella had been beaten, the British championship gone, the glittering Lonsdale Belt no longer adorning that slim waist. Out there in the centre of the ring, Lord Lonsdale himself was fastening the belt around the man of the moment, Seaman Tommy Watson, but his words were drowned by a chorus of booing that rose above the cheers as the men of Merseyside let their hearts rule their heads.

"I was rather surprised at the Liverpool crowd not taking the verdict like sportsmen, for they booed both the winner and the referee," wrote Norman Hurst in his ringside report for the Kemsley papers. "To my mind there was never any doubt when the boys entered the last round but that the Novocastrian was a winner bar accidents, and I think that the referee's decision was a perfectly sound one based on the work done."

Like most of the ringside experts, Hurst was surprised by Watson's triumph, writing, "I have seen Watson in many contests and I never thought he was class enough for the Liverpool performer, but it was evident that Watson was imbued with the championship spirit. He had something to fight for, more than just a purse, he was fighting for a title of Great Britain and Lord Lonsdale challenge belt, something he's been hoping for for a long while."

Although Tarleton was generally regarded as the defending champion, it could be argued that the fight was for the vacant title. Board of Control General Secretary Charles Donmall told the press that the Board had taken no action in regard to the re-instatement of Tarleton as champion.

"The fight will decide the question once and for all," he said before taking his seat at the ringside, "for whichever man wins will be recognised as official champion."

The weigh-in at two o'clock that afternoon, attended by a huge crowd, saw both men pronounced fighting fit, Tarleton scaling 8st 13½lbs with Watson tipping the beam at 8st 12lbs. Later that afternoon a train-load of Geordie supporters made their way to the Stadium, many of them eagerly snapping up the odds of four and five to one still being laid against their champion.

Born and bred among the boxing booths that toured the North of England, Norman Hurst had the gloves on with such luminaries as Jim Driscoll, Spike Robson, and Billy Marchant, before he began writing on boxing for the Sporting Chronicle in 1920. He was reporting contests for the Kemsley Newspaper group that November night in 1932 when he sent out the following round-by-round report from Liverpool Stadium.

"ROUND ONE. With the sound of the first bell Watson shot across and poked a left to Tarleton's face, Tarleton countered with a right and then Watson, tucking his chin well down to escape Tarleton's left hook, went after the champion. But Tarleton was too shifty on his feet and sidestepped the rush of the Tynesider.

"A left swing to the body from Tarleton caught Watson on the edge of his knickers and there was a big oh! Tarleton appeared a trifle wild and missed with a left swing to the head by at least a foot, Watson hooking him with a right to the jaw as he stumbled past. There was hardly any action at all in the last minute of this round and the crowd expressed their dissatisfaction. Neither man had shown anything.

"ROUND TWO. Tarleton quickly went to work but Watson surprised him by jumping in with the left hand. The champion began to fight a defensive battle relying on countering his man as he came in. Even at this early stage it did not bear the stamp of a championship contest, there were too many spells of inactivity. Tarleton was guilty of doing a lot of holding and leaning on his man, he was however jumping in with a wicked left hook to the body, then he nearly fell over himself pulling the blow back.

"ROUND THREE. Watson commenced by forcing the work but at close quarters he found himself tied up by the Liverpool man. Once, when Tarleton grasped his upper arm with his left glove, Watson appealed to the referee and motioned to where Tarleton had offended. Watson had the better of some infighting and pounded Tarleton to the body. The Liverpool man came back with a hail of blows that rattled about Watson's waist line but the Seaman refused to back up an inch and we saw some wonderful toe to toe fighting. They had laid four to one on Tarleton before the first round opened, it looked anything but that in this session. This round ended with Watson pounding both hands to the body while he had Tarleton pinned with his back to the ropes.

"ROUND FOUR. They went into a clinch at the outset. Stepping back quickly Tarleton drove two powerful left arm punches to the body. These must have hurt Watson and the pair were making a good fight of it now. The crowd howled at the Newcastle boy for ripping his glove up when inside, a point which by the way earns disqualification in America. Tarleton was again guilty of holding, grabbing his man by the back of the elbow and pulling him towards him. Tarleton tried a couple of lefts to the face but they were both inches short of their mark. This was an even round and Watson was smiling as he went to his corner.

"ROUND FIVE. Watson made a brave effort to get to close quarters but Tarleton's long extended left was too much for him and he had to try to jump past it to reach his objective. Tarleton was trying to get his man open for a big left swing to the jaw but Watson was wise to this and invariably broke ground just as it was coming. The Tynesider was every bit as good as Tarleton at close quarters. The referee spoke to Tarleton about holding just before the bell sounded.

"ROUND SIX. Watson drove Tarleton into a neutral corner and hurt the Liverpool man with a left to the body and a right to the jaw. This roused Tarleton who showed more action than hitherto in the fight, he came out punching with both hands like a machine and Watson, for the first time, hung on for a breather. The men swapped rights, both landing, but the punches were a bit too high to do any damage. Watson appeared the stronger of the pair and bustled Tarleton around the ring. Watson never gave Tarleton any rest and although the champion looked to have the better style he could not overawe the terrier-like tactics of his challenger. Changing feet rapidly, Tarleton brought over the best punch of the fight, a smashing right to the point of Watson's jaw, and the crowd roared expecting him to go down. But the Seaman was built of tough stuff and even while Tarleton looked to see what damage was done the Seaman was at him again.

"ROUND SEVEN. Watson started out as usual by carrying the fight to his man with Tarleton lying in wait with ready counters. Although Nel looked good he failed to back up this with really solid work and the plodding Newcastle man was continually doing something. Whenever Tarleton elected to use his good left it was in Watson's face before he knew how it got there, but it was all too rare and the Tynesider kept bustling along with his work getting in close to bang both hands to the body.

"Just before the end of the round Tarleton went flat-footed after his man and shook him with a left and right to the short ribs. At this stage there could not have been a lot in it in the matter of points.

"ROUND EIGHT. Tarleton made Watson miss badly and had him wide open but did not profit by his chance. A clever sidestep by Tarleton in evading one of Watson's rushes caused the challenger to go stumbling headlong into the ropes. In this round we saw a flash of the old Tarleton, really the first time in the fight. Watson again appealed that Tarleton was holding him and the referee broke the men. Tarleton demonstrated his cleverness by making Watson miss with one out of every three punches that he sent along and in reply scored to head and body.

"ROUND NINE. Tarleton immediately cut loose and some wicked uppercuts landed squarely on the jaw and must have shaken Watson but Watson never let up and he persevered with his crouching style and it was invariably Tarleton who was backed to the ropes. A left hook to the body caught Watson off his balance and put him down but he was up immediately. A second later a right by Tarleton caught Watson slightly low, the latter looked at the referee but went on with his boxing. At this point the referee stopped the contest to have a chat with both men. No doubt it was about the flagrant holding that was continually taking place and marring the contest. Watson went red hot after the champion and getting him in his own corner sent both hands to the body with great force. Tarleton slipped out of trouble but right on time Watson swung a nice right to his jaw and Tarleton looked serious as he walked to his corner at the bell.

"ROUND TEN. Tarleton tried to get his left into play but he was either short in his leads or found his punches blocked. As he jumped in to lead Watson crossed him with a right and Tarleton was shaken to his heels.

"Watson tried to finish his man but Tarleton hung on to him like a burr on a blanket and Watson shook his head despairingly to the seconds in his corner to indicate that he could not get loose. The referee had the greatest difficulty in prying the champion away from his eager foe. After a few seconds during which I think Tarleton was foxing he came out with a flurry of blows but Watson more than met him halfway and punished the champion about the head and body. Watson had taken everything that Tarleton could give him and was still crowding him. This was Watson's round by a mile and the champion was wobbly as he walked to his corner.

"ROUND ELEVEN. Tarleton had recovered in the interval and came out fighting, carefully using a left lead to the face but whenever they got to close quarters the Tynesider sewed him up with good body punches. Tarleton was looking anything but like a champion, Watson would pin his man on the ropes and ladle punishment out with both hands. As Watson was going away Tarleton sent out a blow that landed flush on the kidney and the referee spoke to him. What had started out as a slow fight had speeded up tremendously and Watson was showing that he was a worthy challenger. A few seconds before the gong Tarleton ripped a good punch to Watson's heart but the Newcastle man never blinked. Again Watson looked the better.

"ROUND TWELVE. Tarleton's long left was in evidence but Watson was always replying with two hands to the body or one to the body and one to the head and when they came to infighting it was always the champion who broke ground first or clinched. Tarleton laid in wait for Watson's rush and shot over a beautifully timed right to the jaw but Watson turned his head and caught it high up or else he must have been on the canvas. Tarleton with both hands hanging low waited for Watson to attack and ducking under a left lead sent a stiff right to the Tynesider's ribs.

"The Seaman's mouth opened wide and his knees buckled.

Tarleton's seconds urged him to go in and do the job but try as he would he could not do it and Watson was fighting hard at the bell.

"ROUND THIRTEEN. Tarleton, making the body his objective, placed his punches well in this round. A left to the short ribs and a right which landed under Watson's heart made the Newcastle lad break ground but only for a moment. Tarleton was trying hard to make it a long range fight and keep Watson at the end of his left glove but the Seaman would not be denied and came back fighting like fury. Tarleton was guilty of palming his man and the crowd yelled their disapproval.

"Watson appeared to be able to take Tarleton's best blows without a flinch and the champion did not know what to make of his man. A right swing as Watson was going away caught him on the side of the head and half turned him round but it was more him being off balance than the force of the blow that caused this.

"ROUND FOURTEEN. Watson was stung early on with a good left hook to the jaw, Tarleton tried another and was met with a right to the body. Tarleton always looked the better at long range but Watson always more than evened up matters when it came to close quarter work.

"Tarleton made a desperate effort to finish the job towards the end of this round, he threw aside his boxing for wild haymakers that would have been laughed at in a novice bout but they hurt just the same. A big uppercut by Tarleton missed by inches and when Watson, getting his man on the ropes in his (Tarleton's) corner, spread his feet wide and pummelled the champion with a hurricane of blows to the body. Tarleton seemed to wilt then sprang to life again with a counter attack that must have literally dumbfounded his challenger.

"ROUND FIFTEEN. The last round opened with both showing a lot of respect for each other. In a mix-up, a good right from Watson split Tarleton's left eyebrow and with the blood trickling in his eye Tarleton kept shaking his head to try to clear his vision. Watson, seeing the championship in his grasp, tore into Tarleton like a man possessed. Tarleton backed before his challenger, snaking out his left in an effort to stave off the attack. There were times when Tarleton stood stock still in the ring and shook his head as if to clear his eyes and in these periods Watson refrained from attacking. Watson was crowding his man all around the ring and Tarleton was banking all on one big punch. He nearly did it with a right that landed like a sling shot on Watson's jaw but the Tynesider came back for more and received a punch in the pit of the stomach. In spite of this he again proceeded to go after Tarleton and punch him around the ring. Watson had Tarleton on the ropes when the end came and was handing out punishment with both hands."

"Seaman Watson, the winner!" That brief announcement from Referee Jack Smith of Manchester heralded not only the crowning of a new featherweight champion of Great Britain, but the realisation of a dream come true, the dream of a boy from Byker who set out against all the odds to become a champion boxer. The words of Lord Lonsdale as he fastened the glittering belt that bore his name around Watson's heaving waist were drowned in the wave of sound that engulfed the ring. The Geordie fans in the crowd, although greatly outnumbered, raised the roof with their cheers, and Johnny Best's new Liverpool Stadium, erected on the site of the old burial ground in St Paul's Square, had claimed its first victim as the "Graveyard of Champions."

Up there in the ring, Alec Lambert was like a dog with two tails as he fussed round Tommy, tying his dressing gown, while Seaman searched the sea of faces milling around the ring for Kitty. She was there, voice hoarse from shouting encouragement, waiting to embrace him as he came down the ring steps. And then she was gone from his side as crowds fought to shake his hand and policemen had to force a way through the crush so that he could reach the dressing room in one piece.

Kitty eventually managed to get through, to be met by reporters who bombarded her with questions. "I enjoyed it champion," she told them after getting her breath back. "I have been at every fight my husband has been in since he left the Navy, and I saw him fight many times in England when he was in the service. We have been married four-and-a-half years and I hope I will continue to see him in more championship matches."

Over in Tarleton's dressing room, his family and friends tried to come to terms with the fact that Nella had been beaten, he was no longer the champion. They all thought he had won of course but Nel knew it was no good crying over spilt milk, or lost titles.

"The referee gave his decision against me so what is the good of arguing about it," he told reporters. "I have been declared defeated and I will not now go to the United States. My arrangements were to go over as British champion, and I am not the holder now. Well, well, every man has his day."

Soon after breakfast next morning, Seaman, Kitty, and manager Lambert were at the station. "It is great to be champion," Tommy told reporters as he boarded the train, "and I'm glad to have won through. As to my future plans, I am going home to Newcastle to rest, and then we shall see about more fighting. I might even go to America. Who knows?"

WATSON SCORES GREAT WIN!...BOXING TITLE FOR TYNESIDE!

Tommy Watson, the boy who sold newspapers on the streets of Byker, was himself in the headlines when the *Journal* and the *Evening Chronicle* rolled off the presses that Friday in November 1932, and by early afternoon a big crowd had gathered in the Central Station to welcome him home. Family and friends were allowed on to the platform to await the arrival of the train but, as the *Chronicle* later reported, "..the masses were restrained with not a little difficulty outside the platform barrier. All were eager to catch a glimpse of the man who, for the first time, has brought a Lonsdale Belt to Tyneside. When the new champion appeared with his wife, crowds surged around them. Shouts of 'Good old Tommy' resounded through the station and when the Lonsdale Belt was produced the noise was terrific.

"After much pushing and mauling, Seaman Watson reached a place of comparative safety, the top of a saloon motor car inside of which were his wife and friends, and the car moved off with Watson and a colleague perched on top, the Lonsdale Belt laid across Tommy's knees."

A tremendous welcome awaited the new champion when the car reached the New Hawk Inn. Byker Bank, which was bedecked from top to bottom with flags and bunting, was lined with hundreds of people just happy to be there to share in the success story of one of their own.

"When our Tommy won the Lonsdale Belt," remembered Frances, "he brought it up home to Fuller Road and he laid it down on the bed beside our mother, because she was so poorly at the time, and you couldn't lift it. I mean, I had hold of it and I

87

couldn't lift it, you know, and my mother just said, 'Oh, well, son, next time you win it it will be yours.'"

"Nothing, not even a crack at the world title, has given me a greater thrill in my whole career than that fight," Tommy would say, recalling the first Tarleton fight. "From the eleventh round on I felt quite confident. I'd taken the best that Tarleton could give and I still felt strong enough to take the fight to him.

"'Seaman Watson, the winner!' When I heard the referee make that announcement and confirm my opinion that I had beaten Tarleton and captured the featherweight title, I thought I was on top of the world. For quite a long time I had heard of the big money which a champion could make and it had always been my ambition to make enough out of the boxing game to ensure the comfort of my wife and children. Well, my end of the purse for winning the featherweight crown was £200, but after I had paid my expenses I was left with considerably less than half!

"Nevertheless, I was quite happy in the knowledge (as I thought at the time) that I should be able to take part in plenty of fights as the champion and pick up 'canny' purses in various parts of the country. I never thought then that I should be almost forced to make the trip across the Atlantic to engage in a fight which promised (but only promised, as I found later) a worthwhile purse. Looking back, I am glad that I rigidly adhered to the advice I received from an old timer many years ago. 'Never get a swollen head when you win a fight, Tommy.' It does not pay in any walk of life to get a swollen head, and particularly in boxing."

In the week following his triumph over Tarleton, Seaman Tommy could have been excused for letting success go to his head, but his hat still fit him comfortably the night he took Kitty along to the Hippodrome Theatre in Nelson Street. Top of the bill was Gracie Fields, the Rochdale songbird and comedienne who brought the house down with the crowd's favourite, "Sally."

But the cheers for "Our Gracie" were eclipsed by the roar that greeted "Wor Tommy" when he climbed on to the stage carrying his Lonsdale Belt. They posed for a photographer, but the modest, shy lad from Byker was uncomfortable with the extrovert stage star as she mugged for the camera. Tommy's daughter Kath ("don't call me Kathleen") says that, "Dad didn't like her at all. I know she presented him with the belt and they had a photo taken, but he didn't like the way she went on."

Seaman was much happier being introduced from the ring at New St James's Hall on the night Jack Casey met Glen Moody. He was given a terrific reception and made a modest speech saying how proud he was to bring the first Lonsdale Belt to the North East and he hoped that both Jack Casey and Mickey McGuire would bring further honours to Wearside and Tyneside.

13

NEW YORK, NEW YORK!

Shortly after beating Tarleton, Tommy went to London for a conference with manager Lambert and promoter John Mortimer, who would recall, "We mutually agreed that I should use my influence to get Tommy a fight for the world title with Kid Chocolate in New York. Tommy laughed at the idea, and when I said to him, 'Don't you want the fight?' he replied with a boyish laugh and in his Geordie tongue, 'I'll fight two Chocolates if you like!'

"Then, after weeks of burning up the cable wires to Charlie Harvey in New York, who was associated with me when Tom Heeney fought Gene Tunney for the heavyweight championship, Harvey eventually cabled to MINSTREL, PORTSMOUTH, my telegraphic address, "Have arranged with Madison Square Garden for Watson to box Kid Chocolate for the world title.' Oh, boy, this was one of the most pleasing telegrams I have ever received. Was I at last to get my heart's desire in being associated with a world champion?"

While all this was going on, Watson was anxious to get back in the ring, a firm believer in the axiom that rest breeds rust. He had promised John Paget that his first fight as champion would be at New St James's Hall and it was announced that he would meet previous victim Julien Verbist on Monday 5 December over twelve rounds at 9st 2lbs. But a training injury to the Belgian brought Luigi Quadrini into the Gallowgate ring as an able substitute.

The Italian was a former champion of Europe but Luigi could do nothing with Seaman Watson, and he was thrown out in the fourth round by Referee Tom Murphy after landing a low punch that caused Watson to cry out in pain. Manager Nick Cavalli protested loudly but ringsiders agreed it was a correct decision.

Two weeks later Tommy scored an easy six rounds knockout over Billy Wyper on a Sunday afternoon show at Middlesbrough's National Sporting Club and Paget booked him for his first bill of

90

the new year, 2 January 1933, against local rival Benny Sharkey. But by this time the papers were carrying the news that Watson was to fight Chocolate for the world championship in New York on 27 January.

Before Tommy could pack his bag however, reports reached Britain that the New York State Athletic Commission had vetoed the proposed fight on the grounds that the British champion had not yet proved his ability to take on an opponent of Chocolate's standing. In New York, Charlie Harvey attacked the Commission, accused them of being tactless, and threatened to take the fight to another city if they persisted in their ban. The Commissioners promptly had second thoughts and agreed to watch Watson in his training, stating that if he appeared to be of championship calibre they would allow the Chocolate fight to go on as planned.

Tommy received a telegram from Mortimer and telephoned the promoter straight away. "Everything is arranged for America," he told Seaman. "Don't take any notice of the cables to the British press. Can you get out of the Sharkey fight?" Assured by Tommy that he could, Mortimer told him to come to London as soon as possible to arrange his passport. "We sail on the Leviathan on 29 December," he said.

Seaman was on the next train to London and after making all arrangements, returned home to spend Christmas with his family. "What a wonderful thing it would be if I brought a world's title to Tyneside," he told the *Evening Chronicle*. "I feel that when I am in the ring in New York, I am fighting not only for myself and the family, but for thousands of people on Tyneside.

"I know they will at that time be saying to themselves, 'I wonder how Tommy is going on.' Well, of course, I do not know how I'll be going on, that depends upon me and also upon the other fellow. I can only assure everybody interested in me that I will do my very best to uphold the best traditions of British boxing."

In releasing Tommy from the Sharkey fight, John Paget announced, "I was looking forward to this fight attracting a big crowd, but it would have been absurd for anyone to stand in the Seaman's way for a fight like this, even if one could. I wish Tommy every success, and I have his promise that, win or lose, his first fight on his return to this country will be at the New St James's Hall against Benny Sharkey."

On Wednesday night, 28 December, Tommy caught the 10.45pm train for London. Next day he boarded the US liner Leviathan at Southampton together with John Mortimer, and a few hours later the former sailor was on the high seas again, this time as a passenger bound for the New World.

Strolling around the deck was not for this Geordie lad however. Tommy spent most of his time in the ship's well-appointed gymnasium with Mortimer keeping an eye on his workouts. This was his big chance, he wanted to be ready...

Delayed by rough seas in the Atlantic, the Leviathan was two days late when she docked in New York Harbour on 7 January 1933. "No one was better pleased than your humble servant than when we were off Sandy Hook," recalled Mortimer, "and when we tied up to the pier in New York, my wife says that I danced an Irish jig! Here were Charlie Harvey, Tom Heeney and his wife, and when they came on board to greet us accompanied by a bunch of irrepressible Yankee pressmen and photographers, old Charlie gently drew me to one side.

"'What kind of a boy is this Watson?' he asked. I quickly replied, 'If you mean his fighting ability, he'll give any boy his own weight a great fight.' But Harvey replied, 'I don't exactly mean that, but since you sailed for New York, the Athletic Commission has decided that they will not permit any foreign boxer to go direct into a title contest till he has proved himself. That means he will have to box in some of the small clubs and give proof of his ability to box for a title.'

"This, after a two-thousand mile journey under such trying conditions, was a bombshell to be informed that the fight was off. I said, 'Don't say too much to the Seaman,' and Harvey said we'll go up to Madison Square Garden to see the boys. Apparently the fight with Kid Chocolate was off unless we agreed to box in one of the small clubs. Naturally I very strongly protested and said, 'We would rather return to England without a fight.' But Tommy was pulling at my sleeve, saying, 'Don't say that. I will fight whoever they like.'"

Watson's treatment by the New York boxing authorities did not go down too well back home. In a front page article headlined, "Play The Game USA!" Mr S W Ackland, the Editor of *Boxing*, wrote, "What unfair procedure is this? Surely our champion had proved his worth by his victory over Tarleton, who was adjudged, even by those in the States, to be the one outstanding Britisher with really bright prospects of securing a world's crown...Watson is a fellow who has attained to titular honours despite the fact that his chances of success were considered slender by the critics.

"He is not a star of the most brilliant order. Rather is he a box-fighter of strong and sturdy type, sound and reliable and a true sportsman. A family man, with a business which he has proved competent of managing profitably, he appeared to have approached that period of life when he was likely to settle down. But no, he fought his way to the top of the fistic tree in this country, and was then successful in his claim to recognition as a contender for the highest honours. And now the solons in New York decree that all his hopes and aspirations shall be squashed, that is until he has proved his worth...So we do make this strong protest on behalf of Watson and we ask those responsible in USA to play the game!"

However, it would appear that the members of the Boxing Commission in the Big Apple had taken more notice of influential New York sportswriter Dan Parker. "Almost six years ago," wrote Parker in the *Daily Mirror*, "the State Athletic Commission passed a rule, 'for the protection of the public' requiring that henceforth, any foreign boxer coming over here must fight at one of the smaller clubs to prove his skill before being permitted to engage in a main bout at the Garden. What brought about the adoption of this new rule was a farcical bout at Madison Square Garden on the night of January 21 1927 between Fidel LaBarba and Elky Clark.

"The Scotsman was billed as the European flyweight champion, had beaten every flyweight in Europe, and came here highly touted. No one on this side of the pond had seen him fight, though, and there was no proof that he could, except a raft of clippings from European papers. The phenomenal Elky hadn't been in the ring more than a minute when light-hitting Fidel had him on his back. He took a count of eight and then resumed his pitiful attempt to fight. Elky was game enough, as he proved before the one-sided dreary affair had run its course, but he simply didn't know anything about his craft. In the third round Elky was on the mat three times and the customers began to walk out. In the eighth round he was floored again. Even left jabs were knocking him down...The result was that the fans filed out of the Garden vowing they were through with boxing.

"To cover up its culpability in the matter, the Boxing Commission thereupon ruled that thenceforth all foreign pugs would have to submit to a test in the small club crucible to prove their right to show on the big time. Since then the Commission has broken this rule whenever the exigencies of politics required that it be broken. And now it's going to suspend the rule again to let Seaman Watson make his American debut at the Garden this month against Kid Chocolate.

"Watson was unheard of on this side until he beat Nel Tarleton recently. One assumes that it takes a pretty good man to beat Nel Tarleton, just as one assumed that anyone who could lick every flyweight in Europe, as Elky Clark did, must be a good scrapper. In the Clark case the assumption was all wrong. Why can't it be just as wrong in the Watson case? I think the Boxing Commission owes it to the boxing fans of New York to reconsider its action and order Watson to fight a first class opponent, not a diver, at a small club before permitting him to appear in the Garden."

On 12 January, under the headline, "Newcastle Boxing Champion To Be Tried Out," the *Evening Chronicle* asked, "Will the New York State Athletic Commission think ex-Seaman Tommy Watson, the British featherweight champion, 'class' enough to meet the world's champion Kid Chocolate? Watson will be put through his paces on Monday before several Deputy Commissioners who will then decide as to his worthiness for the title bout."

"Monday 16 January 1933 is a day I shall never forget," John Mortimer recalled a couple of years later. "The New York Commission selected three of the toughest featherweights in New York for the test and there were present, besides the three Deputy Commissioners, about forty press and cameramen and some thousand-odd spectators to see the plucky little Britisher on his trial. I am sure there are hundreds of men beside myself who are keenly interested in professional boxing who would agree that no-one but Tommy Watson would have submitted to such a test. But to his everlasting credit he did and nobly and well and he once more placed British boxing on the map in America."

Harry Grayson wrote in the *World-Telegram*, "The trial is over, the evidence is in the hands of the jury, and tomorrow, at the offices of the State Athletic Commission, Seaman Watson, English featherweight, will get the verdict. After Chief Justice William Muldoon reviews the transcript of the evidence, he can give one

94

of four possible verdicts. If the Seaman is found guilty of being a good fighter or he is found not guilty of being a bum, everything will be okay for him and Madison Square Garden, for the Commission will then sanction the 15rds bout involving Kid Chocolate's claim to the featherweight title on 27 January. But if Watson is found guilty of being a bum or not guilty of being a good fighter, the show is off and the Englishman can go back to his ship and his beloved sea.

"Whatever the verdict, boxing men agree that Seaman Thomas Watson was victim of a most unfair trial. In this country only ten days with practically no preliminary boxing, Watson was called to the St Nicholas Arena court this afternoon to prove his case. Danny Ridge served as Clerk of the Court as third man in the ring, and the jury was composed of Deputy Commissioners Dan Skilling, Chick Goodman, and John T McNeil. They collected the evidence and adjourned without giving an official or unofficial verdict. The spectators however felt that Watson couldn't possibly lose after a hurried review.

"The Seaman gained a few points with a good left jab and a desire to mix furiously at infighting. He was obviously different from the customary English fighter in that he was rough and tough in close quarters. Mazza, Comforti, and Bedami, are three good boys. Bedami, who seemed the best of the three today, was very good for a couple of rounds, in fact Bedami has been known to step along on even terms with Kid Chocolate in the gym. He is something of a clown, and gave Watson a chance to prove his statement that he has had nearly two hundred fights."

Tommy's big test was held in the basement gym of the St Nicholas Arena at 66th Street and Columbus Avenue and *Boxing's* New York correspondent Peter Varley was one of the reporters present. "The Seaman was plainly nervous," he wrote. "He was being put on a spot and nobody knew it better than he. As this writer saw it...he was a rugged hard-working fighter. He revealed a pronounced weakness against the left hooks to the head and body, and was tagged by many a straight left. His best work was done at infighting. He ripped both hands to the body well. He took punches well, kept his head, and never lost heart. Of one thing you may be certain, there was no pulling of punches by the three youngsters selected to try out the Seaman.

"They were out to do the best they could, realising that if they

95

could knock over the visitor it would mean plenty to them in publicity. Jerry Mazza, who went the first two rounds, is a sturdy youngster. He was shaded by Watson. Joe Comforti, who came next, did too much grabbing to make his two rounds interesting. Charlie Bedami, who went the last two frames, outpointed Watson by ripping left hooks to the body and head.

"The original programme called for Mike Belloise to serve as one of the trial horses, but he showed up with a bad hand and was excused. A better line on the Seaman's chances with Chocolate could have been had if Belloise had been in there, as Mike is a boxer of the same general type as the Keed whereas the three who did spar with the Britisher all are fighters rather than boxers. The trial attracted the largest gathering that has been in the St Nick gymnasium this season, about three hundred turning out. They gave the Seaman a nice hand but it is doubtful if any of them will bet on him as a result of what they saw. Watson's chief objection to the whole affair was that they kept running in new opponents."

"It takes a few rounds to get on to a man's style," said Tommy, "and they put in a fresh bloke every two rounds. Just when I was set to get busy the right way on the bloke, they took him out and put in a new one. Then, too, I have had only a few rounds of boxing since I reached New York. I've easily beaten much better boys than these...It is a peculiar way of doing business, but I want to be a good sport, and so I won't complain."

Watson and Mortimer did not have to wait long for the verdict. At a special session of the State Athletic Commission the following afternoon, it was announced that the British champion had "satisfied the jury at his trial" and would be allowed to challenge Kid Chocolate for his title in Madison Square Garden on Friday 27 January.

"I admit I made a very bad show in my opinion," said Tommy, "and I would not have been surprised if I had not been given the fight. I was worried to death with questions during the rest periods while the flashlight photographers were busy the whole of the time. I must have satisfied them, though."

However, the joy of Watson and Mortimer was short-lived. With Tommy's date with destiny now just a week away, the bottom fell out of the big fight. Kid Chocolate was ordered deported to Havana after a hearing before immigration officials at Key West, Florida, because he had no permit from the Secretary of Labour to enter the United States. Chocolate's manager Luis Guiterrez, before returning to Havana with his charge, told reporters it was the Kid's 25th trip to the United States and on no previous trips had he been required to present a Department of Labour permit. He said he would cable Jimmy Johnston, the Garden matchmaker, requesting him to intercede with the Department of Labour in order that the permit could be issued, but there were now grave doubts that Chocolate would be able to keep his date with the British champion in New York.

"By this time," said Mortimer, "both Tommy and I were getting sick of the whole business, were fed up, and suggested going home. We were on the point of retreating very disgusted when Jimmy Johnston asked me if we would agree to fight Fidel LaBarba, ex-flyweight champion who had recently fought Chocolate. Seaman readily agreed and contracts were signed at the offices of the Boxing Commission for the contest at the Garden, with William Muldoon, the veteran chairman of the Commission, assuring Tommy that should he defeat LaBarba he would definitely meet Chocolate for the title in New York on 17 February."

14

FIDDLE THE BARBER

The letter, postmarked New York USA-11 January 1933, winged its way across the Atlantic to arrive in Newcastle a few days later. It was from Seaman Tommy Watson and it read, in part, "Well, I am properly fed up with this place. It is not half as good as England and I won't be sorry when I set sail for home...I am staying at Tom Heeney's. He is a really good fellow and his home is twenty miles away from New York, which is a wonderful place...I have started proper training and am feeling in good shape. Roll on the 27th of January."

If Tommy was fed up when he wrote that letter, he was even more so in the days that followed. First came the gym trial to see if he was "good enough for the Garden," then the shattering news that the world champion had been refused entry to America. Now he had to beat LaBarba knowing that defeat would blow his world title fight out of the window.

The events in New York were mirrored in the local press back home in Newcastle, with such headlines as, WATSON IN RUN ROUND...LABARBA BARS WAY TO TITLE FIGHT...SEAMAN FED UP. "Seaman Watson has been side-tracked in his quest for the world featherweight championship in the United States," wrote the *Chronicle* boxing writer. "He has been 'diddled' just as many of us thought he would, and again a British boxer is being made a laughing stock for the benefit of the Yankee sporting public."

When news of the Watson-LaBarba fight broke in New York, Fidel was immediately installed a favourite, with odds of three to one against the British champion being offered by the smart money boys along Broadway. "Uncle" John Mortimer was said to have backed Watson for a considerable sum, and in the week leading up to the fight, so much did Seaman improve in his training that the odds tumbled to 7 to 5 against the boy from Byker.

In his first session in a New York gym, Tommy boxed with

three featherweights, one of whom was Billy Humphries, a London boy who had been in the States for the past eight years. Watson concentrated on the body, and also got home some good left jabs to the face and rights to the head. Skipping and shadow-boxing completed his forty-minute workout which appeared to make a favourable impression on the onlookers.

Seaman finished his heavy training three days before the fight, boxing eight fast rounds, impressing the crowd with his footwork and willingness to mix it. For the rest of the week Tommy confined himself to light work-outs of three rounds sparring, shadow-boxing, and skipping. *The Journal* reported, "The British champion appears in excellent condition, fine spirits, and is confident, although he admits that he will have a very tough opponent in LaBarba, a clever, crouching, and weaving boxer with a dangerous left hook to the body and strong uppercuts."

Early in the week of the fight, Dan Parker's 'Broadway Bugle' column in the *New York Daily Mirror* had carried the following item, "A few days before the Seaman Watson fight, Fidel LaBarba, with tails and topper, spent the night in a fashionable speak in the early West Fifties with a beautiful young thing as his companion. They checked out at 9.00am."

But Parker still considered Fidel a good thing over the British title-holder. "LaBarba knows the ropes and it's likely to be a pretty rough sea for the Seaman," he wrote the morning of the fight. "Though LaBarba has dropped decisions to Kid Chocolate and Tommy Paul since he returned from Australia, he figures to make the Seaman walk the bleeding plank, being far too experienced and clever for the rough and ready British tar, whose speciality is infighting. I figure Fidel should romp home with the duke."

Parker's opinion was generally reflected in the New York press, for although they had been impressed by Watson's ability to mix it in the Kid Berg style, the majority of the critics favoured the chances of the more experienced LaBarba.

Born in New York City, Fidel LaBarba grew up in Los Angeles. "We were the poorest people around," he told author Peter Heller in his excellent book, *In This Corner.* "My mother died when I was five years old, when we first came to California. We never had enough to eat. My father worked like a son of a bitch, God rest his soul. He was a labourer, he did anything when he came here from Italy.

"My elder brother Ted began boxing, he was a pretty good fighter but he never contributed any dough. All he was good for was to go out with dames after he got paid. My father was working up there in Bakersfield, I don't know what the hell he did.

"He used to send Ted money to pay the rent but Ted used to go out and spend it on a good time. My brother Joe and I and Tony never saw a dime of that money. We had to go out and hustle after school to sell papers. After I'd get through hustling papers, I'd go down to the bowling alley to set pins till twelve o'clock. I learned to fight here as a newsboy.

"Then I began to box at the Athletic Club quite regularly until they ran out of opponents. Then Mr Blake, the coach at the Los Angeles AC, would have to go out and find opponents for me...I won the National championship and automatically they put me on the Olympic team. In Paris I beat four or five guys and got to the final where I had to fight this tough, rugged guy from Great Britain. I was just a little punk and he looked so goddamn big! But I fought him and I beat him and won the Olympic Games and, Jesus Christ, I stood there and they played the Star-Spangled Banner, it was the greatest thrill in the world.

"Now it was a question of whether to become a professional and make enough money to help my family, or whether to go to Stanford University. I had the marks. So I talked it over with Mr Blake and he said I should fight pro now. 'Your education you can get later.' Mr Blake agreed to become my manager on one condition, we didn't sign a contract. 'If we can't deal honestly and shake hands,' he said, 'then there's no use in even writing a contract.'"

Fidel's Olympic gold medal earned him a fifteen-hundred dollar purse for his first pro fight and he was on his way. A handsome kid with wavy black hair, he became a great favourite with the Hollywood fight crowd and the ringside was always studded with movie stars when LaBarba was on the card. Fidel had three terrific battles with Jimmy McLarnin, an Irish kid from Canada who was destined for ring stardom.

LaBarba's rise was meteoric, his big chance coming in August 1925. World flyweight champion Pancho Villa had died tragically, leaving the throne vacant. Frankie Genaro promptly claimed the title, having beaten Villa shortly before the Filipino took the championship from Jimmy Wilde. But it was decreed that Genaro would have to fight LaBarba for the title. Genaro wanted the fight in New York, his hometown, while Fidel plumped for Los Angeles. George Blake made Genaro an offer he couldn't refuse...fight LaBarba in Los Angeles and bring your own referee! Frankie agreed and named Harry Ertle of New Jersey as third man. Imagine Frankie's feelings when, after ten hard rounds, Ertle awarded the decision and the title to LaBarba!

"Mr Blake knew Frankie Genaro and had been in Genaro's corner in the 1920 Olympics, and he knew Frankie was a good fighter," LaBarba told Peter Heller. "He knew he could move and jump in the air and hit you three times before his feet landed on the ground again...We went up in the mountains and I got myself in great shape, wonderful shape.

"Now I'm fighting Frankie Genaro for the title. It's about the second round and we're both trying to feint each other out and Frankie says, 'C'mon, c'mon.' As soon as he says that, bing! bing! bing! bing! bing! Blake told me whenever a fighter's saying 'C'mon, c'mon,' go in fast, smash him fast, because his mind is not on defence, it's on what he's telling you. I remembered, see! I had a good sharp mind and, Jesus Christ, I smashed him. The crowd roared because I popped him about three or four good hard smashes on the nose. I won the fight. There was no question about my winning the fight and I'm the flyweight champion of the world."

But Fidel was only champion in American eyes, and it wasn't until January 1927 that he won universal recognition with an easy victory over European champion Elky Clark in Madison Square Garden.

In the short space of two-and-a-half years, LaBarba had gone from an Olympic title to the professional championship of the world, a remarkable achievement. A few months later, having fulfilled one ambition, Fidel set about his other aim in life, to attend Stanford University. He had visited Stanford as an amateur boxer and said later, "I fell in love with the place. I promised myself that if I got anywhere as a pro fighter, I would go to college there. Mr Blake sat down and wrote the New York Boxing Commission, not the California Commission. New York was the big shot. Mr Blake sat down and he wrote them a letter telling them that I was going back to the university, that I was going to matriculate at Stanford, and that I decided to give up my championship and quit the boxing game."

But LaBarba found life tougher than the fight game. "I got married, then my father died. Everything was happening, left and right. I was going in the brokerage business. That's where I lost my money. I lost a quarter of a million dollars like that, overnight. Remember that 1929 crash? It took me. I went to bed with a quarter of a million dollars and woke up the next morning, didn't have five cents!"

Fidel was a bantamweight when he came back to boxing, still only twenty-two. Kid Chocolate beat him with a flashing left hand, a trip to Paris resulted in a defeat by Kid Francis, Eddie Shea beat him in a bloody brawl in Cleveland. But he got back to winning form, beating guys like Earl Mastro, Bushy Graham, Bud Taylor, Petey Sarron, and Chocolate in a rematch. He beat Tommy Paul four times then challenged Battling Battalino for the world featherweight title. Fidel lost that one but by December 1932 he had fought his way back to another crack at the title, this time against the Cuban hotshot Kid Chocolate. They fought in Madison Square Garden and nine of eleven newspapermen thought LaBarba won it.

Referee Willie Lewis saw them even after fifteen rounds, but judges Sam Austin and Eddie Farrell cast their votes for the winner and still champion, Kid Chocolate. A storm of booing rocked the Garden as Joe Humphreys tried to make his announcement, holding Chocolate's glove aloft as tears streamed down the Kid's ebony face. LaBarba was stunned, his victory smile wiped away as he realised his fight had been in vain. Next day, *The Brooklyn Eagle's* Ed Hughes caught the seasonal flavour in his column when he wrote, "Santa Claus gave Chocolate his gift prematurely last night. I gave LaBarba nine rounds, Chocolate four, and called two even."

"Accidentally, boxing with this guy, my sparring partner," Fidel told Heller, "I came too fast and bingo! My left eye went right into the point of his elbow, and I let out a scream, you don't know! We stopped everything. That eye popped up, in five minutes got this big. This was on a Tuesday, the second day I got into town. Friday night is the Chocolate fight. I began to put hot and cold applications on my eye night and day, until finally, by the day I went for the weighing in, you couldn't tell that I had anything wrong with me, that anything was wrong with my eye. But a film had come across my eye about halfway, and below I couldn't see. The retina is on the screen, like a movie screen, and you rip into it, it's beginning to tear. I had a tear there. That blinded me.

"I remember that championship fight. I remember very well, because, as we were boxing, Jesus Christ, I was nailing him some pretty good belts, left hooks, in the belly. That was my good shot, then bang to the jaw. Then all of a sudden this film begins to come up. My vision was completely black below. It was like cut in half. The retina was tearing down more. When I was fighting Chocolate, it got to the point where I couldn't see at all out of that eye. Personally, I thought I won the fight."

Some twenty days later, LaBarba was back in the ring, fighting Tommy Paul, a squatty little Italian from Buffalo who was recognised as featherweight champion by the National Boxing Association. It was a non-title bout at the Chicago Stadium with Fidel getting away to a fast start over a guy he had beaten four times. But Paul came on strong to grab the lead with deadly counter punches and LaBarba had to take a few stiff belts on the chin. At the end of ten rounds one judge saw them even but the other two officials gave it to Paul. The day after the fight, Fidel was to have left for Buffalo where he was scheduled to meet Tony Sciolino but the fight was postponed and he stayed in Chicago, training at Trafton's Gym. He never did get to fight Sciolino. A couple of weeks later he was back in New York City to fight Seaman Tommy Watson at the Garden and they said if he beat the Limey he would get another crack at Kid Chocolate for the title.

Friday 27 January 1933. Fight night in the Garden. A noisy crowd of 11,324 fans, having paid $13,992 to come through the turnstiles out of the biting wind that blew along Eighth Avenue, sat impatiently through the undercard fights waiting for the main event. Slowly the ringside seats were filling up with the guys and dolls from Broadway, millionaires from the business world, producers and stars of the entertainment world, mob guys from the underworld. The big guns of the New York papers took their seats on the press bench, guys like Paul Gallico, Damon Runyon, Dan Parker. To most of them, LaBarba's opponent was still Tommy Who?

Murray Lewin's preview in the *New York Herald Post* typified the general opinion of his colleagues. "Watson impressed one as a plugger, pure and simple. Unlike the majority of English fighters, the former member of the British Navy knows exactly how to handle himself in close quarters.

"Instead of playing it safe by attempting to tie up his opponent he continually pumps both hands to the body. Unfortunately for the invader he appears easy to hit with a straight left jab, left hook, or right uppercut. I use the word unfortunately for the main reason that the three blows mentioned are LaBarba's best assets and those with which he has always raised so much havoc. Thus it looks as though Watson is in for a rough night."

Fighting off an attack of tonsillitis, the British champion had already had a rough morning. "To the consternation of Harvey and myself," said Mortimer, "Watson was three pounds overweight. The weigh-in was at two o'clock and there was a 2,000 dollar weight forfeit. I had arranged for Tommy to go to the Turkish Baths, but he left us and went to the hotel where we were staying, and there, working and sweating in the bathroom all on his own, he took the weight off in time to go to the scales. Tommy made it by a quarter of a pound. While Harvey and I were worrying about the forfeit, Seaman's chief concern appeared to be the Union Jack that he wanted sewn on the leg of his shorts!"

"What a different atmosphere Madison Square Garden in New York presents in comparison with St James's Hall in Newcastle," Watson would recall. "Or any other British boxing hall. There were more than eleven thousand people there on the night I fought LaBarba and you can imagine how many Americanisms I heard as I walked to the ring. 'Say, buddy, the Britisher looks a tough guy.' 'Oh, yeah! Fidel will lick the Limey bum!' But let me say at once that I was pleasantly surprised by the reception I got as I stepped into the ring, with one object in mind, to beat LaBarba and so pave my way to a world title fight with Chocolate, and also avenge the defeat of a former British champion, Elky Clark, whom LaBarba had beaten a few years ago."

The wise guys were nodding their heads in the first round as LaBarba set a blistering pace from the bell, hammering both hands to head and body. Watson, who enjoyed advantages in both height and reach, stood his ground and punched back but he was jolted by solid right and left hooks and almost went through the ropes. Towards the end of the round a left to the body knocked him to the canvas. A roar went up from the crowd but Watson was back on his feet before it had died away and he rallied strongly. But it was LaBarba's round.

"Throughout the first round," remembered Tommy, "I was weighing up the American, his style and more effective hand, and soon saw that he was one of those very fast boxers who rush at you and have a go from the very first gong. The crowd was roaring when we went to our corners at the end of the round. All kinds of advice was being shouted at both of us, but I did not hear it. One of the chief things to remember when you are engaged in a fight is to concentrate not only during the rounds but between them and it is a point I never forget."

Watson did better in the second round. They rushed to close quarters and Tommy got home a number of blows to the body. Fidel backed off but the British champion kept after him and a solid right hook to the jaw shook LaBarba. Fidel came back with both guns firing and Tommy was knocked off balance when he got his feet crossed. He came right back at the American and a smashing right to the jaw shook him to his heels and brought a roar from the crowd. The round looked pretty even.

The big crowd began to warm to the British champion in the third as Tommy went straight into the attack, pounding both hands to the body to have LaBarba shaken several times. The American fought back desperately but at the bell it was Watson's round.

"LaBarba had acquired a big reputation for his left hook," recalled Tommy, "a devastating punch that had put many good men on the canvas, and I made sure that he never got a chance to put it on my jaw. It became a battle of scheming, LaBarba trying to fence me off and make an opening for his famous left hook while I forced the fighting and used every blow I knew."

Round four and both fighters were showing respect for each other. Fidel was dancing over the canvas, trying to feint Tommy into leaving an opening for the left hook. The American did find a way through to Watson's jaw with a ramrod straight left, a beautiful punch that took Seaman's legs away from him. But Tommy was up straight away and straight back into the fight and just before the bell he caught LaBarba with a solid left to the head that knocked him into the ropes. It was Fidel's round by a shade.

They battled on even terms through the fifth with the crowd yelling for both fighters. Those who had expected the Limey to fold up at the first tap on the whiskers were standing up cheering for Seaman Watson. This guy knows how to fight! LaBarba took the sixth round but he was more cautious now, countering as Watson led, and he scored several times with hooks and uppercuts to the body.

Into the seventh and Seaman began to take charge as LaBarba tired. The British champion rushed to the attack and Fidel went into reverse, stabbing out a tentative left hand, but he couldn't keep Watson at bay. Tommy forced his way inside and hammered the body with lefts and rights and again the American was sounding retreat as the invader piled on the pressure. Vicious left and right hooks rocked Fidel across the ring and the big arena was a bedlam. They clinched and Watson slipped to the floor, but he was up straight away and it was his round by a country mile.

Coming out for work in round eight, LaBarba knows he has a fight on his hands and he opens up, banging his favourite left hook to the head and to the body, but Watson is as strong as an ox and absorbs the punches like an Everlast bag, firing his own searing uppercuts into Fidel's body to finish the round all square. Watson is fighting all out now, no pretence at boxing, going to his man with both hands ripping to the body, then to the head, smashing away to have the Garden fans comparing him with Kid Berg, that other British guy who fights like an American.

Round ten, Watson coming forward, taking the fight to LaBarba, slamming in left and right uppercuts, Fidel countering beautifully with the left hand, jabbing, hooking, desperately fighting for his professional life but being swept aside as the sturdy British Seaman steams into him with both guns firing, raking the American amidships.

"In the tenth round," remembered Watson, "the crowd seemed to be for me to a man. Their enthusiasm was probably aroused through seeing the unexpected, for I know they expected me to be knocked out by their man."

Round eleven is a bad one for LaBarba. Both fighters meet in ring centre like two stags in the rutting season, heads down, fists locked in combat, pounding the body. LaBarba breaks away, seeking an opening for his pet left hook but Watson gives him no rest, chasing him across the ring until the ropes are at his back and he has to try bobbing and weaving to avoid the avalanche of leather that threatens to swamp him. A vicious left from Watson rips a cut over Fidel's left eye and the crowd is roaring for the Britisher as he goes to his corner. Twelfth and final round, both men out fast throwing punches, ringsiders on their feet screaming encouragement as the gloves cut through the smoke haze hanging over the ring, thudding against tired flesh. LaBarba is hanging on when the bell ends his torment.

"The winner, Watson!" The simple announcement brings a storm of applause from all over the Garden as the New York fans give the British champion a tremendous ovation. He has earned it! Now he faces another fight, to get through the crowd to his dressing room. Hands reach out to slap his back, to touch him, to shake his hand.

"Helluva fight, Seaman!" yells one guy.

"You showed 'em, Tommy!" shouts another.

Two burly cops finally get Tommy to his dressing room but there is no peace there. The room is full of reporters, the same guys who picked LaBarba to stiffen the Limey in their morning columns. Looking surprisingly fresh and unmarked, Seaman answers their questions politely as 'Uncle' John Mortimer and Charlie Harvey stand in the background grinning like Cheshire cats with their own bowl of cream.

"I am glad I did not let my shipmates down," says Tommy, "I did my best. Well, Chocolate is the next."

Over in LaBarba's dressing room it is not so crowded. Fidel, his handsome face bearing the marks of battle, is gracious in defeat. Naturally disappointed, he does not question the decision. "It was a fine, clean fight," he says to a couple of reporters. "I hope I may be able to fight in London some day."

That night, Tommy Watson slept like a baby, and when he woke up he was the talk of the town. Mortimer had the New York papers spread all over the floor and the boy from Byker was the toast of Broadway, his name in the headlines of every sports section.

"Watson made the fistic wiseacres look very foolish," wrote Hype Igoe. "He was quite willing to mix it throughout and he beat one of our best cleanly, fairly, and decisively. As a boxing treat, it was a beauty!"

Jack Kofoed in the *Evening Post*, "...the wired-muscled awkward

Englishman boxed his way to victory. He is a much better man than his style would indicate. This fellow will cause trouble among our featherweights, you can count on that."

"Seaman Watson starts like Phil Scott and finishes a la Jim Driscoll," said Harry Grayson in the *World-Telegram*. "Virtually unheard of until he was brought here by Squire John Mortimer, he was forced to undergo an absolutely unfair trial by jury but now has the big laugh on several boxing officials. He received an ovation such as no little foreign fighter has had in America since the days of Jim Driscoll."

"Watson's victory over LaBarba came as a shocking upset to those who had backed the American," the *New York Times* commented. "Watson's win was earned because he was a better boxer than LaBarba, and a better two-fisted fighter whose rapid-fire tactics compare favourably with those of Kid Berg."

The sports pages also carried a report from the Press Association correspondent in Havana. "I am glad to hear of Watson's convincing victory," said Kid Chocolate. "As soon as I can go to New York I shall be very glad to give him a chance of winning my title."

The Sporting Chronicle's New York representative cabled this glowing report to his London office, "When all was over, Watson was given a splendid greeting as a real fighting man after New York's pugilistic heart. LaBarba was booed, not only by those who had backed him, but also because of his several attempts to rough, attempts which Watson very cleverly turned against him without even glancing at referees or judges, just smiling to himself. Contrary to all expectations, he outfought LaBarba at his favourite game of infighting.

"I think everybody expected to see the usual English style, standing straight up, boxing excellently well with the left jab, correctly developed, and were surprised to find a swift-moving, cool-headed lad smartly getting inside his opponent's guard with pistol-like lefts, to rip into the body with telling lefts and rights, thus escaping trouble in boring in against a lad of LaBarba's known calibre, being now regarded as a masterpiece of offensive boxing. So the ugly duckling that was rated to lose to the first good man he met, came through as a fistic swan."

"My most lasting impression of my fight with LaBarba,"

reflected Tommy later, "was the enthusiasm and sportsmanship of the New York crowd at Madison Square Garden, they were splendid and rose to me so overwhelmingly I did not know where I was. While I do not want to take any undue credit on myself they certainly do recognise when a man has guts. All the things I'd heard about the New York boxing fans and all the criticisms were unfounded as far as I was concerned. I was rather nervy when I went into the ring that night but that was not from any fear of LaBarba. I was full of confidence and although I was down in the first round I never thought of defeat. It was probably because I was in strange surroundings fighting before a strange crowd that I did not find my feet at once. But afterwards I knew just where I had got LaBarba and with all due deference to a very fine boxer, I think he knew too."

15

HAIL, THE CONQUERING HERO!

Even though it was only a quarter-to-four on that cold Saturday morning in January 1933, Kitty Watson was not asleep. She was waiting for the sound of the taxi bringing the reporter from the *Chronicle* offices with the result of Tommy's fight in New York. Good or bad, she had asked that the news be brought to her as soon as possible, and now she could hear the taxi pulling up outside the New Hawk Inn on Byker Bank and she was down the stairs and opening the door as the reporter climbed out of the cab.

"What happened?" she asked breathlessly, her heart pounding.

"He won! He beat the Yank!" came the answer she hadn't dare hope for, and now the tears came freely as she dashed back upstairs into the living room. Then, wiping her eyes, she begged details of the fight...was Tommy all right, had he been knocked down, was he cut, had he knocked the Yankee fellow out, did the people like him?

In between answering the door to neighbours, anxious to hear the news, Kitty calmed herself to say, "This is good news you have brought me. I received a letter from Tommy yesterday in which he said he was coming home soon after the fight. Of course, this victory may mean that Tommy will alter his plans. That, however, depends upon him. I would like him home as soon as possible, but he knows best what is good for the bairns and myself. I expect a cable from him today and I need not say he will not be long in getting one from me."

Tommy's cable to Kitty arrived from New York at 9.20am that morning, stating simply, "WON MY FIGHT. BE HAPPY. TOMMY." Within a few hours the *Evening Chronicle* was on the streets with the news of the Byker lad's great victory. The front page headline told the story:

SEAMAN WATSON DOES THE ALI BA(R)BA TRICK...OPEN
SESAME TO A WORLD'S CHAMPIONSHIP...NEWCASTLE
BOXER'S NEW YORK TRIUMPH.

110

Like all North East sportsmen, Newcastle promoter John Paget was over the moon. "After witnessing Seaman Watson's victory over Nel Tarleton at Liverpool, I had no doubt in my mind that, given a fair crack of the whip, he would not let the old country down. I cabled him yesterday, 'Best of luck tonight. Hope to see you in St James's Hall as champion of the world soon.' Watson has gone a long way towards realising my hope."

Old time fighter Will Curley said, "Splendid! Few people yet know how good Tom Watson is."

Mr Tom Steckles enthused, "I think Tom Watson has struck a fine blow for British boxing by this victory. He has more decisively than ever brought to the notice of national boxing critics, and the British Boxing Board of Control, that we have men in the boxing game on Tyneside and Wearside at the present time who simply cannot be ignored."

The next day, the *Chronicle's* sister paper, the *Sunday Sun*, carried glowing tributes from leading personalities in the fight game. Well known referee Mr C H Douglas stated, "I was always impressed by sailors. I have seen Watson on several occasions, and I know he is a very game boxer. When he beat Tarleton I made up my mind he was capable of beating anybody. I believe he will beat Chocolate for the title, too. Good luck, Watson!"

Unstinting praise came from Ted Broadribb, manager of Nel Tarleton. "He prevented Tarleton going to America and fighting for the title, but I can easily forget that in face of Watson's great victory over LaBarba, and I wish him luck. It was an achievement to beat such a man."

Another top manager in Dan Sullivan was quoted as saying, "I am very pleased indeed. I had more than an ordinary interest in Watson. I was warned some time ago to keep an eye on him. I watched him fight at Newcastle and immediately made up my mind he would be heard of in connection with a championship. A real trier usually goes a long way. I think Watson will."

That Sunday evening, a *Journal* reporter visited Kitty at the New Hawk Inn. "I found nothing," he wrote, "to indicate this was the home of a now world famous pugilist. There was no fuss, no excitement. Mrs Watson was attending to her household duties as calmly as if nothing had happened. Nevertheless she is quietly proud of her husband's achievement. She said that she was so pleased he had won but felt disappointed that it was LaBarba he had fought instead of Kid Chocolate. 'I have had no news from my husband since I received his cable on Saturday morning. Unless he is to stay in the States to meet Chocolate, he should return home immediately. I see from the papers that he has an attack of tonsillitis but I know nothing about it except that he has been troubled with these symptoms before.'"

As Newcastle prepared to welcome the Geordie hero home, New York was saying its own farewell to the salty little ex-seaman who had overcome every obstacle placed in his way in a quiet, modest, and determined manner backed by enormous self-belief. Although the LaBarba victory had firmly established Tommy's right to challenge Chocolate for his title, the fight seemed no nearer, and the proposed date of 27 February no longer appeared viable. Seaman told Mortimer he wanted to go home and Uncle John agreed to stay on in New York until the Chocolate fight was settled.

The night he was to sail for England, Tommy was guest of honour at a dinner thrown for him at the George Washington Hotel by a group of Englishmen living in New York. They had been delighted by his victory over LaBarba, none more so than Mr Donald Nevill-Willing who shared his time between New York and London where he had a home in Park Lane. Later that night, after the dinner, Tommy was due to board the Norddeutscher-Lloyd liner Europa for the voyage home. His friends made sure that he didn't miss the boat!

"Police patrols and shrieking motor cycles scurried through the streets of New York," recalled Tommy, "clearing all the traffic out of our way. It was the fastest bit of work I have seen in my life, and when I got to the boat I found that not even Sir Ronald Lindsay, the British Ambassador, who was travelling in the Europa to England, got such a send-off."

On the voyage home, Tommy had time to read again the pile of cables and telegrams of congratulation he had received after the fight. There was one from someone signing herself, "A canny lass frae Newcastle." The most poignant however was from Alderman Richard Henry Millican, the former Lord Mayor of Newcastle who had taken a fatherly interest in the boy from Byker since presenting him with a certificate for saving a pal from drowning.

Alderman Millican had given Tommy his first job, helped him become a boy sailor in the Royal Navy, and taken a keen interest in his boxing career, always sending a telegram of congratulation on his latest victory. But the message Tommy received in New York would be the last. Alderman Millican had died on 31 December, two days after Watson had sailed for New York, and before his death he had left instructions with his son to send Tommy a cable if he won his fight. "That is something which I shall always appreciate," said Tommy.

When the Europa berthed at Cherbourg before sailing for Southampton, a reporter from the *Sporting Chronicle* boarded the ship and interviewed Watson in his cabin after handing him a letter from Kitty who, in Tommy's words, "though far away in Newcastle, has been my best pal since I set foot in New York. Everyone is naturally anxious to know about my next big fight. It was my original intention to remain in New York to meet Kid Chocolate for the world title but fate in the shape of the immigration authorities stepped in and Chocolate finds that he is debarred from entering the USA. The reason for this ban is none of my business but I am disappointed nevertheless, because it may mean that I will not have a chance of meeting the Cuban and I do so want to have a crack at him.

"I expected that I would be fighting Chocolate in New York in March but now it appears that efforts are being made to match me with Tony Canzoneri who is willing to make 132 lbs for me. This fight would be for Canzoneri's world lightweight championship. I wish I knew definitely what is going to happen, otherwise I will have to hang fire for the next six months. When you consider that I can get three times as much money in America as in this country and that I have struggled for years on the smallish purses for the fights I have had, you see my viewpoint."

One of the first things Tommy did when he came off the Europa at Southampton was to buy a gold wrist watch for Kitty. "Just a little appreciation of a very good wife," he muttered quietly to a reporter at his side. Then he was off to London by car to meet with manager Alec Lambert in Edgeware and to a welcome reunion with Kitty who had travelled down from Newcastle rather than wait for her husband to arrive back on Tyneside. Next morning they were up bright and early to catch the Flying Scotsman from Kings Cross at ten o'clock. They were going home.

Long before the train was due in Newcastle, crowds began to gather at the Central Station, taking up vantage points on the walls and on the bridge to platforms 9 and 10, and when the train steamed in at three o'clock it was estimated that some 10,000 people were there in a pushing, shoving, heaving mass of humanity that spilled over into Neville Street. On the main platform were relatives and friends, among them John Paget, Tommy Steckles, boxer Norman Dale, a regular sparmate of Seaman's and, as the *Newcastle Journal* reported, "the diminutive but singularly penetrative Mickey McGuire who seemed as pleased with Watson's performance as though it had been his own."

There was a little boy there also, two-and-a-half year old Tom Watson Jnr, who kept saying, "I want my Daddy, I want my Daddy." Seaman had sent a telegram asking that his son be brought to the station and Billy Laws, a nephew of his mother's, was there early with little Tom in his arms. As Tommy stepped from the train to a tumultuous welcoming roar, his eyes swept the sea of faces for sight of his son. First to greet Watson was Tommy Steckles and he led Seaman to where Laws was standing with the boy. Taking his son tight in his arms Tommy kissed him as the cameras flashed and reporters pushed close for an interview.

"I'm glad to be home," said Tommy, always a man of few words. Kitty, looking flushed with excitement, her arms full of parcels, could only say, "I'm glad we are here. It's wonderful."

A pipe band played a welcome and every few minutes a cheer went up from the crowd as Watson, Mrs Watson, McGuire, and the rest of the group gradually worked their way through the throng to reach the taxis waiting to take them to Byker. Even then it appeared that they would not be able to leave the station and it was only when mounted police aided by policemen holding on to the car and standing on the running boards cleared a way that the vehicle was able to move out into Neville Street for the tour of triumph, preceded by mounted policemen and a car with a newsreel cameraman perched on top.

Byker Bank had never known a day like it. Since early morning people were busy making preparations to welcome Seaman home and the street was festooned with flags and bunting. In front of the New Hawk Inn stretched a great banner bearing the legend, WELCOME TO OUR HERO! Knowing Watson's shyness, the local people were determined in spite of his dislike for any fuss, to give him a reception worthy of his achievement.

"I knew Tommy when he was a bairn," said Mrs Annie Telfer, who kept a fruiterer's shop on the Bank. "I used to dangle him on my knee, and sometimes when he was naughty I used to smack him. But I would not like to risk that now!"

Later that afternoon, a cry went up from the crowd, "He's here, he's coming!" As Tommy's taxi appeared at the top of the Bank, the Byker Juvenile Jazz Band struck up and, with great difficulty, led the procession through the jubilant, cheering throng, eventually reaching Tommy's pub where he was mobbed as he stepped from the taxi.

"When our Tommy came home from America," recalled Frances, "that day stands so vividly in my mind. He had the Hawk Inn, down Byker Bank, and my mother and all of us were hanging out of the Hawk windows, waiting for the jazz band bringing him in from Newcastle, and I suppose you couldn't get moved at the Central Station for police on horseback. He came home like a champion, because he'd beaten LaBarba, I mean he was made a god of in Byker. There is no disputing about that!"

The crowds wouldn't go away from outside the pub, cheering their heads off and shouting for Tommy to make a speech. Eventually a roar went up as he appeared at an upstairs window. Looking terribly embarrassed and shy, he said, "Thank you very much. I went out to fight for the world's championship but I had to do the next best thing, I beat the best man available. I hope to fight for the championship soon."

Only when he had disappeared back inside the room did the crowd begin to drift away, happily telling each other how they had known Tommy since he was a bairn and how they had always known he would be a champion. One thing they were all agreed upon. "Wor Tommy is a canny lad!"

16

MARKING TIME

A few days after Tommy Watson's triumphant return from America, a *Sunday Sun* reporter found him working hard alongside wife Kitty at the New Hawk Inn. Between pulling pints, Seaman gave his impressions of New York

"Byker an easy winner on points," he said. "Broadway is big and flashy, but over all the place is far inferior to the Bank. I didn't get around much. Before the fight it was mostly training and sleeping, and after the fight dinners and suppers. I saw the tall buildings, of course. They're very fine, but I like Byker better. I did get to one night club after the fight. It was all right, but I didn't touch any of the liquor, it is poison!"

"Watson is one of the most reserved men I have ever come across," observed the reporter, "but he did admit he was sorry he just missed meeting Jack Dempsey."

In just three months and two fights, against Tarleton and Fidel LaBarba, Tommy Watson had shot from virtual obscurity to fame, if not fortune, although the *Daily Mail* reported his purse for the LaBarba fight as being £500 after paying all expenses, easily the biggest payday of his career. But while the North-East was literally bursting with pride over their Geordie hero, it seemed the rest of the country was still trying to come to terms with Watson's success.

Just a few days after the LaBarba fight, as Watson set sail from New York, an English newspaper quoted Ted Broadribb as having sent a cable to the Madison Square Garden people suggesting that the supporting card to the forthcoming Kid Chocolate-Seaman Watson title fight be made up of Anglo-American contests, i.e. Nel Tarleton v Fidel LaBarba, Phineas John v Tommy Paul, Tommy Hyams v Baby Arizmendi.

"Tarleton, I feel, was extremely unfortunate to be deprived of the chance accorded to Watson in fighting for the title," said Broadribb, "and I think he could beat LaBarba even more decisively than did Watson. If he did so, I don't doubt that the Americans would be ready enough to recognise his claims to a title match."

"Very nice, too," said the *Newcastle Journal*, springing to Watson's defence. "But how on earth does Broadribb assume that Tarleton would beat LaBarba more decisively than did Watson? The whole scheme suggests that Broadribb wants to get at Watson in a roundabout way, and hopes that if Watson becomes world champion, Tarleton will be the first to be considered as the Tynesider's challenger. The real trouble with boxing people in this country, at any rate outside the North-East, is that they have not yet got over Tarleton's defeat at the hands of Watson, and the latter's great success in America."

"Watson has his enemies," wrote journalist T S Phillips, "professional, not personal. Lancashire has never forgiven him for unexpectedly and sensationally beating Nel Tarleton and depriving the cotton county of the British featherweight championship. Lancashire, let the truth be told, is championship greedy. Lancashire wants a corner in titles, in all the best fights. Lancashire will never rest until a Manchester or Liverpool featherweight is wearing Watson's featherweight crown, but I don't think the Seaman will worry about that."

Mr Jeff Dickson, the American promoter based in Paris, was reported to have made an offer to Chocolate for three fights under his banner. The first would be in Barcelona against Jose Girones, the second in Paris with Kid Francis, and the third in London versus either Watson or Tarleton. The suggestion was that the Cuban would not be defending his title in any of these contests and indicated that the prospect of Watson fighting Chocolate for the title in America was not at all bright.

However, a news agency report from New York dated 9 February 1933 stated that Jimmy Johnston, the Garden matchmaker, had been informed by the American immigration authorities that it was most likely Kid Chocolate would be able to enter the United States again within a couple of months. After receiving this news, Johnston told the Press Association that it was now expected that Seaman Watson would get his world title fight sometime in May, and on that cheery note, "Uncle" John Mortimer booked passage on the s.s. Leviathan, sailing from New York for dear old Blighty, promising to bring Watson back in good time.

At this news, Watson announced that he was to relinquish his post as manager of the New Hawk Inn and take up private residence with his family, "until my American affairs are settled."

Shortly after returning from New York, Tommy was the guest of honour of the Rotarians at a luncheon at their Newcastle city headquarters, where he received the following welcome from President Mr S Addison Smith. "Rotary's sixth object is the promotion of international friendship, and if travelling in another country and giving one of its nationals a good hammering is a means of promoting friendship, then we have a real ambassador of peace in Mr Watson. We congratulate him and wish him further success."

A few nights later Tommy appeared on the stage of the Royal Theatre at Wallsend to make an appeal for funds for the Newcastle Dispensary, and while collection boxes were being passed around he made a short speech expressing his regret in being unable to bring back the championship from America but believed he would have better luck now that the Chocolate fight had been re-scheduled.

Arriving back in England, Mortimer announced that Watson would probably get his world title shot in late March, but Tommy was still waiting for a definite date when reporters contacted him, in fact he was still not sure that when his big chance came Kid Chocolate would be in the other corner. A letter he had received from Charlie Harvey in New York stated, "Can always arrange match for the world lightweight championship between Tony Canzoneri and yourself, but I have positively refused to consider such a proposition until we definitely dispose of the Chocolate match."

Mortimer had written to Watson on similar lines. "Jim Johnston, the Madison Square Garden matchmaker, wanted to stage you with Canzoneri at 130 lbs but I think that we must concentrate on Chocolate. I saw the messages from Washington myself, and they will get Chocolate all right."

However, there was a growing suspicion in British boxing circles that maybe Jimmy Johnston and his Garden backers didn't want to get Chocolate for Tommy Watson, having seen how the Geordie handled LaBarba, and that Watson had become a victim of boxing politics in New York City. So who were these men who held the hopes and dreams of the young British champion in their hands?

Jimmy Johnston was the man in the driving seat at Madison Square Garden, a long way from Liverpool where he was born, the son of an iron-moulder. Jimmy was thirteen when the family emigrated to New York and settled in the Hell's Kitchen district of the city. Quitting school to work in a foundry in Jersey City, young Johnston boxed at night to make a few bucks. His biggest purse was 150 dollars when fighting Danny Dougherty, to whom Terry McGovern had willed his bantamweight title. Jimmy was knocked out in round ten. Never weighing more than 105 pounds soaking wet, Jimmy fought for six years before he figured there were easier ways of becoming rich. He jumped at the offer of a job from Broadway fight manager Charlie Harvey who specialised in importing foreign boxers to the States, among them top Britons Owen Moran, Jim Driscoll, and Ted Kid Lewis.

When Moran fought Abe Attell in California, Harvey sent Johnston along to look after him. Sometime after the fight, Jimmy arrived back in New York without Moran. "He's in the hospital," Johnston told Harvey. "Doctors say he won't be able to fight for a couple of months." The tough little Birmingham battler had a fractured jaw, a broken left hand, and assorted lumps and bruises. He had fought a gruelling draw with Attell but his injuries had not been suffered at the talented fists of the world featherweight champion.

They were the result of an argument with Johnston in the hotel lobby! When he was sober, Moran was a nice little fellow, but when he was drunk, he was a holy terror who beat up his wife if there was nobody else around at the time. Harvey told Johnston to keep Moran off the booze but when Jimmy found him it was too late. Moran swung a punch, Jimmy ducked, then tripped Moran, bit his nose and jumped on his stomach with both feet. Then he grabbed Owen by the hair and was banging his head on the tiled floor when the hotel detective pulled him off. Moran went to the hospital and Johnston went back to New York.

Only a little guy, Johnston feared no man and was soon known for his explosive temper. In 1912 he leased the old Madison Square Garden and ran fight shows there for three years. He did well, but knew he should have been doing better. The cheap seats were selling out but his ringside patrons stayed away. Jimmy discovered that East Side gangsters and their cronies were commandeering the best seats in the house and scaring off the carriage trade. One night, he marched down to the ringside, yanked a startled hoodlum out of his seat, gave him a good kicking and threw him out! He had no more trouble after that. While running the old Garden, he liked to tell how he leased it to Tex Rickard who wanted to stage the Jess Willard-Frank Moran fight in New York. Johnston, who leased the place for $1,000, charged Rickard a staggering $15,400 for the night!

Jimmy handled burlesque shows, marathon runner Johnny Hayes, staged six-mile bicycle races and auto racing in New York, but it was in the fight racket that he blossomed. *Herald-Tribune* sports editor Bill McGeehan called him the Boy Bandit, tribute to a youthful appearance and a gift for larceny. Jimmy was a hustler, always working the angles, looking for a way to make a fast buck.

Running fights at the St Nicholas Rink in New York, he had the press boys all steamed up with his new headliner, Ah Chung, lightweight champion of China! When he fought, the place was packed with people from Chinatown, businessmen, restaurant owners, laundry workers. Chung won a few fights but spoiled everything one night when he got into an argument with a cab driver and forgot he wasn't supposed to speak English. At the police station he turned out to be Paddy Mulligan from Philadelphia. Noting Paddy's slanting eyes, Johnston had dressed him up at a theatrical costumier, had his hair cut, his skin coloured by a make-up artist who owed him a favour, told Paddy to keep his mouth shut, and presented him to a New York media hungry for colourful copy.

Then there was George Boer Rodel, a big South African heavyweight who was too courageous for his own good. Johnston handled Rodel in New York and gave the press stories of his tiger's heroic exploits in the Boer War, overlooking the fact that Rodel was only thirteen when the war ended! After being bounced off the canvas nine times in ten rounds by Gunboat Smith, the Boer was matched with Jess Willard. The Kansas farmer had just beaten Bull Young, who died after the fight, and Johnston knew Jess was still upset over the tragedy. Before the fight with Rodel, Jimmy managed to get Willard alone long enough to whisper to him that Boer had a weak heart and to take it easy. It was a ten rounds No Decision bout and Rodel was still on his feet at the final bell.

Welshman Danny Thomas started fighting as Young Daniel. In 1920 he found himself in New York and walked into Johnston's Broadway office looking for fights. Noting the lad's dark, swarthy appearance Johnston marched him off to the nearest Woolworths store where he dressed him up in cheap earrings, brass bracelets, and a brightly coloured bandanna.

Then Johnston took his new boy on a tour of the newspaper offices, introducing him as Gipsy Daniels, next heavyweight champion of the world! Daniels got some publicity and he won five out of six fights around New York, but packed his bag and sailed for home after receiving a letter from his father disowning him for posing as a "dirty, thieving gipsy!" Daniels was actually a pretty useful scrapper. In 1927 he beat Tom Berry to become British light-heavyweight champion and a few months later he went to Germany and knocked out Max Schmeling in one round.

Jimmy Johnston reached the pinnacle in October 1931 when he was installed as promoter at Madison Square Garden by Colonel John Reed Kilpatrick, one time American football hero who gave Jimmy the ball and let him run with it. One newspaper article on the Boy Bandit called him "The High Priest in the Temple of Swat!" He had come a long way since starting out as Charlie Harvey's office boy all those years ago.

Harvey seemed to spend most of his life waiting on the dockside in New York City for his next champion to get off the boat. As well as Moran and Driscoll and Ted Kid Lewis, Charlie had many English boxers, among them Joe Conn and Johnnie Brown, and he had Australian Fred Fitzgerald and New Zealand heavyweight Tom Heeney. Like all fight managers, Harvey dreamed of finding a heavyweight champion and he thought his dream had come true when Heeney stepped ashore in New York.

John Mortimer and his brother Bernard, who were promoting and managing fighters around Southampton, heard of Heeney through a friend and invited him to come to England. Tom travelled on a meat boat, arriving with all his worldly belongings jammed in the pockets of his one and only suit. Short for a heavyweight, Tom was strong and rugged, and when he flattened Phil Scott in the gym they were matched over twenty rounds.

Scott won on points and repeated his victory a couple of years later. In between the Scott fights, Heeney beat Tom Berry, Johnny

Squires, Charley Smith, and Jack Stanley, and lost to George Cook. Mortimer advised Heeney to go to the States and fight his way across to the Pacific Coast, earning enough to get a passage home. In New York he was met by Harvey who soon put him to work. Tom lost to Paulino Uzcudun, drew in a rematch, and beat guys like Jim Maloney, Johnny Risko, and Jack Delaney. He fought a draw with Jack Sharkey and Charlie Harvey's boat came in...Gene Tunney, who had shocked the world by taking the heavyweight championship off Jack Dempsey and climbed off the deck to win the return, told Tex Rickard he was making one more defence and hanging up his gloves. Gene selected Heeney as a safe opponent rather than the erratic Sharkey. It was a sound choice, as Heeney was no match for Tunney's brilliant boxing skills and he was cut to ribbons before the referee led him back to his corner in the eleventh round.

Paul Gallico, who worked on the *New York Daily News* as sports editor, columnist, and assistant managing editor from 1922 to 1936 when he settled in England to become a novelist, recalled that fight in his book *A Farewell To Sport*, endorsed many years later by the *Daily Mail's* Ian Wooldridge as "An incomparable classic of sustained sportswriting."

In a chapter dealing with fight managers which he titled "Pigs At The Trough" Gallico wrote, "I remember particularly one kindly old gentleman, a veteran fight manager by the name of Charlie Harvey. He was a mild, sweet-looking old soul with innocent blue eyes and a walrus mustache. And I watched this man one night pick his beaten half-conscious fighter up and shove him out to destruction. The fighter was Tom Heeney and his destroyer was Gene Tunney, then heavyweight champion of the world. Harvey had neither the courage nor the decency to stop that fight.

"Years later he let another of his boys, Steve Hamas, take such a brutal beating at the hands of Max Schmeling that Hamas went to the hospital when it was over and never has been the same since."

Charlie Harvey and Jimmy Johnston handled the extensive American campaign of Ted Kid Lewis, and some of the strokes they pulled against one of Britain's greatest ever fighters are described in the brilliant book Morton Lewis wrote about his father. Of their first meeting, in 1914, the Kid would recall, "Johnston invariably smiled, even when the smile did not spread to his gimlet eyes. Here was a shrewd man, or a sharp man, depending on whether he was on your side or not...Harvey proved a charming man with whom it was impossible not to feel at ease from the moment one met him. During the whole time I was under his wing we never had a written contract. His word was his bond, or so I thought at the time."

In 1915, with Harvey and Johnston unable to fix Lewis up with any fights, the Kid took a fight in Havana on the Jess Willard-Jack Johnson card for a promised $2,000 plus expenses. "In the end I was lucky to finish with $200 as there wasn't money left over when Johnson was paid," he would recall. Back in New York, Harvey was unforgiving. "He seemed to have found out that we had been promised $2,000. 'We get a cut of that,' he said, referring to the fact that Johnston and he were still our managers. I was dumbfounded but what could I do. Not only were we broke, we now owed money, and no amount of argument would convince him that we had not received at least some of the cash. All he would agree to was a regular deduction from future purses." The Kid had no luck with another trip, this time to Buenos Aires in 1916 which Harvey and Johnston lined up for him. Three fights with a ten grand guarantee for each one and a good percentage. Five grand up front and the rest after each fight plus first class return tickets.

"After a week's training however, the bad news broke. The promoters had overlooked the fact that boxing had been banned in Buenos Aires and all contracts were off. It was pretty plain that we should not get our money. Eventually Billy Gibson sent tickets and we all returned home from yet another foreign fiasco, with a lot of wisdom but no money."

The Kid's first visit on his arrival back in New York was to his manager's office, he had to know how he stood financially. Yes, Harvey had collected the first $5,000 but he had got into trouble and had to borrow it. He promised to deduct it from his manager's share of the next few fights. Turning to Johnston, the Boy Bandit, Lewis said, 'By the way JJ, I hope you got the dents on my car's mudguards fixed like I asked you. Where did you take it, I'd like to pick it up now.'

"There was a moment's silence. This time it was Johnston's turn to look embarrassed," Lewis recalled. "He figured that as I was going to be away for about four months, and as there was a lot 'of work to be done, and garage rent to be paid, that it would be a good idea to sell it and that I could buy a new one when I came back. I asked him if he had got paid and he said yes. Where was the money then? He really squirmed. 'I had to use it, Ted, I was in a hole. Of course we'll pay you back, won't we Charlie? We'll see that you don't lose a cent. You know that. Would Charlie or I cheat on you? Would we? You know we wouldn't.'

"Well, I never got paid back. Somehow they talked me out of it, and as a matter of fact I never even found out what he got for the car. I didn't get paid for my car and I got gypped out of my guarantee which had persuaded me to make the trip in the first place. They had taken a real liberty with me and as you can imagine I felt real mad about it all. Still, in the fight game you have to forget and forgive a whole lot."

In 1918, Lewis was upset by the news that his two managers had fallen out, and that in future his affairs were to be handled solely by Johnston. Although Charlie Harvey had cheated him after his South American escapade, the Kid still had complete faith in him as a manager. However, as usual, he didn't argue, he just shrugged his shoulders and accepted the Boy Bandit as his mentor.

By this time, America had entered the war in Europe and Lewis thought he should be doing his duty, but Johnston was critically in debt and amongst his main creditors was Lewis himself. Lewis at the time was world welterweight champion and Jimmy's only chance of avoiding bankruptcy, if he went to Europe as a soldier Johnston would lose his only regular source of income.

Lewis listened to Johnston's pleadings in a surly mood. By his fists he had raised Jimmy Johnston to the top of the boxing world, he had part-financed his manager's gambling, and in reward had been cheated out of his purses. So why should he consider Johnston's interests at such a time? The great Benny Leonard stated that he would never fight Lewis as long as he was handled by Johnston. The Kid began to think that Johnston, far from being his guide, was much more of a load upon his back.

In a return contest with Tommy Robson which was made at 147 pounds, Lewis made the weight without taking his clothes off. When Robson scaled a few ounces overweight, the Kid told Robson not to worry, he wouldn't claim the forfeit. "Robson looked at him with an expression of contempt. 'That's a change,' he said.

'You were quick enough to claim your pound of flesh last time.' 'I don't get it,' said Lewis. Robson laughed. 'You don't get it, but you did. You claimed every last cent when I was over before, so don't give me any of that sportsman kidding now.'

"Lewis made no reply. He hadn't received any forfeit from their last contest. There could only be one answer, the Boy Bandit had done another of his strokes and had first claimed the weight forfeit, then calmly pocketed it for himself. Lewis won the contest with ease, but shrugged off his manager's congratulations."

A few weeks later, the Kid called on Harvey. 'I've had enough of Johnston,' he said. 'He's done me forwards, sideways, and backwards. I'm going to tell him to jump in the lake.'

"Harvey smiled sympathetically. 'I knew you'd get wise in time,' he said. 'The things that man would do. He sure lets down the whole sport.' This from a man of no higher principles might have irritated a more experienced person than Lewis.

"In September 1920 when Lewis returned to America to fight Mike O'Dowd, he discovered that Charlie Harvey and his former partner the Boy Bandit Johnston had buried their past disagreements and were working together again. He had thought himself free of JJ's tentacles but it was not to be. The octopus of the American fight game had him tied once more to a manager of dubious repute."

When Seaman Tommy Watson landed in New York in January of 1933, little Jimmy Johnston was the big man in Madison Square Garden, and Charlie Harvey, the man who had given Johnston his start in the fight business and who had worked hand in glove with the Boy Bandit down through the years, was the man John Mortimer entrusted with Tommy's immediate fistic future. Harvey lost no time filing a one-year contract with the State Athletic Commission, making him Watson's manager and as such, legally entitled to one third of Tommy's earnings.

It was in December 1932 that *Boxing's* New York correspondent Peter Varley wrote, "It was leaked that James J Johnston, the Garden promoter, who already manages a large stable of fighters through his brother Charley and who has never been noted for his magnanimity except in matters concerning himself, his brothers, or his sons, has acquired an interest in Kid Chocolate, the champion according to the New York Commission. It was announced that the Kid was booked for two fights in the Garden which bears out the story that Johnston has been declared in, for only his own fighters get work in the Garden as often as Chocolate has been getting... Until last summer, mobster Little Augie, uncrowned king of Brooklyn, owned a ten percent share in the Kid. He is now out, and it is presumed his share is held by the Garden promoter."

The fight game in America at that time was the playground of the underworld. Rich from the rackets in those Prohibition days, big time gangsters would bankroll promising fighters who were managed by front men, and the mob would gamble heavily on the fights. Of course many of them just loved the raw excitement of the fight game, like Owney Madden, born in Leeds, raised in Wigan and Liverpool, and known in New York as the "Duke of the West Side" and to the police as a master of organised crime.

"Everybody loved to watch Owney at the fights," said Ray Arcel, who trained many of Madden's fighters. "He would stand up at the front, shadow-boxing, throwing punches, and shouting instructions. He used to get beside himself until someone pulled him back into his seat. He just loved boxing."

Madden was said to have a controlling interest in at least five world champions including Max Baer and Rocky Marciano, but is best known for master-minding Primo Carnera into the heavyweight championship of the world in 1933, with his partners Big Frenchy DeMange and Broadway Bill Duffy.

Little Augie Pisano, or Anthony Carfano to give him his real name, had been a gunman for Frankie Yale, and after Yale was murdered in 1928, Little Augie took over his bootlegging and gambling operations in Brooklyn. He became a top lieutenant for Frank Costello and Joe Adonis but got a little ambitious and Adonis had a friendly chat with him in 1932, suggesting that Florida was a nice place to retire to. Pisano had purchased control of a swank hotel in Miami and in 1933, having turned over his rackets to Adonis and given up his ten percent interest in Kid Chocolate, he quit New York for a quiet life in the sun.

So if we believe that Johnston had acquired Little Augie's interest in Chocolate, then we can believe that Johnston.would do all that he could to protect that interest. Like reminding the New York Commission of their rule on foreign fighters making their debut in the Garden.

Like putting through a telephone call to the US Immigration

authorities to tell them that a certain Cuban named Eligio Sardinas, better known as world featherweight champion Kid Chocolate, would be attempting to enter the United States through Key West, Florida, without a labour permit. Remember that when Chocolate was refused entry, manager Luis Guiterrez protested to reporters that this was the Kid's twenty-fifth visit to the States and the first time they had been asked to show a permit!

Like bringing in Fidel LaBarba as a substitute for Chocolate to take care of the British champion, then after Watson upset the applecart by whipping LaBarba, offering him a world title fight in a higher division with one of America's finest champions, Tony Canzoneri. Tony was willing to scale 130 lbs, five pounds inside the lightweight class limit but four pounds over the nine stones featherweight poundage, Watson's best fighting weight.

To concede weight to a fighter of Canzoneri's class would have been foolhardy indeed. Lightweight champion of the world, former featherweight and Junior welterweight titleholder, the American was a formidable fighting machine who had beaten Chocolate, Billy Petrolle, Benny Bass, Andre Routis, Bushy Graham, Bud Taylor, and Johnny Dundee. He had knocked out Al Singer in one round to become world lightweight champion and flattened Jackie Kid Berg inside three rounds. Mortimer was right to turn him down, and Charlie Harvey was instructed to push for the title fight with Chocolate.

As Tommy trained in Byker, awaiting his date with destiny, the *Chronicle's* GJO asked him, "about these challenges on behalf of Parker and Sharkey."

"Now you have already said that you do not expect them to come off before I go to America," Tommy reminded him. "And you are quite correct. I don't really believe that either of the lads personally want to fight me at present. I think they are both too fair to do so. I have beaten both of them. Why should they want to spoil my chance of bringing a world's title to Tyneside by, perhaps, luckily beating me? At the championship weight by the way, I am certain they could not, but I would sooner see them go out to do what I have done than pester me. Take it definitely from me that I am engaging in no further contests except directly through my manager. If I am beaten for the world's championship, then we might see whether Duggy or Benny can beat me."

It was a far cry from Madison Square Garden to the Majestic

Theatre at Ferryhill in County Durham, yet that was Tommy's next professional engagement after the LaBarba fight. Having left the New Hawk Inn, he became joint partner with Mr Percy Boydell, the Newcastle producer who was running non-stop variety shows at the theatre.

Tommy was one of the "turns" and appeared nightly on the stage giving boxing exhibitions with Billy Wyper of Swalwell as his sparring partner, but he smiled and shook his head when asked if he intended to pursue a stage career when he hung up the gloves. "This is just a sideline to keep my mind off the more serious business of boxing," he said, adding, "may as well fill in the time by earning a little dough."

On Friday 31 March 1933, it was back to the serious stuff when Tommy appeared at the Connaught Drill Hall in Portsmouth against August Gyde, the former featherweight champion of France. John Mortimer was the promoter and Alec Lambert had arranged the fight to show his and Tommy's appreciation for Mortimer's assistance with the New York fight.

"Gyde is one of those muscular little men who put their faith in the big punch," commented the *Daily Mail*. "Although he is unlikely to beat our champion he will certainly give him a battle. In 150 bouts Gyde has never once been beaten inside the distance."

Nor was he on this occasion, though he was beaten. "Gyde was very strong," reported the *Evening News*, "and it says much for his ability to assimilate punishment that he finished a gruelling contest as freshly as he had started."

Watson set the pace in the first round, jumping in with a left to the jaw and the Frenchman promptly covered up. Gyde landed a left swing to the head but Watson was untroubled and came right back with two smart lefts then a heavy right to the jaw. Another right to the head sent Gyde into his shell. Seaman took the second with right hands and when the Frenchman tried to open things up in the third he was steadied by accurate jabs. Tommy was easily outboxing his man and when Gyde forced his way inside Watson was still his master.

In the seventh the Frenchman mounted a furious attack and Watson took more punches than he had in the preceding six rounds. The *Evening News* reporter marked the round even and gave round eight to Gyde, observing, "The Frenchman was again aggressive and actually punched harder than Watson in this round. He hurt Watson twice with swings to the jaw and was obviously making a desperate effort to land a finishing blow."

Over the last two rounds however the British champion took charge again, boxing beautifully to finish a clear winner. The fight did Tommy the world of good and he was in the right frame of mind when the news came a few days later. Mortimer had received a cable from New York stating that Watson's fight with Kid Chocolate for the world's featherweight championship had now been fixed for 12 May or 19 May. The Cuban had secured a permit to re-enter the United States and was leaving for New York to make arrangements for the fight at Madison Square Garden.

Seaman's wife Kitty was as thrilled at the news as was Tommy, for good reason. She was going to New York with him, she wanted to be there on his big night, the night he was crowned champion of the world! The children, Kathleen, Tommy, and Joan, by this time four-and-a-half, two-and-a-half, and seventeen months old respectively, would be cared for by Tommy's aunt, Mrs Laws, at her home at 106 Mowbray Street in Heaton.

There were tears all round that Monday, 10 April 1933, when Tommy and Kitty said their goodbyes at the Central Station, where a crowd of friends and relatives had gathered to see them off on their big adventure. Among them was a man hailed as the pioneer of the fight game in Newcastle, old Jimmy Lowes, who used to run a tough boxing school at the Percy Cottage in Percy Street. Mr Lowes had taken no interest in the sport for many years and his presence was greatly appreciated by the Seaman.

Tommy and Kitty were met in London by manager Alec Lambert who travelled with them to Portsmouth. They stayed overnight with John Mortimer at his home in Southsea and next morning, Wednesday, were on the 8.09 train that pulled out of Town Station bound for Southampton. Berthed at one of the piers was the beautiful White Star liner Olympic, sailing soon for New York. All aboard!

Tommy and Kitty negotiated the gangway together but became separated on the ship as friends and admirers jostled Tommy away from the cabin in their excitement, and it was a somewhat flustered Mrs Watson who was brought back to Tommy's side as he finalised arrangements with Mortimer for the trip.

"I'm awfully excited about this trip," Kitty told reporters. "This is my first journey to America and I have been looking forward to it immensely. There is a good reason why I should be with Tommy. He is fighting for the greatest prize of the ring, and for the sake of Old England. I think I should be with him."

"My wife is going to be my chief advisor on this trip," said Tommy, "and you know that's just how it should be, don't you think? My fight? I'm going to give of my best as I did when I beat Fidel LaBarba and no lad can do better than that. When I was in America before I got fair rations and there is no doubt that I shall get it again. I shall never forget the great reception the Americans gave me before and I know I shall be welcomed. May the better man win."

As the great ship moved slowly away from the quayside, the band was playing Mendelssohn's Wedding March. Seaman Tommy Watson would soon be walking down the aisle again, this time for the biggest fight of his life.

17

THE CUBAN BON-BON

The Cuban was good, even better than they said he would be. The big Madison Square Garden crowd knew that as early as the first round, and at the final bell they sensed that they had just witnessed a glimmer of true greatness. The ebony-skinned, small-boned man in the ring was the fastest, most graceful boxer they had seen in years. His style and movements were velvet-smooth, reminiscent of two earlier masters, Benny Leonard and Joe Gans. The word had flashed up from Cuba, this kid is a wonder, and so he was.

When the bout was over and the Cuban sensation had won by an overwhelming decision over his stocky opponent, the old Manassa Mauler, former world heavyweight champion Jack Dempsey, leaned over and shouted into the ear of his ringside companion, "Bobby, you saw a great fighter in there tonight."

Fight manager Bobby Gleason, his eyes glued on the jubilant young fighter who danced victoriously around the ring, a towel draped over his head, said to Dempsey, "That's right, Jack. That guy is great. I bet that there will never be another Cuban fighter like this Kid Chocolate."

There never was. Like many of boxing's great champions, the Cuban Kid was the product of a poor family scratching a living in the ghetto of a great city. Born in Havana's El Cierro district, he was the fifth child, third boy, and was named Eligio Sardinas. Just ten years old when his father died, the skinny, happy-go-lucky kid became a newsboy for La Noche, one of the city's evening papers.

Parking himself on one of Havana's busiest street corners, the boy was doing a roaring trade when a bigger lad told him to move on, or else! Words were exchanged, and when young Sardinas was shoved off the kerb, war broke out. He flew at his tormentor, tiny fists hammering furiously, and he didn't stop until the other lad was lying in the gutter, beaten bloody

One keenly interested observer of the street fight was Senor Luis Felipe Guiterrez, Sports Editor of *La Noche*. To boost a flagging circulation, he dreamed up the idea of a newsboy boxing tournament with the kids selling more papers in their neighbourhoods when their name appeared in the sports pages. He introduced himself to young Sardinas, gave him his card, and invited him to come and see him.

Thus began one of boxing's legendary partnerships as the young street fighter became an amateur boxer with Guiterrez as his manager. He was a sensation from the first bell, racking up 100 straight victories with an incredible 86 knockouts. With flashing, pearly-white teeth and a natural flair for showmanship, the kid soon became a tremendous favourite around the city, and Guiterrez knew he had captured lightning in a bottle!

An older brother had boxed as Big Chocolate, so Eligio became known as Little Chocolate. He would often spot other kids as much as twenty-five pounds in weight and beat them out of sight. At the close of the newsboys' tournament, Chocolate spent a couple of years learning the art of boxing as he was still too young to become a professional fighter. Guiterrez got hold of some old fight films of former champions George Dixon and Joe Gans and the kid would spend hours studying the grainy old films as Luis explained the different styles to his protege. Gans became the boy's favourite and he practised his every move until he looked like a carbon copy of the legendary Old Master.

From time to time Chocolate would fight in semi-pro bouts which were allowed by the Boxing Commission, for which he would be paid two or three dollars a round, and when Guiterrez figured the boy was ready for tougher competition, he matched him with Soldier Diaz, featherweight champion of Cuba. Little Chocolate was a revelation as he destroyed the veteran inside six rounds, and Luis sat down and wrote a letter to Jess McMahon, matchmaker to the great American promoter Tex Rickard in New York.

The sun-drenched island of Cuba was the Pearl of the Antilles, but New York City was the Mecca of the fight game and Luis Felipe Guiterrez knew he had to take the boy there, the boy he called Kid Chocolate, if he was to become a great boxing champion. But it was tough getting started. Trainer Moe Fleischer told me how the Kid got his first break when I talked to him at the Fifth Street Gym in Miami Beach many years ago.

It was back in 1927 and Fleischer was in the gym that became the famous St Nicholas Arena at 66th Street and Columbus Avenue, when in walked former bantamweight champ Eddie "Cannonball"

Martin who was on the comeback trail and looking for some sparring.

"The only one around right now," said Moe, "is a little Cuban kid who just got here and hasn't had a fight in this country yet. There he is, shadow boxing over in the corner."

"He looks like just a kid," growled Martin, "but I gotta use somebody."

So the seventeen-year-old Cuban boy climbed into the training ring with the ex-champ and after two rounds everyone in the gym was asking Fleischer who the kid was, the kid who had just made a monkey of Martin!

"His name is Kid Chocolate," smiled Moe.

When we talked that day in the gym in Miami, Moe smiled again as the memories came flooding back. "I had ten per cent of the Kid, made all his matches," he said. "He was a born fighter, one of the best of all time. Every move was natural to him."

The Kid's first fight in New York came on 1 August 1928 at Mitchell Field where he faced up to Eddie Enos for a forty dollar purse. Those flashing ebony fists had Eddie on his way home inside three rounds and the kid from Cuba was on his way, to the top!

He won eleven straight fights before Guiterrez made him with Jackie Schweitzer, a young Jewish boy from the East Side who had blazed his way to 29 wins. They fought at the St Nick's Arena and after a tough three rounds Chocolate was all over Schweitzer. The Kid finished it in the sixth with a smashing right to the body and a week later he was in Madison Square Garden to fight Joey Scalfaro, the Harlem Druggist. At the opening bell Joey roared across the ring and caught the Kid high on the head with a thudding right hand. Chocolate dropped like a shot rabbit but he beat the ten count and fought back so well that most of the capacity crowd thought Scalfaro lucky to get a share of the verdict.

In those Prohibition days, New Yorkers developed a taste for hot Chocolate, and they packed the fight clubs to see the Kid go unbeaten against guys like Fidel LaBarba, Chick Suggs, Vidal Gregorio, and Bushy Graham. Sports columnist Joe Williams wrote after one of his fights, "My favourite fighter, bar none, is Kid Chocolate." Damon Runyon described him as "...exquisitely handsome." Jim Jennings of the *New York Graphic* compared the Kid to an ebony statue come to life.

Life was something the Cuban Kid had plenty of. He lived the way he fought in the ring, at a terrific pace. His rapid rise to fame and fortune found him ill-prepared, ill-educated, still immature. He did what any fun-loving young fellow would do in similar circumstances, hitting the night club circuit, going home at dawn after picking up the tab for the hangers-on who flocked like bees to a honey pot.

"I made a million dollars in the ring," the Kid would recall years later in Martine Barrat's book, *Do Or Die*. "I shared what I made. So even though my pockets were empty, I felt like a million dollars. Because I shared my happiness."

Ring Magazine publisher Nat Fleischer wrote, "In Kid Chocolate, the sport of pugilism had its first big Negro money-maker since the halcyon days of Jack Johnson. There were many other fine Negro fighters in the lapse of years between Jack Johnson and Kid Chocolate, but none carried the gate appeal of this ebony-hued lad from Havana, a human magnet who found little difficulty in continuously breaking attendance records in whichever club he appeared."

When Chocolate fought Al Singer on a warm August night in 1929, a huge throng of some 37,000 paid a then record gate for little guys of $215,266 to see the fight at the Polo Grounds in New York.

Unfortunately for the fans, it wasn't a very good fight. For a while the Kid's natural ability had been enough to carry him through, but the night life was beginning to erode his great talent, he looked jaded in the ring and his boxing lacked the sparkle that had made him box-office dynamite. He still won his fights, but the fire was gone.

"The Kid didn't only burn the candle at both ends," remembered Moe Fleischer, "he broke it in half and burned all four ends!"

The Singer fight rang the alarm bells for the fighter they called the Cuban Bon-Bon. While the Kid did his roadwork along the primrose path, Al Singer was hammering his way to the fore and the sportswriters were hailing the young Jewish kid from the Bronx as another Benny Leonard. Bring on Kid Chocolate, they cried in their columns.

But the box-office hit was something of a miss in the ring.

Chocolate contented himself with boxing his way to victory, building an early lead as Singer's punches fell short. Al finished like a train and a storm of booing filled the night air as the decision was announced...for Chocolate. In the dressing room afterwards, Luis Guiterrez gave his boy a tongue-lashing, and in the papers next morning the press slammed the Bon-Bon for a sloppy performance.

Maybe the critics got to him, maybe it was that big crowd booing him up at the Polo Grounds. Whatever it was, Moe Fleischer was happy, he had his fighter back in the gym training like a demon and when he got back in the ring his blazing fists whipped Allie Ridgeway and Mickey Doyle and Vic Burrone and Harlem's great Italian prospect Dominick Petrone. The old Kid Chocolate was back and in August 1930 some 36,565 fans paid their way into the Polo Grounds to see him fight another kid, Jackie Kid Berg, the British fighter who had taken American rings by storm.

This was a fight half won before the first bell had sounded. Berg was a lightweight, in fact he had won the world Junior welterweight championship (140 lbs) six months earlier and defended his title five times going into the Chocolate fight. Berg's manager Frankie Jacobs demanded a contract for the fight at 135 lbs, the lightweight limit. Guiterrez held out for a weigh-in at 131 lbs but he got nowhere and Chocolate, who weighed 124 lbs on fight day, went into the ring at least ten pounds lighter than the man they called the Whitechapel Whirlwind. Luis Guiterrez would later admit it was the biggest mistake he ever made in managing Kid Chocolate.

Even so it was a tremendous scrap, one of the finest seen in a New York ring. Chocolate's opening punch, a hard right to Berg's nose, brought the claret flowing but the English tearaway backed the Kid up with a body attack. The second round was all-action as both fighters hammered away and already the huge crowd was on its feet. Round three saw Chocolate put on a sensational performance, smashing at Berg with terrific punches until it seemed he must go down. But he didn't!

He fought back from the fourth through the seventh, his gloves cutting red arcs through the steamy night air as the crowd maintained a continuous roar, and it was obvious that the weight was telling on Chocolate. The Cuban Kid threw everything into the eighth, smashing lefts and rights at his tormentor in a desperate bid to bring the Englishman down, but at the bell Berg was still there and Guiterrez knew then and there his boy was beaten. Two rounds later it was official.

When veteran announcer Joe Humphreys held Berg's glove aloft in token of victory, Kid Chocolate broke down and wept in the ring and he couldn't be consoled at any price. It was a new experience for him, his first defeat in 168 amateur and pro fights.

"Kid Berg was the bravest fighter I ever met," the Cuban would recall years later. "Round after round he would come at you. The first time we fought I was terrified! We fought twice and the judges gave it to him both times. The first time I cried. It was my first loss."

The Bob-Bon went back to Havana for a rest and when he drove through the streets crowds shouted and waved to him. He was still their champion, still unbeaten in their eyes. The bars and clubs were open all night and the girls were pretty and when he went back to New York a few weeks later Fidel LaBarba licked him in the Garden and again the sports pages were saying that Kid Chocolate had burned himself out.

Then Guiterrez signed him to fight Battling Battalino for the featherweight title in Madison Square Garden and the Kid knew this was his big chance. He buckled down in the gym and Moe Fleischer brought him into the Garden ring in superb shape. The Kid outpunched the tough little champ from Hartford through fifteen rounds and at the final bell he looked a good winner. The Associated Press reporter scored it nine rounds to six for Chocolate as did boxing writer Hype Igoe, but the decision of all three officials was unanimous...for Battalino!

"Chocolate was the challenger," said judge George Kelly when reporters queried the decision, "and if he wanted that championship it was his job to go out and get it and not to wait to counter Battalino's assaults."

Six months later, in July 1931, the Kid did get his championship, but he had to move up a division, fighting Benny Bass for the Junior lightweight title in Philadelphia. The Cuban outboxed and outpunched Bass through the first three rounds with Benny hammering the Kid's body to take the fourth. But his left eye was cut in the next round and the referee was forced to stop it in the seventh. The Kid was the new champ.

In November 1931, Chocolate tried to take Tony Canzoneri's lightweight title in a fight that kept a capacity crowd at Madison Square Garden on the edge of its seat throughout. The champ was just too strong for the Cuban and the ringside pundits agreed with the unanimous decision for Canzoneri, even if the fans didn't. The Bob-Bon was beginning to look jaded again but he had been fighting strong lightweights in Berg and Canzoneri when he was a legitimate featherweight himself.

By this time Jimmy Johnston was in control at the Garden and, having acquired a piece of the Cuban Kid, was able to match him with Lew Feldman for the world featherweight title vacated by Battalino. The New York Commission gave its blessing and the fight was scheduled for 13 October 1932. Feldman, a highly-touted Jewish boy from the Brownsville section of New York, had, according to the *New York Times*, "a stout heart and a willingness to fight," but he had been beaten twice by the Cuban Kid and Chocolate made it a hat trick with a lop-sided victory, Referee Patsy Haley stopping the contest in round twelve.

Feldman waded in from the first bell as Chocolate made a slow start and in round five Lew caught the Kid with a right swing to the jaw that jellied his legs for an instant. But Chocolate picked up the pace and took the next three rounds. In the ninth he floored Feldman with a sizzling right to the jaw for a nine count and the Brownsville boy was well beaten in the end.

The fight had been disappointing however, and former featherweight champion Abe Attell, who was a ringside spectator, was so disgusted that he offered to climb in the ring and fight the both of them! Be that as it may, Kid Chocolate was now the world featherweight champion according to the all-powerful New York State Athletic Commission.

Author Martine Barrat mined a deep seam of warmth and affection for the charismatic Cuban in New York's Harlem when researching her book *Do Or Die*. Frankie Richardson, who used to manage the Renaissance Ballroom, had fond memories. "Oh, Kid Chocolate! Those were some good days. Him and his buddy Al Brown would go to the famous tailor Mr Orye on 125th Street, who used to dress the performers of the Apollo. They'd have their suits cut in the same pattern, but different linings. They both drove the same model car too, a silver Packard.

"Whenever the Kid and Al Brown showed up, everybody would

hang out with them beneath the Tree of Hope in front of the Lafayette Theatre, their headquarters. They always refused to fight each other because one of them had to lose. They were two nice, lovely fellows. And they both could fight."

Lenuel Hamilton recalled, "Kid Chocolate was my very first hero. Now I don't go to the fights, it would tarnish my memory of those days when Kid Chocolate and Al Brown used to hoist their bodies over the sidebars of the silver Packards and go into Frank's Famous Steak House, where only white people were admitted at that time. Frank's made a special exception for celebrities like Kid Chocolate and Al Brown, just like the Cotton Club."

Actor Robert Earl Jones, who founded a theatre group in Harlem, said, "People would be talking for days on end about how the Kid had won. He was a real talent. After his fights, he would say from the ring, 'Hello everybody! I am glad I win.'"

Then there was Mr Reid who rented tuxedos to the stars from the dry-cleaning shop he ran for fifty years. "I dressed them all, Count Basie, Duke Ellington. Kid Chocolate, he was my man, a hell of a fighter and a heavy dresser. He had a style of his own."

Another Harlem old-timer, Frank Haywood, told author Barrat, "The Kid would lure his opponent into the corner and then he would score a lot of fast punches. And the next thing you know he was killing him. He was very artistic with his legwork and punches. I used to sell newspapers as a child so I'd always find a way to his fights. Sometimes he would give me a ticket. I remember that even though he was a big star, as a black person the Kid couldn't stay in the Theresa Hotel. Black people could only stay at the Braddock or Woodside."

A couple of months after winning the featherweight title, and just two weeks before Christmas 1932, Chocolate put his crown on the line for Fidel LaBarba in Madison Square Garden. It would be their third fight with the score one-all, Chocolate winning a close decision in their first match at the Bronx Coliseum and LaBarba taking the nod in the rematch at the Garden. Now they were fighting for the title.

Moe Fleischer had the Kid training at Gus Wilson's place where one reporter observed Chocolate to be, "in superb condition, working eight rounds with sparmates Johnny Alba and Frankie Rinaldi after doing four miles roadwork in the morning. The Kid stepped around his helpers at terrific speed, continually poking a straight left to the face from long range and using short hooks and uppercuts to head and body when inside."

It was just as well Chocolate was in good shape, for LaBarba gave him a helluva fight for fifteen rounds and a lot of people thought the man from California was a good winner. He rocked the Kid in the fifth with a steaming left hook to the chin, and by the seventh, Chocolate's lip was puffed and bloody. Round nine saw LaBarba crease the Cuban with a left hook to the body and in the twelfth Fidel had Chocolate all over the ring as he poured in the left hooks.

At the final bell, Referee Willie Lewis called it a draw while judges Sam Austin and Eddie Farrell both voted for the Cuban, much to the disgust of the Garden crowd. The press boys favoured LaBarba but there was praise for both men. Ed Frayne in *The American* saw it for LaBarba 10 rounds to 5 ...Harry Grayson of the *World-Telegram* called it, "a rank decision. I credited 12 rounds to LaBarba and 3 to Chocolate." Sid Mercer in *The American,* tabbed it for Fidel 9 to 5 with 1 even.

There was support for the champion from Jack Kofoed in the *Post.* "I think it was a fair verdict," he wrote. "LaBarba won 7 rounds and Chocolate 8 the way I saw it." Francis Wallace in the *News* agreed, "It was very close. My score sheet gave Chocolate 8 rounds with 7 for the challenger." For the final word, the *Herald-Tribune's* Richard Vidmer reported, "The battle was too close to take away a man's title, as I saw it, each man won 7 rounds with the other round even."

Kid Chocolate went home for Christmas but his Harlem friends knew he would be back among them in a few weeks time. The Garden had signed him to defend his title on 27 January 1933, this time against a Limey ex-sailor called Watson. There was suddenly a problem however, when the Kid tried to land at Key West, Florida, on his way to New York. It was Thursday 19 January when US Immigration officials detained the Kid and the following day he was ordered deported to Cuba after a hearing conducted by Deputy Inspector A S Caviness who declined to give out the reason for deportation. The fight with Watson would have to wait...

18

BACK TO BROADWAY FOR THE BON-BON

When the s.s. Olympic berthed at the White Star pier at the foot of West Eighteenth Street in New York, little Charlie Harvey was pacing nervously back and forth along the dockside. The worried expression on his face was quickly replaced by a smile however as he spotted Seaman Tommy and Kitty coming down the gangway, and he soon had them in a taxi speeding uptown to their hotel. That night they spent a pleasant evening with Tom Heeney, the former heavyweight contender from New Zealand, and his American wife at their home on Long Island.

Soon after breakfast next morning, Harvey collected the Watsons and took them over to Madison Square Garden on Eighth Avenue, to the office of Jimmy Johnston where the press boys, photographers, and newsreel cameramen had gathered for the ritual signing of the contracts by Seaman and the champion, Kid Chocolate.

Just after a week later, patrons of the Paramount Theatre in Newcastle upon Tyne cheered as the British Paramount News flashed on to the big screen:

SEAMAN WATSON SIGNS UP. BRITISH FEATHERWEIGHT CHAMPION AND KID CHOCOLATE MEET FAMOUS PROMOTER JIMMY JOHNSON TO ARRANGE BOUT

Johnston was shown seated between Chocolate and Watson, Kitty at his side, behind them little Charlie Harvey and the tall, lean figure of Luis Guiterrez, Chocolate's manager. Johnston passes the contracts to Watson, saying, "Now, Seaman Watson, put your John Hancock there. Remember, I'm watching you."

"I'm watching you, too," says Kitty, rising from her chair to prod Johnston with her right hand.

"Who's doing the fighting here?" growls Johnston.

"My wife," says Tommy with a smile as he hands the contract

140

back to the promoter. Facing the cameras, Johnston says, "Well, I'm glad that match is made. Seaman Watson is the peer of any European featherweight, in fact he's the third English featherweight champion that Charlie Harvey, his manager, has handled during my time, and I look forward to seeing one of the greatest featherweight contests ever."

Wilbur Wood reported in the *New York Sun*, "'He looks big for a featherweight,' commented Luis Guiterrez as he got his first peek at Seaman Watson in Johnston's Garden office yesterday...Watson does look big for a featherweight, his large head heightens the impression that he is too big to be a natural featherweight. However, the Seaman takes a salty oath that he will do 126 pounds without any ill effects. He scales 134 right now... Mrs Watson by the way is not a wife who cannot bear to watch her husband trade punches with somebody in the ring. 'I have seen him in most of his fights,' she said, 'and I'm going to see him in this one. That's why I came over with him.'"

Ed Frayne, Sports Editor of the *New York American*, wrote in his column, "Seaman Tom Watson has retired from the bar...A bit sadly, the Seaman said that he had resigned his $17-a-week job in the Newcastle pub, he has thought the matter over a great deal and decided it would be best to abandon his profession for a time...Mrs Watson, a pretty little woman, accompanied her husband to the Garden offices to meet James J Johnston and the newspapermen. Johnston was born in Liverpool, England, and one of the interviewers thought it would be apropos to have Mrs Watson say something nice about Jimmy's hometown. He asked her how she liked Liverpool. Evidently, Mrs Watson is not acquainted with the Johnston history. She stared incredulously for a moment and then with an expression of deep distaste she said, 'Oh, that's an awful place. Really, it's the dumping ground of England!' Was Mr Johnston's face red? In fact it will probably be a bit pink for days."

As well as the fight, Johnston had other things on his mind at the time, such as what to call the latest addition to his growing family! "It's a boy, 7lbs 7ozs," reported one paper, "and it's at the Fifth Avenue Hospital with Mrs Johnston where it arrived early yesterday. This makes the twelfth offspring of the Madison Square Garden boxing director and when a man has used up eleven names he has about run out of ideas. There are seven girls and this is the fifth boy."

Watson's chances of lifting the Kid's crown were perhaps best summed up by the news that Guiterrez had Chocolate tied up for two more engagements with the Garden. He would go against Tony Canzoneri, the lightweight champion, late in July or early August, scheduled for the Long Island Bowl, and he would then defend his own title against Freddie Miller, the champion according to the National Boxing Association.

In the event of Watson beating the Kid however, he was committed to defend the title for the Garden within sixty days. A similar contract had been signed by Eugene Criqui of France when he won the same title from Johnny Kilbane in 1923. He was required to meet Johnny Dundee within sixty days, kept his agreement, and lost his title.

The 22 April issue of *Topical Times* carried an article under Seaman Watson's byline entitled, "How I'll Tackle Kid Chocolate! Who's been spinning this yarn that I have some secret plan to beat Chocolate? Everybody is asking me what my plan is, next time anybody asks me I'm going to slosh him! I've no secret plan, as a matter of fact I've no plan at all. I've not seen this fellow Chocolate and know him only by repute. How on earth can I have a plan to beat him? It is the height of silliness when you want to talk about a plan for beating the unknown. I haven't the faintest idea of how he will fight nor can he have the faintest idea of how I am going to fight. Everything for the moment is in the hands of the gods, maybe Chocolate will win, maybe I shall win, you know the Scottish poet's lines about the best laid plans of mice and men, take it from me, I've got no plans. Anyway, if I had any secret plans, do you think that I would divulge them?"

Seaman had his first public workout at the St Nicholas Gymnasium and made a big impression on the assembled newsmen. So did Kitty! "Mrs Seaman Watson is in town with her two-fisted husband," wrote Jack Lawrence in the *New York American*. "Mrs Watson is a lass who loves her tea as it is brewed in the British Isles. Jimmy Johnston took her to a restaurant where she could get the real thing. Mrs Watson was so overcome with gratitude that she took her husband into a Broadway shop and bought him a new hat, and she sent the old one to Jimmy Johnston!"

A few days after arriving in New York, Watson, Kitty, trainer Archie Watson (no relation) and a couple of sparring partners, left the city for Dr Joseph Bier's training camp on the shores of Pompton Lake in New Jersey.

"He trained for LaBarba in a stuffy indoor gymnasium," said Harvey, "and such surroundings hardly soothed his nerves or quieted his troubled mind. Now he is out where he can relax and I look for a far better fighter than caused such an upset by beating the Californian. I don't hesitate to predict a surprise for those who are picking Chocolate to win easily."

Life in a training camp certainly seemed to agree with the Geordie champion. In a letter to Newcastle sportsman Tom Steckles, Tommy wrote, "I am settled down now in a training camp belonging to Dr Joseph Bier, MD. Gee! It is sure a nice place to train at, and I am beginning to feel fine now. My weight is round about 9st 6lbs and I have still another sixteen days before the fight, so by the time it comes round I should be OK. We are having fine weather here and my wife is enjoying herself a treat. Give my regards to all my friends."

One thing that Tommy and Kitty could not come to terms with was the great American love of coffee, the national drink. Reported one New York paper, "Information trickles in from Pompton Lakes, where Seaman Watson is in training, that the English titleholder must have his tea and egg at one o'clock in the afternoon or else he will not shed his street clothes in favour of gym togs.

"The tea thing is something brand new in Dr Bier's bailiwick. Mrs Joseph Bier has been serving coffee and what have you to other ring gladiators over a stretch of years so when the Seaman up and commanded tea, she gasped. To please the Briton, Mrs Bier yesterday installed a big pot on the kitchen stove to make tea for him."

A facet of American life that the Watsons found disturbing was the segregation of black people. Their daughter Kath remembers, "My Dad had a sparring partner who was a coloured lad and at that time they were segregated. Well, my mother, being my mother, anyhow, they were in this restaurant, her and Dad and whoever was with them, and this lad was at another table because he was coloured and she wanted him to come over and sit with them. She didn't understand it, they weren't allowed to, so there was a bit of a do."

On Monday 1 May, Charlie Harvey took Seaman off to Philadelphia to see a fight. Just eleven days before his date in the Garden with Watson, the Cuban Kid was in the City of Brotherly Love to meet Johnny Farr at the Arena, scheduled for ten rounds or less, with Chocolate's Junior light-weight title on the line. Farr, an Italian-American from Cleveland, was thirty a couple of days before the fight but all he got from the Kid for his birthday was a belated beating.

Hype Igoe noted in the *New York Evening Journal*, "Harvey is a thorough fellow. He and the little English featherweight journeyed to Philadelphia recently to see the Kid fight Johnny Farr. It was the fourth time the Kid met and thrashed the Farr person. Harvey explained that it was a soft touch for the Kid and not to bank too strongly on what his eye told him. After the fight, Harvey didn't mention Chocolate. He was happy when he saw Seaman thinking intently, with a little nudge of one shoulder, then the other, on the way back to New York.

"'I didn't speak of the fight Chocolate put up until the next day,' said Harvey. 'Seaman never jumps at the moon, he studied the whole thing over in his mind, and was ready for me when I asked him what he thought of the Bon-Bon.'

"'Well, if that is ALL he's got,' replied Watson, 'I'm sure that I will beat him.' 'And I think he is just the type who will concentrate along those lines,' said Harvey. 'I'm sure that the English boy's body attack will bring Chocolate right into his lap. Fidel couldn't stand it and I know this fellow can't. I'll have a little quid on the result myself, and I'm not a betting man.'"

Charlie's belief in Watson received a boost from Alfred Drayton's column in the *New York Sun*. "There is a feeling gaining strength every hour in fistic circles concerning the chances of Watson in his assault upon Chocolate and the featherweight title which marks the return of boxing to the Garden. When the match was made shortly after Watson beat LaBarba, the Englishman was given a chance to annex the 126 pound crown. But then after reflection, the majority of investors in the Sock Market concluded that LaBarba had encountered a bad night and Watson would not get far with such an accomplished boxer as the Cuban.

"Lately though there has been a swing back to the Englishman and while he hardly will be favourite the odds will be much closer than anticipated a fortnight ago. All of which pleases Charlie Harvey, who now is looking after Watson's interests in this country. Harvey stroked his mustache nervously as the match was discussed yesterday, and when odds of three-to-one were quoted, he was unable to remain out of the conversation any longer. 'Jiminy goodness me!' Harvey exclaimed, using one of his favourite expressions. 'Chocolate shouldn't be any better than an even money choice.

"'They say LaBarba was not himself. Well, neither was Watson for that matter. My gracious, I never saw a fighter so annoyed before a match. What an ordeal they put him through. I mean that test showing, gymnasium tests are ridiculous anyway.

"'In that one he didn't have a chance, being tossed in with three opponents whose identity was revealed only when they stepped into the ring. Can you imagine a fighter signing to meet anyone they might produce? Then, when this nerve-wracking ordeal was over, a report went back to the Commission that he should break in at some club other than the Garden. On top of this he was panned in many of the papers and by the time he met LaBarba he was so nervous and upset he didn't know what he was doing.

"'In the first round he was caught by a left hook that wouldn't dent a balloon. Still at sea, he went down again in the second. I hardly knew what to do, I hadn't seen him before he landed on these shores and I looked for the worst. Friends at the ringside yelled, 'Hey, Charlie, another Limey palooka!' and I was afraid they were right. But I encouraged him between rounds and from the fifth round onwards he had everything all his own way. The way he steadied himself after a bad start won me over completely. That is why I fancy his chances against Chocolate.'''

Watson's training programme intrigued American observers who visited the camp on the shores of the lake. A report dated 8 May noted, "While Seaman Tommy Watson is no model of grace and finesse at Dr Bier's gymnasium here, he is storing up a supply of stamina for his bout for the world title with Kid Chocolate at the Garden Friday night. There is a marked difference in the training methods of English and American fighters. The boxers here put in much of their time in boxing while Watson is concentrating on getting into the peak of physical condition. He believes stamina and rugged hard fighting will win for him. Watson has been doing more boxing in his preparation for this fight than he has ever done before but he does not consider gymnasium boxing as important as getting into the best of physical shape.

"The British champion did his last boxing this afternoon, two rounds with Frankie Klick, the clever Californian, and George Reilly, negro boxer from Detroit. The latter acts as a counterpart of Chocolate in Watson's preparation. Watson did not attempt to match Klick's boxing cleverness but he was punching incessantly throughout the three-minute rounds. He kept his left popping into the body and his right was hooking its way to his sparring partner's jaw. This attack was not marked with a great deal of technique but it resembled perpetual motion. The Briton weighed 127½ lbs after coming off the road this morning and should have no trouble making the 126 lbs limit Friday afternoon at 2.00pm. Watson has so much energy that when he came here he wanted to have three training sessions a day, one in the morning, one in the early afternoon, and one in the late afternoon."

Kid Chocolate was in camp at Orangeburg in New York State. His final workout two days before the fight did not impress a crowd that included Jimmy Johnston. The Cuban worked only four rounds, two rounds of shadow boxing and two rounds sparring with Joe Dougherty which showed him still as fast and clever but gave no indication as to his stamina. Manager Guiterrez spent most of the time quizzing the sportswriters on Watson.

"What do you think of this fellow Watson?" he asked.

"He's rugged, aggressive, and a fair puncher," replied a reporter, "and counts on wearing his opponent down rather than scoring a one-blow knockout."

"But he isn't clever," said Guiterrez. "Chocolate will whip him easily. Watson will find Chocolate far different from LaBarba. LaBarba is a smart fighter but he lacks Chocolate's speed, nor is he as finished a boxer. I don't think Watson will be able to do much damage, I doubt if he can reach Chocolate with many solid blows.

"They say he is a good body puncher and Chocolate doesn't like to take it in the middle. Did it ever occur to most of you that Chocolate is a master at tying the other fellow up in close, so if he can handcuff Watson, and I'm sure he will, there isn't anything to worry about."

Twenty-four hours later there was something to worry about. "WORLD TITLE FIGHT SENSATION! CHOCOLATE ILL!" Dateline New York, Friday 12 May; Seaman Watson will have to wait another week for his world title shot. His fight with Chocolate has been postponed for a week owing to the Kid's illness. Chocolate was suddenly taken ill yesterday with pains in his stomach and vomiting while putting the final touches to his training at his camp at Orangeburg, New York State. A doctor examined him and pronounced him as unfit to fight. The illness only being temporary the contest will be staged a week tonight on 19 May."

Back home in Britain, the champion's illness was viewed with some scepticism, as still yet another obstacle in Watson's path to the title. The Editor of *Boxing* headlined his front page, "HARD LUCK, WATSON!" and went on to say, "To keep on that thin edge of finest weight for a further week is a tricky business in any case, and with Watson it will present more than ordinary difficulty. Archie Watson, who is training the Seaman out there, will tackle the task in his usual big-hearted fashion, but it does strike one as most unfair to our champion that his chances should be thus prejudiced by the indisposition of Chocolate."

Even in New York there was a suspicion that something was rotten, not in the state of Denmark, but in the state of New York. Under the *Daily Mirror's* headline, "KID'S PAIN IN TUMMY BELIEVED GAG!" Murray Lewin wrote, "The oft-postponed featherweight championship engagement between Chocolate and Watson, scheduled for the Garden tonight, is off again.

"The Bon-Bon is said to have suffered a tummy ache from something or other he ate or drank at his Orangeburg training camp Wednesday night. Senor Guiterrez, who pilots the Kid, explained yesterday that his charge complained of severe pains in his tummy all Wednesday night and again yesterday morning and that he was so weak that there was no alternative but to postpone this evening's party for a week by which time he believes the indigestion will disappear...From what the writer has been able to learn, Chocolate is suffering more from the lack of working activity than he is from indigestion. Chocolate is said to have looked anything but hot in his scrap with Johnny Farr in Philadelphia, according to some who saw the bout, and seemed in dire need of work."

Ned Brown noted in his column, "The Kid looked desperate in his training jousts last Wednesday. If he had fought Friday night your reporter is positive Watson would have kayoed him. Guiterrez used good judgement asking for a postponement."

Another to cast doubt was Jack Kofoed of the *New York Evening Post*, who wrote, "No-one seems to know whether the Kid really had only a slight illness or whether he is actually burned out and ready for the scrap heap. Chocolate is only twenty-two although his eleven years in the ring probably made him considerably older physically."

Even little Charlie Harvey questioned the Kid's reported indisposition. A couple of days later he sent off a cablegram to John Mortimer at his home in Southsea, stating, "Took own doctor to see Chocolate. Match should take place on Friday. Very tough luck for Watson as he was down to weight ready to go. Am in fact keeping him down another week. If in same condition next Friday think he has a chance of upsetting the odds laid on the champion."

The champion appeared to have made a remarkable recovery when he resumed training on the Monday of fight week. "If Kid Chocolate fails to retain his featherweight title when he clashes with Watson in the Garden on Friday night it will be only because the Englishman is a better fighter," said one New York paper. "The picturesque Cuban Bon-Bon is in superb condition, physically and mentally. Chocolate sparred only three rounds today and displayed all his usual form, scoring almost when and where he pleased. His left hook and right uppercut worked overtime and he raised havoc with his helpers when he let loose. If Chocolate retains his present form he should easily outgallop the invader."

Charlie Harvey made the journey to Orangeburg to check on the Kid's condition but he was soon spotted by Luis Guiterrez. Just before the Kid's workout began, trainer Moe Fleischer tapped Charlie on the shoulder and told him there was some lovely rain outside and wouldn't he like to see it. Moe took Charlie by the arm, led him out of the gym, came back in and locked the door. But Harvey had seen enough. "We've been tricked," he complained to reporters. "There was no reason for postponing the fight, there is nothing wrong with him."

Boxing Inspector John T McNeill weighed the champ before and after his workout, he was 127½ going in and 124 coming out. Dr Nardiello of the Commission staff said that Chocolate was in much better condition than when he examined him the previous Thursday, had shown a remarkable improvement, and there was no reason why he should not be in perfect condition by Friday.

Watson stayed on at Pompton Lakes, doing light work, seemingly untroubled by the postponement. "While at the camp," he would recall. "I met Primo Carnera who was training for his world heavyweight championship fight with Jack Sharkey.

"I had several chats with Carnera and he impressed me as being

148

"BOS" sees Seaman Tommy Watson, Newcastle's own featherweight champion, in his world title fight with Kid Chocolate at New York to-morrow night.

a very good chap. I wondered just what I would do if I had to meet him in the ring. It must be like tackling the side of a mountain to tackle Carnera! Tony Canzoneri was also there, he was the lively boy of the camp who was always singing. Tony, the world lightweight champion, was training for his fight with Battling Shaw in New Orleans for the Junior lightweight title, which he won by the way."

A couple of nights before the big fight, Tommy and Kitty slipped out of camp. The local baker, who supplied the fight camp, had become friends with the English couple and invited them along to an amateur boxing show. Harvey had given strict instructions for Seaman to stay in camp but Tommy didn't like living by the book and rebelled. It nearly cost him his life! Two shots broke the night air and two men fell dead just a few yards from Tommy and Kitty. Were the shots meant for him, or was it just another gangland killing in those Prohibition days? Seaman didn't wait to find out. He hustled Kitty into the baker's van and they roared off back to camp. Next day he didn't see any of the newspapers and he didn't inquire into the shooting. Suddenly, Byker seemed a long, long way away.

19

"FOR THE CHAMPIONSHIP OF THE WORLD!"

It was Friday, 19 May 1933, the day of the big fight, and the excitement and anticipation was as intense in Newcastle as it was some three thousand miles away in New York, probably more so on Byker Bank than on Broadway. It was the sole topic of conversation in Annie Telfer's greengrocer's shop on the Bank, the walls of which were plastered with photos of Seaman Watson, his wife and children.

"Yes," said Annie to a visiting reporter, "we women are just as enthusiastic as the men. I have known Seaman for years, ever since he was a boy. He is a great fellow, and although I have not seen him fighting, he is the best man in the world at his weight. We think the world of him round here. He is everybody's darling." A cable on behalf of the residents of Byker Bank had been sent by Mrs Telfer, reading, "Dear Tommy. Wishing you all the very best, with love from Annie Telfer."

That cable was one of many flashed across the Atlantic wishing Tommy every success in his quest for boxing glory, including one from the children, Kath, Tommy, and Joan, who were being looked after by Seaman's aunt, Mrs Laws, at home in Mowbray Street, Heaton. Little Tommy had been troubled by his tonsils but in her letters to Tommy and Kitty Mrs Laws had kept the news from them.

"I have kept it quiet so far and I don't want them to know until they come home again," said Mrs Laws. "It will only worry them." Mrs Laws added that she would be getting up early next morning as Mr Mortimer had arranged to telephone her as soon as he received news of the fight.

From midnight a crowd began to assemble outside the Newcastle offices of the *North Mail*, men and women, some with babies in their arms, taking up their positions on the steps of the Stephenson monument to await the news from New York which would be coming over the wires at about four o'clock on Saturday morning.

"You'll have a long wait," shouted a passer-by, "the fight doesn't start until half-past-two."

"We don't mind that," a man spoke for all of them. "It will be well worth the wait if Tommy wins."

Over in New York however, the bookies were sending Kid Chocolate to the post a firm two-to-one on favourite to retain his featherweight title against the British champion, as were the boxing writers. Joe Williams wrote in the *New York World Telegram*, "The Seaman is one of those sturdy plodders with a vast amount of energy and enterprise who is always swimming upstream and thrashing away with his padded fins. He doesn't give you much time to rest and taking him by and large, fore and aft, is a very annoying person indeed.

"He likes to get in close and bang away at the delicatessen shop or kitchen pantry as it is more definitely known, and because of this fact some of the boys are saying that he is very apt to take the Cuban Kid, who does not like it downstairs, as who does my dear Cuthbert! Should this eventuate it would be a cruel blow to art. The Cuban Kid is a spirited picture of grace and poetry in action, a master boxer with a finished formula of hitting. That it is possible to offset these artistic gifts with bovine ruggedness and uncouth labour is not happy to contemplate."

Big Dan Parker of the *New York Daily Mirror* saw Watson as, "..a rough-and-ready infighter who doesn't pack much of a punch but who keeps an opponent busy trying to tie him up. He's a less dynamic edition of Jackie Kid Berg. In Chocolate, Seaman faces a much harder hitter, and a rangier fighter whose long looping left to the body is exactly what the physician prescribed as an antidote for Watsonitis. Chocolate has had plenty of experience against the crowding, infighting type of pug like Berg and Battalino and should know what to do against the Seaman instinctively. Chocolate, as I see the situation, has entirely too much class for the prosaic seaman and has little to fear from his opponent's light blows."

Writing in the Newcastle *Evening Chronicle*, GJO stated, "Never during a long association with the boxing game have I known a fight that has created such widespread interest in the North, and in Newcastle in particular, as that which will take place at Madison Square Garden, New York, between Seaman Watson of Newcastle and Kid Chocolate, the coloured Cuban, for the featherweight championship of the world. This interest, almost enthusiasm, has been intensified by the postponement of the fight from last Friday until tonight owing to Chocolate complaining of stomach trouble.

"The anxiety of many people was what the effect of the postponement would have on Watson...any doubt on this question, I think, must have been removed by the cheery cable I received from Tommy. 'Still smiling. Feeling all right. Will carry on as usual.' Seaman Watson is in America fighting for a fortune, but I also know that he is fighting for the credit of his native city. His local patriotism is one of his chief characteristics. He told me once, after his LaBarba victory, that when he heard a cheery voice shout, 'Gan on, Tommy!' his mind immediately came back to Newcastle. The cheeriness of Watson's letters to his home folk encourage and stimulate my faith in the Seaman tonight. All we can do at this side is to wait, hope, and wish to acclaim a new world's champion in one of our own."

At the official weigh-in at 2.00pm that afternoon, both fighters were pronounced fit and ready to do battle. Tommy scaled just half-a-pound inside the nine stone featherweight limit with Chocolate two pounds lighter at 8st 11½lbs. The physical measurements of the two men released to the press by the Boxing Commission doctor highlighted the sturdy build of the Briton and brought to mind the initial reaction of Luis Guiterrez when he first saw Tommy, "He looks big for a featherweight!"

Tale of the Tape:

Watson		Chocolate
24	age	23
5' 6½"	height	5' 6"
65½"	reach	68½"
36½"	chest	35½"
38"	chest exp	38¼"
15"	neck	14"
32"	waist	28¼"

The fight drew some 13,836 fans through the Garden turnstiles paying a gate of $31,675, making it the second biggest boxing attraction at the famous New York arena in 1933, topped only by the Primo Carnera-Ernie Schaaf heavyweight fight which drew a capacity 21,935 crowd. There was a tragic aftermath to the bout as Schaaf, who was knocked out by the Italian giant in what proved to be an unlucky thirteenth round, died in hospital five days later. *

"What are one's feelings when fighting for the championship of the world?" Watson would recall some years later. "So far as I was concerned, I felt very calm and confident as I was getting ready in my dressing room. There were times when I felt elated at the prospect of capturing the title, and as I walked from my dressing room to the ring, saw the glaring lights, glimpsed the thousands of cheering people, the contrast to those days when I fought in the Navy struck me forcibly. Once again, the Americans gave me a tremendous reception, and as I sat in my corner during the preliminaries, I was determined to fight as I had never fought before. Chocolate looked a picture of fitness when we were called together by the referee and I did not need to be told I was up against a tough proposition."

The sound of the bell for round one broke the tension hanging over the ring and triggered a roar from the big crowd as the fighters walked briskly from their corners. Gloves cocked, they sparred cautiously for an opening, Watson already trying to reach the Kid's stomach. They clinched, broke free, then Tommy rushed to close quarters, hooking to the ribs. The Bob-Bon ripped an uppercut to the head but missed wildly with a left and right swing. Watson went for the body again, left and right, and the crowd cheered him on, but the Kid was throwing vicious hooks and uppercuts and looked to have won the round.

Out for round two and Chocolate was the first to lead off, but he was wild with a couple of left swings that missed the target. Watson rushed in and they clinched, broke away, and sparred for an opening. Chocolate scored with hooks to the body and as Watson swapped leather with him, the Kid landed two terrific right swings to the kidneys. There was nothing between them at the bell.

Seaman roared across the ring for round three and launched a barrage of left and right hooks to the head and body of the startled champion. The Kid recovered his composure but before he could get back into the fight Watson shook him with a hard right to the jaw. Chocolate ducked his way out of trouble and bounced a left hook off Watson's head before letting loose a tremendous volley of punches that had the crowd in a frenzy at the bell.

153

The fourth round saw the British champion take the fight by the scruff of the neck, forcing Chocolate to the ropes where he hammered away at that slim brown body. The Kid was hurt but he fought back and a right uppercut rocked Watson and gave the Cuban a brief respite. He flashed out that long left hand, the right glove cocked and loaded, but Tommy caught him off balance and a thudding right to the head shook the Kid to his toenails. Left and right swings took him to the ropes and at the bell it was Watson's round and he received a tremendous cheer as he trotted back to his stool.

Round five was another good one for the British challenger. A sizzling right hook bounced Chocolate off the ropes and he had to call on his ring savvy to get out of trouble. As Tommy came forward again, the Kid fired a terrific uppercut but Watson stood his ground and came off best in a slugging match. Chocolate missed a vicious right hook and looked tired. In the *New York Evening Journal,* Hype Igoe would write, "Chocolate backed away for the first time in all his Gotham fights."

Watson answered the bell for the sixth round with a searing body attack but was shaken by a left that exploded on his chin. He paused for a few seconds and Chocolate wondered why he didn't fall down, then Tommy was crowding back in, hammering the body with both hands and the Bon-Bon was not feeling too sweet when the bell sent him back to his corner.

Manager Guiterrez and trainer Moe Fleischer lit a fire under the Kid in the interval and he stormed out for the seventh round like the champion he was. He absorbed a solid left hook from Watson before opening up with a withering two-fisted attack that drove the Briton around the ring. Chocolate pounded the body then fired left and right to the head. He was outboxing Seaman at the bell and it was a good round for the Kid.

Round eight saw both miss their opening shots before Watson hammered a right to the stomach. The Kid replied with a sizzling right hook to the head. They traded long lefts and Watson threw a hard right to the heart, only for the Kid to reply with a left to the ribs. Chocolate landed a right to the head and Seaman was glad to hold on. It was a round in which Hype Igoe observed, "Watson was making the mistake of boxing Chocolate, and there are few who can outsmart the Kid. It was a duel at long range and the Cuban seemed to have the edge."

154

A sturdy young Seaman poses with some of the trophies won boxing for the Royal Navy.

i

Sailor Tom and Kitty on their wedding day 6 August 1928.

Seaman fought tough Belgian Francois Machtens four times and beat him four times. Here they pose with veteran referee Tommy Murphy at the weigh-in for their Newcastle fight 19 September 1932.

ii

Seaman and Kitty (at his left) host a party for the kids of Byker.

*Bringing home the bacon
Kitty and Tommy show off Lonsdale
Belt after Tarlton fight Nov. 1932.*

*Training at St. James's Hall, July
1934 for second Tarlton fight.
Daughter Joan is his second.*

On board the Leviathan bound for New York debut, Seaman works out in the gym as John Mortimer holds the watch.

Hail the Conquering Hero! Crowds at Newcastle Central Station greet their champion on arrival home from New York after beating LaBarba.

iv

LaBarba

Tommy and Kitty hand over another cheque for charity.

A proud father with Kath, Joan(middle) and Tom Jnr.

Tommy and Kitty enjoy a social occasion in 1934.

Manager Alec Lambert (left) and Mrs. Lambert (right) arriving at Southampton to see Kitty and Tommy off to New York for the Chocolate fight.

Kitty and Tommy on board ship bound for New York and the World title fight.

Manager Alec Lambert (left) wishes Tommy, Kitty and John Mortimer the best of luck.

Training in America for the Kid Chocolate fight; Kitty joins Tommy on the road.

Kid Chocolate.

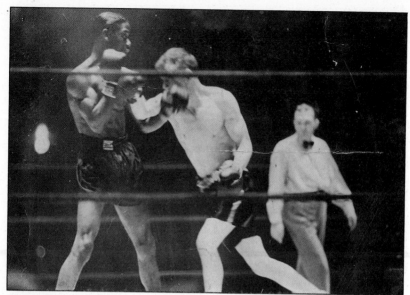

So near and yet so far. Seaman comes within an ace of beating Kid Chocolate for the world title in New York 19 May 1933.

MC Joe Humphreys raises the glove of Kid Chocolate as winner and still featherweight champion of the world, Madison Square Garden, 19 May 1933. In the other corner Watson's seconds share his disappointment.

Tommy shows off his Lonsdale Belt to John Harding (left) and Lieut. Commander E. W. B. Leake, chairman of the National Sporting Club, who promoted the Watson-McMillan fight in Glasgow with Charles Black.

Seaman Watson (right) and Johnny McMillan shake hands after signing the contracts for their contest in Glasgow 21 March 1934.

Watson (left) successfully defends British featherweight title against Johnny McMillan in Glasgow 21 March 1934, winning 15 rounds decision.

The morning after the fight before; Johnny McMillan (right) admires Watson's Lonsdale Belt the day after their fight in Glasgow.

Seaman relates his New York experiences to some young hopefuls as manager Alec Lambert looks on.

Tommy, seen wearing his Lonsdale Belt, was actually an ex-champion when he signed this photo.

Tommy and Kitty enjoy a night out with friends.

Tommy with Newcastle manager and matchmaker Joe Shepherd.

Ex-Seaman Tommy Watson, Newcastle's British featherweight champion 1932-34 in role of referee sends Frankie Johnson to a neutral corner after KO of Jim Findlay at New St James's Hall, Newcastle, August 1952.

Referee Tommy Watson with, from left, Stafford Barton, Jamaican middleweight, promoter Arthur Clarance (in specs) and South Shields middleweight Jim Berry 4 July 1939.

Frances proudly shows off a photo of "our Tommy."

A group of ex-boxers and associates at the funeral of Seaman Tommy Watson: Bob Graham, Billy Farrell, Charel Beart, Billy Charlton, Mickey McGuire, Harry Craster, Joe Sheperd, Billy Sheldon, Joe Corbett, G. Hall, Paul McGuire, Ginger Roberts, Bob Lance, Joe Thompson, Bomardier McLeod.

Between the eighth and ninth rounds Chocolate told his handlers that he was so tired he could hardly hold up his hands. "Go out and bluff this fellow," said Guiterrez as he lifted the Kid off the stool, and Chocolate did just that, fighting in flurries whenever Watson set up an attack and shaking Tommy a couple of times with a vicious left hook. Watson got home to the body again but had to take a beauty himself that jack-knifed him. He recovered to smash the Cuban with a right uppercut to the chin but Chocolate stood up under the blow and was punching back at the bell.

Coming up for the tenth, Watson sent a left into the body, the Kid came back with two lefts jabs then missed with a right uppercut. Watson came forward again and belted Chocolate around the body, but as he switched a left hook to the head he ran smack into a whistling left hook from the Cuban that bowled him over like a shot rabbit. With a roar the fans were on their feet, but so was Watson, almost before Referee Pete Hartley could pick up the count from the timekeeper. Seaman brought another roar from the crowd as he tore back into the Kid and a solid left hook to the chin told the Cuban he had a fight on his hands. Chocolate tried to cash in on the knockdown and raked the Briton with lefts and rights to the head in a furious attack that took him up to the bell.

Watson had a menacing look in his eyes as he answered the bell for round eleven but the slick Cuban danced around the ring and tricked Tommy into a series of clinches before scoring the cleaner shots. Chocolate displayed the smooth skills that had made him the darling of the New York crowds and those ebony fists beat a tattoo on the white body of the lad from Newcastle. At the bell the Cuban Kid had clawed another round on to his side of the scorecards.

He didn't win round twelve! Seaman scored with a right uppercut to the chin, then hammered both hands to the body. He switched his attack to the head and brought a trickle of blood from the Kid's lips. A smashing left hook to the head staggered the Cuban, then a right crashed against his jaw. Chocolate's mouth gaped open and his knees sagged and Watson's handlers screamed for him to finish it. But he stood off and watched the Kid recover and the moment was gone. "I didn't want to take too many chances," Tommy would say later. "Chocolate is a mighty smart fighter and if I'd walked in wide open I might have fared even worse."

Just before the bell the crowd roared as Watson sprawled on the bottom rope but he had lost his balance. He was back on top in the thirteenth with Chocolate desperately shooting the left to the head. Seaman hammered away at the body and not even a terrific left hook that crashed against his head could halt the bombardment. Round fourteen and Watson fenced for an opening, then whacked Chocolate with a left hook to the stomach. As the Kid gave ground, Tommy went after him with both hands, but he had to take two long left hooks to the body. He went to his knees but it was just a slip as he missed the Kid with a right hand.

Fifteenth and final round, and for many in that vast arena the fight was still to be won, many of the rounds so close they could have gone either way. Watson was still unmarked and looked the fresher of the two as they shook hands. This was how Hype Igoe called the round for the *Evening Journal*. "Hard fighting at close range. Watson at his best, he blocked lefts to the body and rocked Chocolate with the right when the Keed missed with a right. A mix-up followed that was a honey. The Englishman was the cooler of the two and he went at it methodically. He hit Chocolate with a right to the heart. Chocolate was well spent and was working furiously. Watson was making every blow count and he practically drove Chocolate across the ring before him. Watson's round."

Igoe saw the fight as seven rounds each with one even, a draw. The official judges were not so generous to the British challenger, calling the winner by unanimous decision, and still featherweight champion of the world, Kid Chocolate! Tommy stood in his corner and smiled as he heard Joe Humphreys announce the decision. Then Kitty was at his side, consoling him, tears streaming down her face, he was still her champion, and Charlie Harvey was shouting to the press boys that Watson had been robbed.

"Well, I did my best," said Seaman ruefully as Archie Watson cut the sweaty bandages from his hands in the dressing room. "I'm sorry I lost of course but it was a good clean fight and the Kid is a fine boxer. But I thought I won easily. The judges thought otherwise so what is the good of kicking. Anyway, that is only the third time I've lost a fight."

Over in Chocolate's dressing room, manager Guiterrez admitted, "Watson is a better fighter than he appears when looking at him from the sidelines. He is hard to hit but even so Chocolate should have won beyond dispute. I'm going to lay him off for a month. We have an offer to take on Watson in London very shortly, and I say that the match will be staged before the summer is over. First, Chocolate has to rest. He isn't burnt out, he is just the victim of too many good times."

Next morning, Tommy had a nice bunch of press clippings to take back home with him. Sportswriter Alan Gould praised "Watson's boxing judgement in the early part of the fray and also for the brisk persistence of his attack to the Cuban's mid-section." Joseph C Nichols wrote in the *New York Times*, "..the Briton forced the fighting up to the ninth round." Harry Cross of the *Herald-Tribune* observed that to many it appeared the Englishman had the better of the infighting in several of the rounds which were given to Chocolate. So ding-dong was the battle, said Reuters, that the ringside experts were of the opinion that at the worst Watson deserved a draw.

Ed Frayne, Sports Editor of the *New York American,* reported, "Thanks to an old ring custom which gives champions the benefit of every doubt, Kid Chocolate retained the world featherweight title at Madison Square Garden last night. Referee Pete Hartley and two judges voted unanimously in his favour after fifteen see-saw rounds with courageous Seaman Tom Watson.

"The crowd thought the verdict was all right and said so in a happy roar. The professional element was not so enthusiastic, quite a large proportion thought Watson had earned the decision and a considerable number were quite vehement about the matter...Watson took the offensive from the first round and had the advantage as long as he pursued that policy. Watson outroughed him at infighting and made Chocolate miss badly at long range. Close rounds every one, but with everything else even an aggressor wins the round. Watson was clearly forcing every round he received. On this writer's scorecard Watson took seven of the fifteen rounds, Chocolate had a clear edge on four, and the remaining four were even. The Briton gave a masterly exhibition of ring generalship and it was a great pity he did not receive a title he richly deserved."

20

BROADWAY TO BYKER!

One of Seaman's greatest admirers was Annie Telfer who kept the fruit shop on Byker Bank. Mrs Telfer was in the big crowd that had started forming at midnight around the Stephenson Monument outside the *Chronicle* offices in Westgate Road to await news of the fight. "He did well," she said. "When he comes back we will give him such a welcome as Byker Bank has never known before. When they told us that Chocolate had won I began to cry. I had felt sure Seaman would win."

Another woman, carrying her thirteen-months-old child in her arms, had been there all night and said her husband didn't know she was there. "I'll have to tell him," she said, "but it was worth it. It was exciting. There was some excitement when a newspaper came out with the announcement that Seaman Watson had won. It wasn't right. A few minutes later we had the correct result in the *North Mail*. Seaman did well."

Dawn was still busy lighting the sky that Saturday morning as the *Newcastle Journal* reporter drove across Byker Bridge on to Shields Road, along Heaton Park Road and into Mowbray Street where, despite the early hour, small crowds had gathered near the home of Seaman Watson and his family. As the car came to a halt, they surged forward, men, women, many youngsters among them, anxious for the news from New York.

"Well, Jack, did he melt the Chocolate?" shouted one man.

"Think the Americans will let him get away with the title?" said another. "Let's hear about it then."

They were disappointed at Seaman's defeat, but not downhearted. "After all," said one, "he has done mighty well to battle his way up to a world championship. It's up to Newcastle now to plan a reception for Tom that will show him that we are still as proud of him as ever."

That weekend the *Sunday Graphic* carried an exclusive interview with Watson, conducted over the OceanPhone between London and New York. "I was the most surprised man in the world when victory in my fight with Kid Chocolate for the world's featherweight title was awarded on points to my opponent on Friday night. All through our fifteen rounds battle I felt that I would finish stronger than the Kid and I still believe I did although I have no grumble against the verdict. I believe however that if it had been possible for the fight to have gone a few more rounds there would have been a different story to tell.

"However, I can tell those friends of mine at home who have so warmly supported me that this affair with the Cuban is not settled yet. Before the fight, my manager Charlie Harvey, and Luis 'Pincho' Guiterrez, Chocolate's manager, had agreed that no matter what the result might be we should have a return bout in London.

"After our battle was over, Guiterrez, Harvey, Chocolate, and myself, again made a pledge that a return meeting would take place. It will probably be at the Albert Hall in August, and by that time I'm convinced that I shall be able to wrest that title from the Kid, ringmaster and clever boxer though he is. I know now exactly how to tackle Chocolate and when we meet again I shall not make any mistakes. Meanwhile, my friends in England and particularly in Newcastle can rest assured that I don't intend to give up my struggle for the title until it is mine.

"The folks in Newcastle are in my heart now, I feel that they are sympathising with me in my effort and I hope they will believe that I put up a good fight. I long to see them all again, and of course my three kiddies in Byker. I have a message for the boys of the Navy, my old pals, many of whom have written me. Here it is; I fight for the Navy as well as for myself and for my hometown. It's only about three years since I left the service but much of my success so far is due to the training I had there. I would like to say that I have a great admiration for the Kid, he is a clean, straight fighter, and although I would have liked the decision to have been otherwise, I could not have found a better man to deprive."

A few days later, James Butler reported in the *Daily Herald*, "Kid Chocolate has cabled his terms for a world title contest with Seaman Watson in London and Mr John Mortimer has accepted on behalf of our champion. Mortimer said to me last night, 'He has a great opportunity which will not be missed. Chocolate is not demanding an unreasonable figure, he is asking for a guarantee of under £4,000 and the National Sporting Club are definitely prepared to stage the match. All that is required now is Chocolate's acceptance, then arrangements will be completed to hold the fight at Olympia during the first week in July.'"

Among the transAtlantic telephone calls Watson received in New York was one from manager Alec Lambert in London. "Well, Tom," he asked, "were you satisfied with the decision?"

"How can I raise a kick when everybody in New York treated me so well," replied Tommy. "They are great sports over here and have given me every encouragement and a good time. Chocolate is a good fellow and gave me his word that if a return fight could be fixed in England he will give me the chance of winning the world title before my own countrymen."

Of course, in Kitty's eyes, her Tommy was already the world champion. In a letter home, she wrote, "All the people at the ringside started to shake hands and congratulate me in the last round, so that will tell you how near he was to getting the fight. I was terribly upset. Tommy had trained so hard for the fight, and it looked good for him. I say that Tommy won fair and square."

A big Watson booster in New York was former world heavyweight champion Jack Dempsey. A couple of days after the Chocolate fight, a newspaper reported, "Jack Dempsey regards Seaman Watson as a great fighter. He says that Watson had Kid Chocolate licked to a frazzle right up to the time the pair started the last round. Many of the ringside critics, he said, considered that Watson would have won if he had not blown up during the last couple of minutes."

Speculation over a rematch between Watson and the Cuban in England was rife in the week following the New York contest. WORLD TITLE FIGHT BID FOR NEWCASTLE headlined a front page story in the *Evening Chronicle* which stated, "A very definite move is being made to stage a return world's championship fight between Kid Chocolate and Seaman Watson in Newcastle (writes our Boxing correspondent).

"From correspondence I have been privileged to read I can state that it will overshadow all promotions ever staged in the North of England. A well known businessman, as well as a prominent Newcastle sportsman, is greatly interested in the proposition. I am not in a position to reveal definite figures, but I can say that they are stupendous...It is expected that a sum of approximately £7,000 would have to be raised, and it is almost certain that the champion's end of the purse would have to be deposited before he signed a contract...There is sure to be great competition for the match, and the Jeff Dickson party as well as the National Sporting Club are certain to bid for it, but as Watson is a Newcastle man there are strong hopes that the match will be staged in Newcastle."

The *North Mail* reported, "Watson v Chocolate in Newcastle was given weight by a local businessman who announced that he could get backing of £6,000-£7,000 within a week if all the other obstacles were overcome. There was some speculation over the possible venue, some doubt whether St James's Park would be made available. Failing that, there were two greyhound stadiums in the area. At Brough Park, the terms of the lease guaranteed a percentage of the gate to the owner of the land. Gosforth Park was also suggested, ideal if the ring was pitched between the 6/- ring and Tattersalls with the great standage there eliminating the risk of bad weather."

Any chance of the fight taking place in Newcastle however seemed to fade with the announcement by John Mortimer that he, "had been in communication with the National Sporting Club with a view to fixing the match. The champion has assured me that if it is arranged quickly he will promise not to fight again until he meets Watson in the ring. If the NSC do not want the match I will negotiate with other promoters."

The NSC did want the match. Mr A F "Peggy" Bettinson, manager for the club, said that negotiations for the fight were almost complete. "Providing that Chocolate accepts our terms," he said, "the match will be staged at Olympia in London in the first week of July."

Meanwhile, Kid Chocolate and Seaman Watson were seeing to business. A few days after their world title epic, they left New York, the Cuban on a boat for Europe where several fights had been lined up for him, and Watson on a train for Toronto to honour his contract for a contest with Bobby Lawrence. This fight, scheduled for Friday 26 May, had been arranged before Tommy's fight with Chocolate, and when that match was postponed for a week, Charlie Harvey told Watson he would ask that the Lawrence fight be put back a week also. Seaman wouldn't hear of it.

161

"I'm going," he said to Harvey, "because if I don't, it will be unfair to Lawrence."

So, just seven days after that tremendous fifteen rounds battle with Kid Chocolate for the world championship in New York, Seaman Tommy Watson climbed into the ring at Toronto's Maple Leaf Gardens to box Bobby Lawrence for ten rounds or less, and a crowd of some 4,000 fans gave him a terrific reception. Lawrence had only recently won the Canadian championship and he jumped at the chance of a fight with Watson.

Sadly he was no match for the Seaman who hammered the youngster from pillar to post to score an easy decision. Lawrence reeled helplessly around the ring in the closing rounds as the Briton hit him when and where he pleased, and at the final bell Bobby's face was covered in blood from Watson's short, chopping blows. Whenever Lawrence tried to get to close quarters he was foiled by the speed and hard punching of Watson, who showed great ringcraft and landed his punches accurately.

On the rare occasions when the Canadian youngster landed a scoring punch, Watson just smiled grimly and retaliated with solid blows from either hand. When the decision was announced, Lawrence congratulated Watson who patted the boy's head as the crowd roared its approval. Next morning however, a local sportswriter called the fight, "one of those tragic matches between a much too clever, too fast, and too hard-punching boxer, and a youngster who is just mounting the pugilistic ladder."

Another ringside observer saw the fight as, "One of the fastest, cleverest, most pleasing exhibitions seen here in quite some time...They were both at the same weight but the Englishman looked pounds heavier. He was strongly built, fast on his feet, quite as quick with his left lead and hook and his overhand right swing...While he received no great amount of punishment last night, the Englishman looked and acted as though he could take plenty and in the midst of it keep on coming in with something in return. He had every mark of that stamp of fighter who is never beaten until he is laid out and until then remains dangerous...Watson is fast, clever, a good boxer as well as a game fighter, and that makes a combination that is hard to beat. Seaman Tom Watson is the classiest fighter England has sent to Canada since Jimmy Wilde and Jimmy was all but through when he showed here, while Watson has every appearance of being at his best for some time to come."

162

Back in New York, with the Lawrence fight out of the way, Charlie Harvey was eager to cash in on Seaman's excellent showing against Chocolate and arranged a three-fight package that would see Watson take on Tommy Paul, the former champion of the National Boxing Association, in Buffalo on 9 June, George Reilly in Pittsburgh on 15 June, and finish in Chicago on 23 June against an opponent to be named later.

Some newspaper reports still referred to Tommy Paul as the NBA featherweight champion in the days leading up to the match but in fact the Buffalo Italian had lost his claim to the title some months previously when beaten in ten rounds by Freddie Miller in Chicago. In any case, Paul sustained a badly cut eye in a gym workout and the Watson fight was cancelled. A week later, on the eve of his Pittsburgh fight with George Reilly, the clever coloured boy who had been one of his chief sparmates for the Chocolate fight, Seaman learned that Reilly had pulled out of the match. That was enough for the Geordie champion. He informed Charlie Harvey that he was going home and booked passage for himself and Kitty on the s.s. Aquitania, sailing from New York at midnight on Wednesday 14 June 1933.

A week later they stepped ashore at Southampton to be met by John Mortimer and a crowd of reporters. Before they could fire their questions at Tommy however, they had to wait for him to deal with the horde of well-wishers who surrounded him, eager to shake his hand, to congratulate him, and to wish him better luck next time. Among the crowd of boat officials, customs officers, and railway porters, was the American Ryder Cup team who had travelled over on the same boat led by Walter Hagen, in England for his last visit as a Ryder Cup golfer. Hagen's fifteen-year-old son, Walter Jnr, was with him and he was obviously thrilled when introduced to the famous English boxing champion.

"I am glad to be back again," said Tommy when the reporters gathered around, "but it has been a wonderful experience for me. Chocolate is a fine fighter and I hope to meet him in London this summer. If I get a return fight, I can promise I shall go all out for the world title. It was a tough fight last time and it will be a tougher fight on the next occasion. I'm after Kid Chocolate!"

"Yes, we are after him," said Mortimer, "and I hope to fix the fight for London, probably in August. We are ready with the money, up to any amount. I've been in cable and telephone contact with

163

his manager and I think everything will be arranged all right. Chocolate's people want me to go to Barcelona and discuss the matter and I shall take action very quickly for an engagement."

Next morning, Tom and Kitty boarded the Flying Scotsman at Kings Cross. They were going home, on the last lap from Broadway to Byker, and when their train steamed into Newcastle at three o'clock that afternoon, there was a big crowd on hand to welcome them home despite the fact that it was the middle of the Race Week celebrations in the city.

"SEAMAN WATSON HOME," reported *The Journal*. "Smiling broadly and waving a light grey American slouch hat, Seaman Watson arrived in Newcastle yesterday after his fight with Chocolate. Watson, looking very fit, was accompanied by his wife. On alighting from the Flying Scotsman they ran forward to embrace their three-year-old son, then returned the greetings showered on them by relatives. Watson had all his time cut out dealing with welcome home kisses.

"A crowd of about two hundred friends from Heaton and Byker were awaiting the boxer and his wife on the main platform of the Central Station. They gave the pair a warm cheer as they dashed for a waiting motor car. Watson cheerfully returned the greeting before climbing into the car. 'It was hard lines,' he remarked to a *Journal* reporter, 'but it's good to be home again.' As the car turned into Neville Street, the crowd moved across the road and formed into two lines through which the car had to pass. A number of friends and supporters were also awaiting Mr and Mrs Watson when they reached their home in Mowbray Street, Heaton."

"I was not sorry to leave the States and return to the old country," Tommy told a reporter a few days after coming home. "In my opinion no place compares with 'canny Newcassel' and I have never felt so happy as the day I stepped out of the train at the Central Station. The dazzling lights of New York, its high-speed night life and its ultra-modern theatres did not make a hit with me. Give me good old Byker Bank every time!

"My supporters at home probably think I derived some satisfaction from the 'small fortune' I received as my end of the purse. It was some small fortune I arrived home with! The £1,000 I got was swallowed up by all kinds of expenses which had to be incurred. There was passage money, training expenses (which are

164

exceptionally heavy in America) first class sparring partners to pay and keep. My American manager got his share of the purse, one third, and then the income tax authorities came along and scooped the remainder of the pool. You want a purse of considerably more than £1,000 if you are going to show any profit when you go across the Atlantic to fight. When I arrived at Southampton from New York I had exactly one dime in my pocket!"

21

BATTLE OF BYKER

"Britain owes a National Debt to Newcastle," clarioned an article in the *Sunday Sun*, penned by T S Phillips. "In America, British boxing has regained its old prestige. Once again British boxers are treated with the respect which is their birthright. No longer are British titleholders sneered at by the Yankee critics as horizontal champions. A year ago, any Briton who went to America to fight took a return ticket. If he didn't, there were the breadlines...

"What a different tale today! And the man who has done it is a Tynesider! Let us announce him in true ring fashion: Ladies and Gentlemen, Seaman Tom Watson of Newcastle, featherweight champion of Great Britain! Tommy Watson of Byker, ex-seaman, ex-publican, has just returned to 'canny aad' Newcastle from New York, defeated, but neither disgraced nor discouraged, in his attempt to wrest the world title from Kid Chocolate.

"Tommy returned in the luxury liner Aquitania. Just before she berthed at Southampton I wonder if he remembered how, a few years ago, he often saw the glory of the English Channel on an early summer's morning, not from the deck of a floating palace, but from one of the ships of the King's Navy? When he was a Jack Tar, no one knew or cared about him. Yet for more than an hour one morning recently, the trans-Atlantic cables were buzzing with his name, telling of how he mercilessly punished Kid Chocolate's ribs or how the Cuban speared him off with his left. For more than an hour Tommy Watson kept journalists working on both sides of the Atlantic to give the public the news. For hours, in Newcastle, he kept thousands up out of bed, standing in the streets outside the *Newcastle Chronicle* offices waiting to hear the result. And though he did not win, did they regret their vigil? No! 'Good old Tommy!' they said, and went home to bed. They knew he had done his best. If that is not romance, what is?"

Back home in Byker, reality replaced the romance. Local rival Benny Sharkey was hoping to get his promised shot at Tommy, put on the back burner when Watson made his first trip to New York six months previously. In this respect, the 14 June issue of *Boxing* carried the following letter, "Sir, In this week's Flotsam and Jetsam column it mentions: Benny Sharkey (Newcastle) is hoping Seaman Watson will keep his word and give him a return at any weight agreed on his return to his native city. May I respectfully ask Benny Sharkey if he has ever known Seaman Tommy Watson to break his word? Will you be good enough to give this a par in fairness to Watson? Yours, etc. Alec Lambert, 39 Burne Street, Edgware, London, NW1."

A fortnight later however, it was announced that Watson's next fight would probably be in London, staged by the promoting syndicate at Lea Bridge Speedway, against an opponent to be named later.

"However," observed GJO in the *Newcastle Chronicle* on 27 June, "most interest in the northern area is taken in the proposed contest between the featherweight champion and Benny Sharkey of Newcastle...I would think that it would have to be on percentage terms, for which there will have to be negotiations, while I am asked to state that the Sharkey party are willing to take £100 to £50 that Watson does not beat Benny at 9st 2lbs.

"Well those are probably the odds that Sharkey would get if he invested his money at the ringside. Some people with whom I have discussed the question think even bigger odds would be laid on the champion, but in view of the atmosphere that the match would undoubtedly engender, I am not going so far. We must not close our eyes to what Sharkey has been doing during Watson's absence abroad. A lot of people still think that he was unfortunate to have the decision against him in the final of the Manchester featherweight competition against Phineas John, while against Farrell last week he used his hands more quickly and more accurately than I have ever seen him do before. I saw the Seaman yesterday and he told me that he was quite willing to box Sharkey in the open air and would lay £100 to £60 on himself, but the date of course must be conditional upon that of another contest between Watson and Kid Chocolate."

That was the fight Tommy wanted more than any other and every day the sports pages speculated on when and where. Meanwhile, the Cuban Bob-Bon had discovered the fleshpots of Barcelona and Madrid and was acting more like a kid in a sweetshop than a Kid in a sweatshop. He was reported as having accepted an offer of £3,500 from a London syndicate to defend his title against Watson, while Spanish promoters were trying to make a match between Chocolate and Jose Girones, the Spanish and European featherweight champion, whose record included a string of 34 straight knockouts.

The Girones fight fell through when it was pointed out that Chocolate's title claim, although recognised by the all-powerful New York Commission, could not be recognised by the International Boxing Union as they had a working agreement with the National Boxing Association of America and their champion was Mr Freddie Miller!

The Cuban Kid had really captured the fancy of Spain, and on 15 July a huge crowd paid their way into the bull ring in Madrid to see him make a fool of Frenchman Nick Bensa in a ten rounds bout. Chocolate said he expected to win easily and he did, and he also said he was confident of repeating his victory over Watson when they meet again in London. John Mortimer was having the utmost difficulty pinning the Cubans down to a date however, which was understandable. They were having too good a time in Europe for one thing, and hadn't Luis Guiterrez himself stated that his boy Chocolate took more punishment in his fight with Watson than in any other fight in his career! In any case, Chocolate was already signed to fight in Barcelona on 2 August, against the rugged Belgian Francois Machtens, a three-time loser to Watson.

Manager Alec Lambert had more bad news for Tommy. The fight arranged for 23 July at the Lea Bridge Speedway had been cancelled. "I had agreed with Mr Joe Morris to let Watson box Dick Corbett, the former British bantamweight champion," said Lambert. "Then, when everything was agreed by phone, he called everything off." The Lea Bridge people had also proposed a match at nine stones between Watson and Panama Al Brown, the world bantamweight champion, to take place on 20 August for a purse of £2,500. Tommy stated that, as always, final word would be left with Lambert, but he ventured the opinion that should he and Brown meet before his return bout with Chocolate, a much bigger purse than £2,500 would be required.

It was local pride rather than purse money that mattered most when Watson agreed to honour his promise to John Paget and Benny Sharkey and fight his Byker rival at New St James's Hall on Monday 31 July 1933. The match, over twelve rounds, was made at 9st 2lbs, and two weeks before the fight Tommy set up his training camp at Whitley Bay. He ran six miles every morning around the sea front with a salty breeze off the North Sea blowing in his face as he ran. In the afternoons, from two o'clock until half-past-three, he worked out in the splendidly equipped gymnasium of the Rockcliff Football Club, skipping, mat exercises, bag punching, then brisk sparring sessions with Billy Sheldon and Vic Foley, wearing twelve-ounce gloves.

In the first week of his training, Seaman welcomed Mickey McGuire to his camp at the coast. The little giant-killer from George Street was to fight Jackie Brown at Manchester on Monday 24 July. British and European flyweight champion when he dropped a 15-rounds decision to McGuire at Newcastle, Brown had since become world champion, but the Manchester bout would again be a non-title affair.

Nevertheless, Mickey was looking forward to meeting Brown again and he sparkled in some fine sparring bouts with Watson. After twice being told not to pull his punches, McGuire opened up and was able to get past Tommy's longer reach on several occasions. A few days later, Mickey beat the champion again, but in fairness to Brown, when he was disqualified in the seventh round for a low punch he was generally considered to have a good points lead over the Novocastrian.

Although Watson's British title would not be on the line in the Gallowgate ring, Benny Sharkey trained as though he were fighting for the championship of the world. The winner would not only be best in Byker, but best in Britain!

"I was very much impressed by Benny Sharkey's showing in the gymnasium at Byker yesterday," wrote GJO in the *Chronicle* five days before the fight. "I have certainly never seen him look in a better physical condition. Biceps, shoulder, thigh, and stomach muscles are splendidly developed, but in spite of the fact that he has been hard at work preparing for the fray for almost a month, he is very free and lissom in the use of his arms. He is now only a pound above the 9st 2lbs he has to scale at 2 o'clock on Monday, but still his work is of a very strenuous nature. He had half-a-dozen fast bouts while I was present, and he only confirmed what Tommy James, who is one of his sparring partners, had told me...that Benny is hitting exceptionally hard.

169

"His bout with Alec Tennant, a Scotsman who has only been on Tyneside a fortnight, was an exceptionally strenuous one. Tennant is a hefty fellow with a long reach, and he set about Sharkey as though a championship was at stake. He was not as particular as he might have been in punch delivery, and during a clinch Benny looked over to me and observed, 'A bit of a dangerous fellow this.'

"At the same time he evidently realised that attack in this case was the best defence, and before time was called Tennant knew that he had been boxing, twice going to the boards from high blows delivered with great force and accuracy. If less robust the rounds Sharkey had with Jim Vickers and Tommy James were none the less brisk.

"From the signing of the contract I have been enamoured of this contest: I am even more so after seeing Sharkey in training. I am looking forward to one of the keenest battles of the season, and one of the cleanest. So, apparently, are thousands of others, for the bookings are very heavy."

Fight fever gripped Newcastle that Monday and there was almost a capacity crowd at New St James's Hall when the men appeared for the official weigh-in at two o'clock. Both received a tremendous welcome as they stepped on the scales and although actual weights were not disclosed it was announced that both men were inside the stipulated poundage. Seaman was in a happy, jocular mood, while Benny, never one to reveal his inner-most feelings, was quietly confident.

On the eve of the fight, the *Sunday Sun* had carried the views of Douglas Parker, the Sunderland man who had fought both Watson and Sharkey. "Watson's special virtue was coolness and generalship," Parker stated in recalling his three losing bouts with Seaman. "This, I would say, will be the big difference between Benny and Watson when they meet, unless people have not overestimated Benny's improvement as shown when he stopped Billy Farrell. Sharkey was apparently so dominant in this contest that probably we can scarcely take it as a criterion. It should not be forgotten, however, that Farrell's style makes him generally one of the most difficult men to hit, and all the reports say that Benny never missed him.

"If Sharkey has mastered his wildness he has certainly got rid of his greatest fault as a fighter. He carries a good punch, especially

170

his hooks, and has pluck and strength enough for two men: but when he loses his head his frequent misses are bound to be taken note of by a referee, and very often call for the ridicule of the crowd. Yes, steadiness may be the deciding factor in a fight that is sure to be an exceptionally keen one. I see Watson allowing Sharkey to do all the swinging he cares to, but you may be certain that the champion will not allow anyone make him fight except the way he wants to, while he is cute enough to make his opponent do the things he ought not do.

"Now to sum up the chances, as the tipsters say. I have been much impressed with Sharkey's form recently, but we cannot get away from what Watson has done in his last three principal fights...beat a 5 to 1 on Tarleton for the British championship, beat LaBarba with practically the same odds against him, and then just failed to beat Chocolate for the world title. On this form I think Watson will win, but in saying so I want to impress upon readers that I still want the better man to win. They are both pals, and two of the cleanest fighters I have ever met."

The big fight was scheduled to begin at 9.30pm and by that time New St James's Hall was packed to suffocation. Parked cars filled every street in the vicinity of the hall while a big crowd still milled around the entrance hoping to gain admittance.

"There is nothing that appeals to boxing enthusiasts of any fighting centre like a good local duel," wrote Norman Hurst for the Kemsley papers, "and in matching Tom Watson and Benny Sharkey promoter Paget had given his public a contest they had long been waiting for. Both the British champion and the dour, determined Jewish boy who aspires to championship honours had trained hard for the fight. Both boys were wonderfully fit and at the weigh-in scaled inside the required weight of 9st 2lbs. Referee for the contest was Mr Tom Murphy.

"Watson had a decided advantage in height. This fight clearly demonstrated that it requires something more than a ton of pluck and a desire to fight to be a champion. No one could deny that Sharkey had those two great ring assets but it was in the finer points of the game that he failed to measure up to the champion. Watson's short-arm punching to the body was a treat to watch, his blows were crisp and thrown with the knuckle part of the fist.

"Once, Sharkey had his chance when, in the tenth round, pulling

171

back from a left lead by the champion he swung in again to smash a right counter to the jaw and amidst a thunder of cheers the champion went to the canvas. Watson was more surprised than hurt but he was too old a general to jump to his feet immediately while his head was still singing from the punch. The wildly excited crowd saw the slugging Sharkey try his utmost to pull the fight out of the fire, but Watson weathering what had been his hardest round, went on to make the fight safe and beyond quibble. No one in the hall needed the pointing finger of Referee Mr Tommy Murphy to tell them who had won. Nevertheless it was a smashing fight between two great little battlers with the champion proving to the satisfaction of everyone present that he is a worthy titleholder."

There was nothing in the opening round as Benny forced his way inside and Watson smothered his attacks. The champion did land one good right to the body and they were working in close at the bell. Round two and Watson opened the scoring with two fast lefts to the face before Sharkey drove both hands to the body. Benny slipped a left and slammed a right to the heart, then Watson planted his feet and hammered both fists at the body to make his rival clinch. Once, when Benny slipped to the canvas, Tommy sportingly helped him up again.

As Sharkey attacked in round three, Watson stopped him in his tracks with a barrage to the body. Realising the champion's strength inside, Benny tried boxing at range and a savage left to the mouth hurt Watson just before the bell. Seaman forced the action in the fourth and Benny's ribs showed red from the punishment they were taking from those hammering blows. In the fifth Benny again signed for two wicked punches to the short ribs and in a heated exchange was cut over his left eye.

As Sharkey faltered and put a glove to the eye the crowd roared for Watson to go in and finish it, but Benny fell into a clinch and survived to the bell. Round six brought him further grief with the champion beating him to the punch time after time, almost anticipating Benny's blows before he threw them! Seaman just got his head inside a smashing right as the round ended. The seventh saw Watson continue his dominance, fierce body punches sapping the strength from Sharkey's legs. Watson took him to the ropes near the end of the session and Benny stumbled over backwards. Tommy again helped him to his feet as the bell rang.

Seaman was out for work early in the eighth round and his

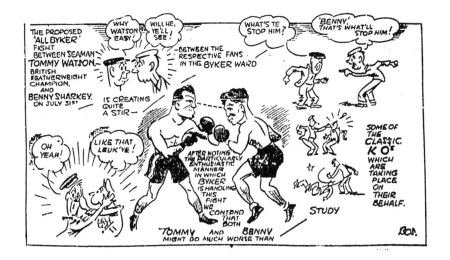

aggressive fighting forced Sharkey to use the ring. Benny however was always dangerous with his counter attacks when he would dive in and send in punches from every angle. Watson timed one of these rushes perfectly and uppercut his man viciously. The punch rocked Benny to his toenails and it looked as though he would fall, but he closed the gap to mix it up with his Byker rival. The ninth was one of Sharkey's best rounds as he succeeded in keeping the champion at a distance with an accurate left hand and following with the right to the jaw.

This was how Norman Hurst saw the tenth round. "Sharkey was doing a lot of swaying and weaving to avoid Watson's leads but the body bombardment he had been subjected to earlier in the fight slowed him up a lot. A beautiful left flush on Sharkey's mouth brought cheers from the crowd but Sharkey, with one of the best counters I have ever seen, dropped the champion to the canvas for a count of six and proceeded to have all the better of the round. Watson fenced his man off in a wonderful manner when he got to his feet but was bustled down in his own corner just before the round ended. This round was all Sharkey."

In round eleven Benny tried to build on his success, but he was telegraphing the right hand and Watson made him pay for every mistake. Solid left leads pulled Benny up in his tracks and a sizzling right cross had the blood pouring again from his injured eye. Sharkey realised time was running out and he launched a fierce attack but there was an old head on Watson's sturdy shoulders and he boxed his man off to the bell.

"Go all out, Benny, last round!" Sharkey tried desperately to obey the words from the corner, charging at Watson, the blood again streaming from his injured eye, hurling punches that would have brought down lesser men. But the man in front of him was a champion and champions are special men in the roped arena. Seaman Tommy Watson was just such a man and in that final three minutes he brought the crowd to their feet with a brilliant display of defensive boxing and at the final bell was a worthy winner. There were cheers too for Benny Sharkey, a great little fighter who would beat six champions, but not this one, not this night, not ever.

John Mortimer was a ringside spectator that night at New St James's Hall and he was delighted with Watson's performance. Due to leave for Spain to see Kid Chocolate fight Francois Machtens in Barcelona and talk to Luis Guiterrez about that elusive return match for the Seaman, Mortimer had received a letter from the British Boxing Board of Control stating that the World Championship Committee had agreed to recognise a Chocolate-Watson contest, should it be arranged, as for the true world's championship.

"I like this lad so much," Mortimer said, "that I am set on his being a world's champion, and I have seen enough of the game to know that if Tom is to achieve the highest honours he will have to make sacrifices for a year or two. I just wish he would stop smoking his bloomin' cigarettes!"

22

DEATH AND DISAPPOINTMENT

Everyone knew Dr Smith who ran the Newcastle Dispensary on New Bridge Street at the city end of Byker Bridge. From about 1928 he had sat in his little consulting room for six, seven hours a day, and the waiting room was always full. There was only one charge, whatever the ailment. Sixpence! For that a patient would receive medicine for a week, a consultation, and a visit if necessary from one of three lady doctors.

Many of the troubles that came before Dr Smith were caused by malnutrition. "In my room sits a child blue with cold and crying with pain," he recorded one day in 1932. "It's a pouring wet morning, she's drenched to the skin and has only plimsolls on. We visit the home and find the mother, the wife of a casual worker, could not come to the Dispensary. She had pawned her boots for food. The family is at tea, seven of them, bread and pease pudding, one pennyworth for seven."

A local reporter wrote after visiting Dr Smith, "When I was there, a little girl of about ten stood before him. She was thin, oh terribly, frighteningly thin, you could see all her bones, she had a little white pinched face and arms like anaemic matchsticks. She had been complaining of a pain over her heart. A nasty pain which caught her breath. She had just recovered from pleurisy. The doctor found her blood was very much under what it should have been and that she was actually running a temperature. And her mother was an ordinary, decent, struggling Byker woman, who so obviously was doing all she could for her children. Poor woman, she was very worried about her little girl.

"The doctor gave her an order for Virol and some medicine, with instructions to put the girlie to bed and that one of the women doctors would call on her. Soon, he hopes to be able to send the lassie away to the home at Shotley Bridge. But the crucial point of this very typical case was that after all the necessary bills, like rent, clothes tickets, gas, were paid, this woman was left with exactly two-shillings-and-ninepence per week per head to feed her family. And her husband was working. He has forty-five shillings a week.

"The other day, the doctor found a man he knows taking home the dinner for his family of seven. The meal was a quarter-pound of sausage. Price, three-half-pence! 'It is no good me advising a spring cabbage,' said Dr Smith. 'That costs sevenpence. Far too much for my people.' He can only deal in coppers. So if ever you feel in need of meeting a real Christian, drop into the Newcastle Dispensary sometime. I guarantee that you will come out feeling that at least you had done a Christian action, because you will not be able to help leaving the grand fellow something to assist him to carry on his mission of mercy."

Tommy Watson was a great admirer of Dr Smith and had often raised money for the Dispensary by boxing an exhibition somewhere or running a raffle when he had the pub on Byker Bank. But he never thought that one day he would need the professional services of Dr Smith.

"My mother was ill in bed," remembered Frances. "Our Nan used to wear those big picture hats and I would put one on with my bathing costume and put a cigarette holder in my mouth and parade for my mother. She would say, 'I'll give you a good hiding young lady when I get out of this bed!' But I never did get my hiding. I was eighteen-years-old, in service with a lovely family at West Monkseaton who had two little girls. I lived in and would come home to see my mother on the half-day a week I was allowed.

"This time when I came home she told me how cold she was and pulled the bedclothes back to show me her legs. I ran for our Tommy who was then living in Mowbray Street and he came back with me. When he saw how she was he got packs of cotton wool and hot water bottles and whatever else to keep her warm. Tommy wasn't too keen on the doctor we had and he went and got Dr Smith who ran the Dispensary on New Bridge Street. Dr Smith was able to get her into hospital and they said she had cancer. She died shortly afterwards, in Fuller Road, lived there till she died. Our Tommy just broke down, as we all did."

According to the death certificate, Jane Eleanor Hunter, widow of Luke Curry Hunter, a ship rigger, died on 11 August 1933 at 26 Fuller Road aged fifty-nine. Cause of death as certified by J K

176

Hope Scott, MB, was a large carcinoma of the stomach. The death notice in the *Evening Chronicle* stated, "Jane Eleanor Hunter, widow of Luke C Hunter and mother of Seaman Tommy Watson, died on Friday 11 August 1933. Funeral leaving 26 Fuller Road 2.00pm Monday 14 August for burial at Elswick Cemetery."

The death of his mother hit Tommy like a knockout punch and boxing took a back seat for a while. Fortunately in this respect he had just taken over The Wolsington Hotel in Shields Road, Walkergate, and the long hours he put in helped him come to terms with his grief. The job was demanding but he was ably assisted by Kitty of course, as well as the dapper Billy Sheldon, one of his regular sparring partners.

John Mortimer and Alec Lambert had always been welcome at Jane Eleanor's table and they shared the deep sense of loss felt by the family. The Portsmouth promoter was even more determined to get Tommy his rematch with Chocolate but kept running into a brick wall. The Kid's manager Guiterrez failed to keep a couple of appointments with Mortimer for the simple reason that the Cuban Bon-Bon was sadly out of condition and would have been an easy mark for the British champion. Still sharpening his footwork in the nightclubs of Paris and Madrid, the Kid had a tough night in Barcelona when he struggled to take a decision over Francois Machtens of Belgium. The spectators protested the verdict and hissed the Cuban before turning their attention to the referee who was only saved from attack by the intervention of the police.

Press reports from the continent had Chocolate linked with half-a-dozen fighters including IBU champion Jose Girones, Italian titleholder Vittorio Tamagnini, and Panama Al Brown, the world bantamweight champion then barnstorming around Europe. The only name not in the frame was that of Seaman Tommy Watson. In the meantime the British Boxing Board of Control announced a series of eliminators to find a challenger for Watson's title. Tommy Rogers (Southern Area champion) would meet Ginger Jones (Welsh champion) and Scot Johnny McMillan would face the winner of a contest between Phineas John and Dick Burke.

At the beginning of September 1933, Alec Lambert was offered a fight for Watson with Tommy Rogers at the Royal Albert Hall on 5 October. The promoter was Jeff Dickson, the Paris-based American who was moving into the London fight scene, and he wanted to bill the contest as being for Watson's British

177

featherweight title. Lambert was also considering fights in Glasgow and Newcastle as well as an offer for three fights in Australia. The hoped-for return bout with Chocolate for the Cuban's world title seemed as far away as ever.

"Kid Chocolate has had all his demands acceded to," said Mortimer, "yet will not fight the Britisher. Why?" A final telegram was sent off, reading, "Guiterrez, Barcelona-Good offer Watson, Australia. Accept unless reply within twenty-four hours. Mortimer." Neither Mortimer nor Lambert expected a reply and a few days later Lambert accepted the fight with Rogers in London. Watson set up training camp at Hexham, a market town in Northumberland some twenty-odd miles from Newcastle.

The lad from Byker did his roadwork on the local racecourse but was short on sparring partners, as noted in Eldon's Northern Outlook column in the *Newcastle Chronicle*. "Seaman Watson wants sparring partners at Hexham, I observe, Well, boxing with a titleholder, even for amusement, is not everybody's hobby, but I hope the gallant Seaman will not lack in his preparation for the fight in London with Rogers for the want of local lads to biff. Watson is training at Haugh Lane Centre and what is more for a small fee anybody can see him doing it. Many have availed themselves of the opportunity with the result that the funds of the Hexham Social Services Centre are benefiting. Social workers raise money in various ways but I would almost wager that this is the first time that a featherweight champion has been the medium."

Tommy Rogers was already in full training at the Waterglade Inn at Willenhall, his hometown, where his chief sparring partner was Peter Nolan, matched with Jake Kilrain on the Albert Hall bill. Holder of the Southern Area featherweight championship, Rogers was born and bred in the hard-living district that was half Black Country and half iron works. He was spotted in a six rounds contest by Mr D W Davies, who promptly gave up his referee's licence and, to quote a Midlands sporting journalist, "took out a manager's certificate in order to start a boxing stable with Rogers as the Hyperion of the occupants."

A recent surprise winner over Tommy Hyams, Rogers was already a big favourite in Paris where Jeff Dickson had featured him against the best nine-stone men in France, Kid Francis and Eugene Huat. Tommy boxed a draw with Francis and gave a masterly exhibition to defeat the former French champion Huat.

Despite those results, the *Sunday Pictorial* noted in its preview of the Watson fight, "Rogers has yet to establish himself in his own country as a featherweight of the first flight. He has already done so in France but as yet he is comparatively unknown here...When it comes to the supreme test give me the man who has taken a long time to arrive. He is the man who usually stays the longer at the top of the tree, that's why I look for Watson to win."

Storm clouds were gathering however. On the day he arrived in London from Paris, Jeff Dickson received a body blow that left him on the ropes. He was summoned before the British Boxing Board of Control and informed that the contest between Watson and Rogers would not be recognised as a championship bout as he had omitted to notify the Board of his intention before making the match.

Under the headline "WHY I APPLAUD SEAMAN WATSON," Norman Hurst wrote, "Let us hand it to Seaman Tommy Watson for being one hundred percent champion. The fact that the BBBC has had it placed on record that the match between himself and Tommy Rogers of Willenhall at the Royal Albert Hall is not for the title has made no difference to the Tyneside battler who holds the featherweight title. 'If Rogers licks me, then I shall consider him the champion,' Watson is reported as saying. That is the championship spirit. We could do with more Watsons!"

Dickson announced to the press that he had definitely signed Kid Chocolate to defend his world title at the Albert Hall on 30 October against the Watson-Rogers winner, and that the Cuban and his manager were due in London to see the fight. "I will have Chocolate introduced from the ring on the night," he said.

The day before the fight however, Wednesday 4 October, Dickson caused a sensation by announcing that he was cancelling the Albert Hall bill, and that Watson and Rogers would now meet in Paris on 13 October. "There are two reasons for my cancelling the show," Dickson told the press. "The first is that the British Boxing Board of Control, in my opinion, killed the Albert Hall programme by refusing to allow me to bill Watson and Rogers as fighting for the British featherweight championship.

"The second is the fact that Kid Chocolate, who was due to fight either Eugene Huat or Kid Francis on 16 October and was due at Croydon today, has at the last moment sailed from Le Havre for America. I arranged for Chocolate's air passage from Paris to London and was going to Croydon to meet him. To my consternation I found that he had simply walked out on me and taken a boat for New York. In view of these circumstances I have decided to cancel the Albert Hall programme."

"Discussing his Paris venture," reported *The Sporting Life*, "Dickson declares that Rogers is as popular in Paris as Marcel Thil, the world middleweight champion, so there will be no question of the attractiveness of the bout over there. We understand that Rogers has agreed to the change-over and that Watson is also expected to fall in with the promoter's scheme. For the bout in Paris there will be a British referee, British timekeeper, and British seconds. The supporting bouts will be between Frenchmen.

"The matter will not end where it is. Mr Dickson, I have good reason for saying, is likely to break away from the Board, in which case he will promote shows as he did five years ago without regard to the governing body. 'We are all rebels now,' remarked his manager Mr Ted Broadribb. 'I wanted Mr Dickson to break away long ago and he would not agree. He has now changed his mind.'

"'The Watson-Rogers fight was absolutely under championship conditions but I suppose I offended the Board by not first asking for its blessing,' said Dickson. 'That was merely an oversight. The taking away of the championship label ruined the match from the point of view of public interest and I had to cut my losses.'

"According to an official of the Board the ban so far as calling the fight a championship was put in force because Rogers had previously been chosen to meet Ginger Jones of Wales in an eliminating contest. That match said the official will now take place in Birmingham. Mr Broadribb however stated that he understood Jones had since informed the Welsh branch of the Board that he was relinquishing his Welsh title because presumably he can not do the featherweight limit and instead was challenging Johnny Cuthbert for the lightweight title."

Watson was disgusted with the whole business. He had just arrived home from his Hexham training camp on the Wednesday morning when an *Evening Chronicle* reporter telephoned with the news that the fight was off. When the reporter called at Tommy's home shortly afterwards he was sat in his easy chair, still shaking his head.

"This beats me," he said. "I wonder if I am ever going to have some luck in the fighting game. This is enough to make a fellow say to hell with the whole business. When I left Hexham this morning I was dead nine stone and as fit as ever a man could be. I was going off to London about two o'clock as confident a fighter as ever lived. And now you bring me this message. Never mind Paris, my contract is to fight Rogers in England and I want that fight to take place tomorrow night."

Referring to the clause in his contract stating that should the promoter break the contract he will pay the boxer £100 damages, Watson snorted, "That will merely cover my training expenses. I looked upon this fight as a preliminary to another world title fight with Chocolate and no-one will really know the sacrifices I made to get this. I refused £300 for a fight with Johnny McMillan, and other contests for big sums to attain my aim. And now we have got this flop. I'll go to London tonight to see the terms of my contract are fulfilled. If Jeff Dickson wants me to fight Rogers in Paris I want a new contract, and the weight will have to be about 9st 2lbs, with an English referee and under English conditions. After all is done and said, I am the British champion, and will be until I lose it to a better man."

"Never mind, Tom, we are not broke yet," observed Mrs Watson. Pointing to the front page of the previous night's *Chronicle*, she added, "and I am a jolly sight better off than poor Mrs Stribling."

The news story was headlined, "FAMOUS BOXER'S DEATH" and read, "Young Stribling, the famous heavyweight boxer, died in hospital at Macon, Georgia, today, from injuries received when he collided with a motor car when motorcycling to the hospital to see his wife, who gave birth to their third child recently."

"Righto, Kitty," replied Tom. "It helps if you look at it that way."

Next day, Tommy was in London, not for his planned argument with Tommy Rogers at the Albert Hall, but for his argument with Mr Jeff Dickson. That it was concluded to the champion's satisfaction must be assumed from the cable he sent to the *Evening Chronicle* that afternoon stating simply, "Fighting Rogers in Paris on 16 October."

"For a trip to Australia," speculated the *Chronicle's* boxing man GJO, "before he left these shores Watson could have had £250 with two first class return fares. Then he would have got £250 on arriving in Australia. After that he had a guarantee of £500 for one fight, plus percentage, and the option of two other fights on a share of the gate. But, as I have said elsewhere, Watson thought he saw in the Rogers contest the best way to get another cut at Chocolate for the world's championship. There are many of Watson's best friends who do not think that he should have gone to Paris, but I am relying, from the brief wire the champion sent me, that the Seaman has struck a sound monetary bargain with promoter Jeff Dickson, and that he will be well paid for his fight."

But five days later the jinx struck again. Watson received a wire stating, "Paris fight off. Letter follows. Dickson." The news did not come as such a shock to Mr D W Davies of West Bromwich, manager of Rogers, who told the *Birmingham Mail*, "I foresaw too many difficulties. Watson was standing out for an English referee.

"The rules of the French Boxing Federation made it definite that two English boxers fighting in France could not be governed by an English referee. Tommy Rogers will fight a French boxer in Paris on 16 October as an alternative and will approach the British championship and a fight with Watson by the route the Board of Control have made clear, that is he will meet the winner of the Burke and McMillan fight which will take place in Liverpool on 26 October."

The French Boxing Managers Association had protested against the Watson-Rogers contest on the grounds that no two Frenchmen could fight a French championship bout in England and consequently argued it was unreasonable to stage an English championship contest in France.

"What can I do?" shrugged Watson. "I need not tell you that I am nearly fed up with the whole business. I had ambitions to win the world title and in persisting in that quest I have probably turned down £2,000 worth of engagements. Boxing is my living and I cannot go on making sacrifices all the time to suit the purposes of promoters. I have made up my mind to fight anyone about my weight, and I would like to meet a real good'un in our own hall in Newcastle. I am not looking for easy jobs. The better the man I meet, the better I fight. I am going to tell Mr Alec Lambert, my manager, that he can get me as many fights as he likes, with whom he likes, and where he likes."

Lambert moved fast and within a couple of days Tommy received word that he was to top the bill for the National Sporting Club at

London's Olympia on 19 December against world bantamweight champion Panama Al Brown in a match made at nine stone. The Geordie battler was elated, but that was December and this was October and there was still talk in Newcastle of yet another fight with his Byker rival Benny Sharkey.

Mr Tom Sharkey announced that his son would fight Watson at New St James's Hall at 9st 2lbs for purse only, or he would fight him at 9st for £100-a-side if he could get the Board of Control to sanction the fight as one for the title and the Lonsdale Belt. On hearing this, Watson said he thought Sharkey's request for a fourth fight between them was absurd for a Belt match at £100-a-side, saying that Sharkey was not even considered good enough to be included in the official eliminators for his title. However he would agree to meeting Benny again at New St James's Hall at 9st 2lbs for £100-a-side. Mr Paget was also trying to book Francois Machtens of Belgium for a fight with Watson at the Gallowgate hall for 30 October.

Meanwhile Tommy Rogers moved a step nearer Watson's title when Welsh champion Ginger Jones confirmed Ted Broadribb's statement and withdrew from the eliminators to box at lightweight, leaving Rogers to receive a bye to meet the winner of Burke and McMillan. And it was the Scottish boy Johnny McMillan who was emerging as the favourite to box Watson for the championship. *Boxing's* Scottish correspondent was already calling him, "without a doubt the greatest drawing card in Scottish boxing circles today. He has been a contender for top honours for years and has a devastating hook in either hand that has been the dismay of the majority of his opponents. He is light-footed, skilful, pleasing to watch, and goes about his business in an extraordinarily cool fashion. No amount of wild attacking or bull like tactics ever upsets his calm. That's Johnny's way. We have not had his like in Scotland for many a day, and his many supporters are wondering when he will girdle himself with a British belt and mark out a campaign for world honours. It is only his due."

23

HARD-LUCK TOMMY

Within hours of the liner Ile de France docking in New York harbour, Luis Guiterrez had called a press conference to explain why he had not allowed Kid Chocolate to defend his featherweight title during their stay in Europe.

"I refused £3,000 for Chocolate's services at weight against Seaman Watson in London," he said. "I wouldn't let him fight a good fighter on the other side for the very good reason that I knew he wouldn't get a decision if he was entitled to it. America is the only country where a foreign fighter gets money, an honest count at the box-office, a square shake, and where crowds have the faintest idea of sportsmanship."

Chocolate, who alleged that he was bombarded with chairs after one of his fights, added his two-cent's worth with the statement, "Any good fighter who goes over there is crazy, plumb crazy!"

The announcement in New York caused no great surprise in Newcastle. In the *Chronicle*, GJO put the matter in perspective when he commented, "I once had a fine little 'pom' named 'Punch.' Whenever I had him out, and we approached a bigger dog, he would walk close to my heels and then, at a safe distance, give mouth to the bigger fellow. I think Luis Guiterrez, Kid Chocolate's manager, in some respects resembles my little dog, for he has waited until he has got to America before he dare bark.

"After the way Watson was messed about when he was in America I think this about the cheekiest bit of Cuban chat that I can imagine. I am prepared to stand by what Mr John Mortimer observed in a letter to me when he was making such tempting offers to get the Cuban over here. 'I am afraid the coloured man has had plenty of Tommy Watson,' he wrote. That is undoubtedly the real reason why Chocolate slipped off home from Le Havre."

Further confirmation came a few days later in a letter received by John Mortimer at his home in Belmont Street, Southsea. It was from Charlie Harvey, who had interviewed Guiterrez in New York, and he quoted the Bon-Bon's manager as saying that Chocolate was so unfit and run-down while in Europe, and his form was so bad against Machtens, the Belgian, that he was afraid to put him up against the hard-hitting Tommy Watson again. He also informed Harvey that he had matched Chocolate with Tony Canzoneri, this fight to take place at Madison Square Garden on 24 November.

That news didn't set too well with manager Pete Reilly who was in New York pushing the claims of Freddie Miller, recognised by the National Boxing Association of America as featherweight champion. "Why talk about a Chocolate-Canzoneri fight?" he asked. "This could only be an over-the-weight-match, meaning nothing and leading nowhere. The Garden complains of a scarcity of attractive matches.

"Well, Miller is ready for Chocolate at any time, and he doesn't want any more than the chance. And I'm willing to take Miller to England for a bout with Watson, but I'd want a suitable purse. Anyway, we want the featherweight title and nothing to dispute the claim, so will fight both Chocolate and Watson if necessary."

The New York State Athletic Commission must have been listening to Reilly for they served notice on Chocolate that he was to defend his featherweight title against Miller, the NBA champion, immediately after his bout with Canzoneri, and should he fail to do so he would be barred from boxing in the Empire State. Since the Cuban was already under suspension by the NBA for failing to honour a fight contract in Detroit, he would in fact be unable to fight anywhere in the United States or Canada.

Guiterrez promptly announced that he was ready to accept the Miller fight provided Chocolate drew the champion's 37½% slice of the purse. Reilly countered that his boy was at least entitled to 25% and offered Miller's services to the *New York American* Christmas Fund if the Chocolate bout could be arranged. Striking while the iron was hot, Miller made his New York debut in a fight with Lew Feldman.

Boxing's New York correspondent Peter Varley would later report, "I'm tipping Freddie Miller as the next world's featherweight champion, and have formed this conclusion after seeing him in action against Lew Feldman, the smart New Yorker, at the Ridgewood Grove club the other night. Miller, who is the

NBA champion, boxes in the southpaw fashion, and he showed enough against the plugging Feldman to give Chocolate a headache, for which purpose Miller is in New York. The Keed and Feldman have met three times but in none of these starts did the New York champion handle Lew as did the Cincinnati youth.

"Freddie, whose most potent weapon is a left uppercut, was handicapped by Lew's running, but he had Feldman's ribs red before the bout was very old, and did not lose more than one round in ten. Frank Rappold, prominent Cincinnati promoter, has offered Chocolate and Miller $7,500 each to meet at his club, which accommodates only 6,600 persons, but it seems that New York is bound to get this clearing-up featherweight championship battle which will probably be staged at the Garden in February."

With hopes of a return fight with Chocolate fading day by day, Tommy was anxious to fight again. The big match with Panama Al Brown was still on but it was weeks ahead, 19 December, time to get in a warm-up bout. Former British bantamweight champion Dick Corbett was lined up to meet Benny Sharkey on the Olympia bill but Watson was the man he wanted.

"It is our hope that a match with Watson matures," the Londoner's manager told the press. "We have long been challenging the champion, and now that there are suggestions that Watson may go to Australia early in the New Year we are more than anxious to fix a fight. We have been offered a date for a match by Mr J J Paget, the Newcastle promoter, in January, and it only remains for Watson to accept."

But Tommy refused to consider such a contest until after he had fought Brown in London. "After that fight," he said, "I will fight Corbett for £100 a side." However Seaman did agree to appear at New St James's Hall for Paget and a match was made against Sonny Lee over twelve rounds at 9st 4lbs for Wednesday 29 November.

Lee was no stranger to the Gallowgate hall. Five weeks previously he had given Benny Sharkey a boxing lesson for the best part of twelve rounds despite a badly cut eye received in the second round, and not many fans agreed with Referee Fred Charlton's decision for Sharkey.

Now he was back to meet Watson and Professor Louis Marks, manager of the Leeds boy, was confident that Sonny would acquit himself well against the British champion. Born at Hunslet, Lee had been apprenticed to the building trade and he was just seventeen when he got into an argument with a big, husky fellow. The youngster amazed his workmates by handing the bully a severe hiding and a few days later one of them took him along to the local gym. So the builder became a boxer. Still only twenty-one, he had crossed gloves with some of the best in the business and now he was meeting the champion.

Eager for battle, Watson took the fight to Lee from the opening bell and the Yorkshire lad joined issue to swap punches. Seaman broke away and threw two left hooks to the body, but when he tried the same shot to the head, Lee ducked low and the punch missed. They were both hitting hard with Watson the more effective and coming up to the bell he chastised Lee with a stream of straight lefts to the face.

Round two and both of them punched away inside before Lee broke off the exchange. Driving his man into a neutral corner, Watson attacked again with a two-fisted barrage of leather that once more had Lee ducking away into a low crouch. Then a left hook to the body from the champion sent Lee rolling on the canvas, his face contorted in agony. Referee Murphy moved forward and waved Watson to a neutral corner before taking up the count.

Then Murphy caused a sensation by pointing to Lee's corner as that of the winner. The arena became a bedlam as the crowd rose to their feet, some of them shouting at the official, "Why did you start to count?" As manager Alec Lambert voiced his protests, Watson, realising that he had been disqualified, left the ring looking disconsolate, cheers and shouts of sympathy following him to the dressing room.

As Seaman changed into his street clothes, a *Journal* reporter entered the room and, in discussing the fight, suggested that as Watson hooked his left to the body, Lee had come up to the punch. Tommy nodded in agreement, adding, "If I hit Lee low, I deserve to be disqualified. It is the first time in my career that I have been beaten on a foul. But I do not think I deserved to be disqualified. I will meet Lee again next week if he will give me a return contest."

A ringsider with more than a passing interest in the proceedings was Mr Lionel Bettinson, manager of the National Sporting Club who were promoting Tommy's next contest at Olympia in London against Panama Al Brown. "I do not think the referee could see the punch from where he was standing," he observed to a reporter, "but I saw it and it was a very good punch to the body."

Asked for his comments a few days later, Referee Murphy stated, "I think that Watson's fine principle in admitting that he may have hit low when some of his chief supporters were endeavouring to defend him, over-shadowed all other happenings. He has always been one of the fairest and straightest men in the game."

But that defeat, only his fifth in 98 fights, rankled with Tommy for a long time. Some years after he had retired, he recalled the contest in a newspaper article, stating, "The bloke I was fighting was doubling up so low when I went into him it was inevitable something was going to happen. I let rip one punch and as I did so he started straightening up. I caught him right in the solar plexus. It was fair enough. But he dropped immediately and started groaning and clutching his middle. The referee sent me away before I realised what was happening. I was very angry about the referee's decision that night."

The summary ending to the Lee fight left Tommy still ring-rusty. It had been four months since his twelve rounds with Benny Sharkey and he wanted to be at his best against Panama Al. He would have to be! A few days later Seaman was on his way to London to finish off his training. Lambert had arranged for him to stay at the Black Bull at Whetstone, an excellent training camp used regularly by Len Harvey. Len had just beaten Jack Petersen for the British heavyweight title and had trained for the fight at Whetstone, his favourite camp.

Boxing headlined its 6 December 1933 front page, "WATSON'S WORLD CHAMPIONSHIP CHANCE..Seaman Watson, now nicknamed 'Hard-Luck Tommy', arrives in London on Friday to continue his training for his great fifteen rounds contest at Olympia on 19 December against Al Brown, bantamweight champion of the world. The winner will be matched against the victor of the Miller-Chocolate world title affair to be staged about the same time in America. If Tommy succeeds in defeating Brown he will then really be in the running for world championship honours. The opportunity to fight for the featherweight title was denied him when Kid Chocolate refused to fight him after coming over to Europe expressly for that purpose."

The same issue of *Boxing* carried a report of Chocolate's

sensational second round knockout by Tony Canzoneri at Madison Square Garden, adding, "Boxing followers hereabouts are inclined to take Luis Guiterrez's story that he has sold his interest in Kid Chocolate for $25,000 with a large grain of salt. Luis says he has disposed of Chocolate's contract to Fernando Eguileor, a Havana boxing promoter. Guiterrez adds that his reason for selling the contract is that he wishes to retire from boxing but methinks he must have gleaned advance information that Chocolate is fast on the slide and got out while the going was good."

Meanwhile, Watson was hard at work training for his fight with another world champion. The *Chronicle's* London correspondent reported, "With his face aglow from the exertion of a three-and-a-half miles walk and a run round Regents Park in the face of a keen east wind, Seaman Tommy Watson of Newcastle looked a picture of perfect physical fitness when I saw him at his London training quarters during his preparation for his great fight with Al Brown at Olympia next Tuesday.

"'I feel fit enough to knock a house down,' was genial Tommy's answer to my greeting. 'This cold weather seems to ginger one up more than anything else. Speaking seriously, I feel very confident about next Tuesday's match. I know I am up against a tough proposition in facing the world bantamweight champion but I feel I can beat any man in the world at nine stone.'

"Seaman Watson then went into the ring for a six-rounds swift practice bout. Among the youngsters acting as his sparring partners is Johnny McGrory, a Glasgow youth of eighteen, and Billy Sheldon of Newcastle, who is the hero of more than one hundred fights in which he has never been knocked out. Watson was a bit of human lightning in the ring yesterday. His practice bouts are all high-speed strenuous affairs but he finishes up as fresh as the proverbial daisy. He is up and out at 7.30 in the morning for his outdoor exercise, and after his ring practice he has a spell at the bag and then skipping and arm and body swinging exercise. This will be his daily programme until Sunday when he will ease up for the big fight.

"'Tommy has learned a lot in his big fights in the last year or two,' said manager Lambert, 'and what he does not know about ring craft and speed is not worth knowing. I am as confident of Tommy gaining the victory on Tuesday as I have ever been in my long experience in the ring.'"

Lambert's confidence was duly justified when Tommy won his big fight on the Tuesday, but it was not over Panama Al Brown. Monday's headlines told the story..."BROWN-WATSON FIGHT OFF! CROWLEY SUBSTITUTE! COLOURED CHAMPION IN ALGIERS! The NSC created a sensation last night when they announced that Panama Al Brown will not be able to meet Watson at Olympia tomorrow night. Instead, Dave Crowley of Clerkenwell has been engaged to fight Watson, the British featherweight champion, over 15 rounds at 9st. A cable was received yesterday by Mr Lionel Bettinson, manager of the NSC, from Brown, the coloured bantamweight champion of the world, who is still in North Africa where a few days ago he beat the Italian Luigi Quadrini. It read, 'Find difficulty in settling matters before tomorrow. Impossible be in London Tuesday.'

"The NSC management were anxious about Brown arriving in time for his contest with Watson and in the middle of last week Bettinson began to communicate with Brown by cable and telephone. 'Brown gave me an assurance personally that if he were enabled to fulfil certain personal financial requirements over in Algiers there would be nothing to prevent him coming over to London to fight Watson on Tuesday,' said Bettinson. 'Steps were immediately taken by the NSC to enable Brown to meet his obligations and complete travel arrangements were made for him. Commander E W B Leake, who is deeply interested in the Club, actually placed at our disposal a private aeroplane in case it should be needed. Apparently there are now complications of which the Club has not been informed.'"

Bettinson had actually begun seeking alternative opponents for Watson a few days before the news of Brown's non-appearance broke. He asked Ted Broadribb to cable Nel Tarleton, then on his way home from Australia, to stand by. Nella arrived in England on Saturday but talks broke down.

Into the breach stepped Crowley, who had lost to Brown in London but had just beaten Dick Corbett. Dave, who was training with his stablemate British Empire heavyweight champion Larry Gains at Market Bosworth, near Leicester, was delighted at the news that he was to fight the champion.

"This is my great opportunity," he told reporters. "I know Watson is good but I think I stand every chance of beating him."

To make the substitute match more appealing, Bettinson tried to get it sanctioned as being for Watson's title. "I understand that I shall be asked by the National Sporting Club to fight for my belt against Crowley," said Tommy. "As far as I am concerned it is okay. My heart and soul is in boxing so naturally there will be no argument on my side. If the National Sporting Club say 'Yes,' well that goes for me."

However, official recognition was not forthcoming. In a hastily convened meeting on Monday afternoon, the Stewards of the British Boxing Board of Control decided to refuse the request for a championship label because, "The final eliminating contest for the right to meet Watson is taking place tonight in Glasgow between Johnny McMillan and Tommy Rogers, and a similar position was created by Messrs Jeff Dickson Sports Promotions Ltd when Watson was matched with Tommy Rogers and the Board refused recognition.

"The Stewards feel, having chosen boxers to meet in eliminating contests for the right of boxing for the title, it would be most unfair to the boxers who have contested the eliminators to be superseded at forty-eight hours notice by a boxer who has not contested in an eliminating bout. The Board appreciate the good sportsmanship of Watson who, in an endeavour to help the promoter, had agreed to put his title at stake provided official recognition was obtained."

Tommy had already sent a message to Newcastle asking Kitty to bring his Lonsdale Belt to London. Tuesday's *Evening Chronicle* reported, "SICK WIFE TO BE AT RINGSIDE! Behind the scenes of the big fight at Olympia tonight there is a human story, a 300-mile dash by a sick woman. Mrs Watson, wife of Seaman Watson, the British featherweight champion, went to London from her home in Newcastle in the early hours of today. Before her husband weighed in for his fight with Dave Crowley she was making preparations to be present at the ringside, despite the fact that she has been ill for several weeks.

"'My wife has been unwell for some time,' said Tommy. 'For the first part of my training I stayed in Newcastle so that I could be with her, but when it came to the strenuous work of the preparation I naturally had to come to London. I have been keeping in close touch with my wife. She is no doubt much better, otherwise the journey would have been too much for her. Of course I will not tell her to keep away from the fight. It may be a tonic for her.'"

If Kitty was in need of a tonic, then this fight at Olympia was just what the doctor would have ordered. Apart from watching her beloved husband in action, she would see in Dave Crowley a fighter of whom Gilbert Odd would write, "When Dave was performing it was action all the way, full of incident, sparkling as champagne, a pleasure to watch."

Arthur Helliwell, columnist for the Sunday newspaper The People, wrote in similar vein. "Crowley's style in the ring had a frothy, champagne sparkle. His critics accused him of 'flashiness' but I frankly admit I was a Crowley fan, and the brand of cheeky, audacious ringcraft in which he specialised never failed to fascinate me. Winning or losing, his showmanship was superb."

One of six kids, Dave Crowley started scrapping in the streets of Clerkenwell, a tough East Central area of London. The death of his soldier father in the Great War left him as the breadwinner and he got a job as a pageboy at the Savoy Hotel. Then he signed on as steward on a boat sailing for Australia and while Down Under made his debut as a boxer. In a fight at Rushcutter's Bay in Sydney, site of the famous Jack Johnson-Tommy Burns world heavyweight championship bout, young Crowley was bounced up and down like a yo-yo and it was stopped in the second round.

Back home in London he joined the St Mary's ABC and it was a short step into the pro ranks, making his start at Collins Music Hall. A pint-sized puncher, he whipped some good men in the flyweight division, among them champion Bert Kirby. Unable to land a title fight, Dave moved up to bantamweight and after winning the Southern Area title, the cocky kid from Clerkenwell was matched with British champion Johnny King at Belle Vue, Manchester. He lost a close decision and asked for a return with the title on the line. King agreed but was prevailed upon not to risk his championship and Crowley was forced to come in over the bantam limit. "It was very close," Gilbert Odd would write many years later, "and I hold the opinion that had the bantam title been at stake, little Dave would have pulled out just that little extra and brought home the bacon."

Now Crowley was in an identical situation with Seaman Watson. The British champion was more than willing to put his title on the line and strenuous efforts were made over the weekend to force the Board to recognise the fight as a championship affair, but all were in vain. The Board, despite the fact that several members were in favour, resolutely set their faces against it. Officially,

Watson's title was not at stake, morally and in the eyes of every British boxing enthusiast, it definitely was.

Championship or not, Dave Crowley had nothing to lose and he set a fast pace from the opening bell. Watson missed with a left swing but a solid jab from the same hand caught Crowley full in the face. The perky Londoner ducked away from the champion's punches but couldn't avoid a smashing right to the jaw. He closed with Watson and they swapped leather inside before Crowley landed a beautiful left hook to the jaw. He scored to the body and looked to have shaded the round.

Dave was again prominent in the second as Watson took time settling in and he caught the champion with two good lefts to the face. Seaman came back with a heavy right to the body and a short right to the head but when he tried for the body again Crowley danced away across the ring. They were punching away inside when the bell rang and the referee, Mr A S Myers of Manchester, had to break them up.

The London fans had plenty to cheer in round three as their favourite went straight for the champion to score with solid punches to the body and Watson drew a caution for holding. Dave rattled two cracking left hooks off Tommy's jaw and the Geordie slammed back with a heavy right to the body. At the bell Crowley was elated with his success and in the corner manager Harry Levene and trainer Larry Gains sensed an upset in the making.

Crowley was carrying the fight to the champion but his punches were not troubling Watson who came more into the fight in round four, a left slamming into Dave's body to have him desperately gasping for breath. Seaman was also landing his right to the head and Crowley's left eye was showing signs of damage as he went back to his stool. It was Watson's round and he took the fifth, driving the London boy across the ring with a two-fisted body attack. Dave gritted his teeth and fought back but Watson caught him coming in with two beautiful punches to the face.

Round six and everything Watson did bore the stamp of a champion. He forced Crowley back to the ropes and slammed a terrific right to the jaw, then the same fist into the body, one, two, three times. Dave faltered, then came back with a left swing, but Tommy stepped inside the punch to land a hard right to the jaw and Crowley was down. The bell ended the round before Watson could do any further damage.

Tommy came out fast for the seventh and banged two sizzling lefts to the stomach. Crowley fought back gamely, landing a right to the head and the same hand to the body. Another body attack from Watson drew a warning from the referee, so he switched his punches to the head and his hammering fists brought the blood again from Dave's left eye. "His defence was as good as ever in theory," reported *Boxing*, "but in practice he found Watson far too strong and rugged for him. The defence that kept Dick Corbett away was of no use against a man who hit four times as hard as Corbett."

By round nine Alec Lambert figured Crowley was ready for the taking and sent Tommy out to finish his man. But Seaman left himself open in his eagerness and Crowley punished his wildness with stinging left jabs and finished the round with a two-handed attack to bring a roar from his fans. But his success was short-lived.

As *Boxing* reported, "Watson was cunning in the tenth. He played light in the early part, as though Crowley's punching had weakened him. Crowley became too confident and Watson pulled the final shot from his locker. He led to the face and drew Crowley's guard up. He had done the trick. He put all his force into a right that travelled upwards to the solar plexus and Crowley went dead out. It looked as though it would have been a knockout punch at any time. But the champion had paved the way for it in the early rounds. He won as a champion should."

The *Chronicle's* London correspondent reported, "The punch that ended the contest was a great one. It took Crowley just about two inches above the belt and dropped him like a stone. The Clerkenwell boy uttered a gasping sob as he fell and some people immediately jumped to the conclusion that he had been fouled. That the blow was not a foul was proved conclusively by the fact that Crowley actually staggered to his feet and collapsed again and at the actual moment of Watson being declared the winner the boxer was sitting up in the ring, his legs straight before him."

Claims of a foul came from Larry Gains in Crowley's corner but were ignored by Referee Myers as he raised Watson's right glove aloft in victory. Stepping down from the ring, Mr Myers described the knockout punch as a "perfectly legitimate blow, a wonderful right hand punch."

Lord Tweedmouth, a leading member of the Board, visited Seaman in his dressing room shortly after the contest, exclaiming, "Congratulations, Watson!"

"Thank you, sir," replied Tommy, a big smile on his face as Kitty kissed him.

"And congratulations to you too, Mrs Watson," added Lord Tweedmouth.

24

"TOMMY WHO?"

"Because he has not a flamboyant style, a wonderful profile, or curly hair," commented the *Newcastle Journal* a few days after the Crowley fight, "Watson has never been popular with the sensation-loving scribes of the south. But even they are beginning to realise that the ex-seaman is in every way a worthy champion." The man behind the gloves however was still very much an unknown quantity, as the following excerpts from an article in a January 1934 issue of Topical Times illustrated.

"Meet the mystery man of the roped square, the boxer practically nobody knows anything about. He is known in private life as Mr Thomas Samuel Watson but you may have read something about his ring achievements under the name of ex-Seaman Tom Watson. He is not the kind of chap who talks about who he is and if you happen to be one of his most privileged friends you may as well talk to Nelson's Column as ask him questions.

"There are few people who understand him, he hates people who make a fuss about anything, dislikes speaking to strangers, he has roughed life, any lad who spends part of his life at sea has to, there are no easy channels on the seven seas...Tommy is a man of few words and little or no ceremony, he dresses neatly but not loudly, he didn't go crazy over New York, visited very few of its sights, didn't even attempt to go up the Empire State Building, he hates anything that is high!

"He is the proprietor of the Wolsington Hotel, Shields Road, Byker, where Tommy and his wife are always behind the bar to greet customers. He doesn't drink, never makes whoopee after a fight, night clubs are taboo to him. He is a wonderful gym worker, when he is training for a fight he talks even less than ever, he is very frank and will speak his mind, he hates interviews with newspapermen, hates to be recognised in a crowd, and if he is forced to dine out he will go to some desolate spot where nobody will take stock of him.

"A keen follower of the dogs and owns a greyhound named Mighty Hunter that has won a number of races in the north. Follows Newcastle United and is a good friend of Sammy Weaver, never misses a home match and sometimes travels away with the team. He is not a big smoker and drops it altogether when training for a fight, he has travelled a good deal, been to Spain, Greece, Italy, Malta, Algiers, America, and Canada, likes Algiers most of all, loves hot weather. While in Spain he saw a bullfight, didn't like it, would sooner watch a good film. He has never been up in the air, owns a baby car, a cautious driver. An expert climber, learned in the navy on the big cruisers, climb a tree like a monkey, hasn't any mascots and doesn't believe in them, takes everything as it comes and isn't superstitious. He still has a passion for reading twopenny bloods, reads one a day.

"He has a small opinion of golfers, baseball players, and cricketers, ridicules the idea of patting a ball. A good swimmer and diver, a brave fellow, he can't ride a horse and seldom speaks on the phone. He has a gold watch that was presented to him by the Lord Mayor of Tynemouth for organising a charity tournament between the local people and the crew of HMS Valiant...He owes much of his success to Alec Lambert, the man with the goggles, who is always in his corner."

"My father was a quiet man," remembers Tom Watson Jnr, "he never talked about his fights to me. I used to ask my mother what happened, because he'd never tell, he would never decry fighters, he wouldn't talk about them. The fights he had, I always had to ask about them, 'what happened there, what happened with that one,' but very rarely would he tell me."

"He was a nice lad, quiet and ineffective in his own way," Frances recalls, "you never heard him brag about what he did and what he didn't. The only time I ever heard our Tommy, 'cause he and I were very close, I was his youngest sister and I supposed he spoiled me when I was a little lassie and he kept on spoiling me, was when he was feeling sentimental and he would say, 'Frances, I was robbed of that world title.' It grieved him.

"He was a heavy gambler, liked his cigarettes, but he wasn't a heavy drinker. He had a dog running at Brough Park and I was working in the Wolsington for him, and he come in to me and there would be a bundle of money like that, all rolled up, you know, and he'd say, 'Put that on the sideboard for me, Frances.' I

197

would just put it on the sideboard in the bar and I'd say, 'Where you getting all that from?' 'Mighty Hunter did well tonight,' that was his dog. He would go out with the same bundle of money and there would be nothing left, it would be gone the next night. That's the kind of gambler he was."

Publican and punter, family man and fighter, that was Tommy Watson, and as 1934 rolled in it was the fighter making the news. It was reported that negotiations had broken down for his British title defence against Johnny McMillan in Newcastle when Watson refused the purse offer, reported to be £1,000, and the fight looked certain to go to Glasgow, McMillan's hometown, with three promoters putting in bids. This was verified a few days later with the announcement that George Dingley Jnr had secured the fight and was making application to Glasgow Corporation for Kelvin Hall where a crowd of 10,000 could be accommodated. The purse was said to be the biggest ever offered for a fight in the city.

However, according to the *Newcastle Journal,* "Reports that Watson has signed to fight McMillan in Glasgow seem premature as the champion has not yet signed anything. A Glasgow syndicate of sportsmen is in the market versus Dingley for the fight and Watson, who is looking fit and well, is waiting for advice from Alec Lambert. An application for the use of Kelvin Hall was due to come before a meeting of Glasgow Corporation on 4 January but the matter was not discussed. Glasgow Town Council is not due to meet for a fortnight and the fight is in jeopardy as the Board have stated offers had to be in for 12 January.

"Mr George Aitchison, who is McMillan's manager, said, 'It means that we cannot complete our arrangements, however a way may be found. If the fight takes place in Glasgow, it will be a great attraction. The purse will be the biggest ever put up for a featherweight title bout in Britain.'"

In the meantime, Lambert arranged for Watson to meet Jimmy Walsh of Chester in a fifteen rounds bout at Liverpool Stadium on 25 January for a purse of £225. It would be Tommy's last fight before defending his title against McMillan

There was also a glimmer of hope that the fight with Panama Al Brown might be re-scheduled. Dave Lumiansky, Brown's manager, said that he had received a cable from his fighter stating that he was unable to leave Algiers to be in London by 19 December

1933 as he was under contract to fight in Tunis on 26 December and also that he had damaged his right hand in the fight with Quadrini on 8 December. Realising the gravity of Brown's non-appearance, Lumiansky said he decided to go to Algiers to obtain proof and statements from Brown to place before the National Sporting Club. He said that he had verified Brown's statements and obtained the documentary proof including the contract Brown had signed to fight in Tunis, also the receipts for the sum forfeited by Brown when he cancelled the fight. It was hoped that Brown would be able to meet Watson some time in the future.

All through January the sports pages carried conflicting reports of Seaman's title defence against McMillan and the only certainty seemed to be that the contest would take place in Scotland. It was rumoured that the four-figure purse offered by J J Paget on behalf of New St James's Hall in Newcastle had been almost doubled by the Glasgow promoters, keen to get McMillan his big chance in his own backyard.

"Naturally I would have liked to have fought in Newcastle," Watson told the Chronicle, "but I could not see my way to turn down the Glasgow offer. Personally, it does not matter to me where I fight, so long as I get a clean break, but I would have liked to have given as many of my own people a chance to see me perform as possible. I am forwarding the signed contracts to my manager, Mr Alec Lambert, today. Tomorrow I commence training, though so far there is no date fixed for the fight. Needless to say, I look forward to the contest with confidence, for I still think I can beat any nine-stone man in the world."

A few days later, GJO reported in the *Chronicle,* "Seaman Tommy Watson, the British featherweight champion, is undoubtedly one of the most conscientious men in training for a big event. He is the best of all competitors, he gets himself fit without the aid of any manager or adviser. I saw Watson do his workout at a new gymnasium he has erected at the back of his hostelry, The Wolsington Hotel, Shields Road, Newcastle, yesterday, and he was most impressive in all that he did.

"I liked Watson's shadow-boxing as much as anything, for it revealed to me the mentality of a man doing not what he had to do, but what he might have to do at a later date. There is so much more in the shadow-fighting than the average onlooker sees. Jim Bird (the Gateshead fighter who, speaking from his own experience in the ring and as Watson's frequent sparmate, placed Tommy first among the hardest punchers in Britain) was shown the way to go in six rounds that he had with Watson. There may have been an inclination for Bird to pull his punches, but the champion urged him to do his best, and especially to the body. The immediate object of Watson is in preparation for his fight with Jimmy Walsh of Chester at the Liverpool Stadium on 25 January."

On 17 January, a Glasgow newspaper reported, "Negotiations are now complete for the British featherweight championship between Seaman Watson, the holder, and Johnny McMillan. The contest will be staged under the joint promotion of Mr Charles Black of Glasgow and the NSC and may or may not take place in Glasgow. The promoters have submitted to the town council an application for the Corporation Kelvin Hall and should their request receive favourable consideration the bout will probably be decided in February or March. All previous applications for the Kelvin Hall to be used for professional boxing have been turned down."

Two days before Watson's fight with Walsh at Liverpool Stadium, promoter Johnny Best announced, "Walsh came to me on Monday, limping badly, and said he did not think he could fight. The damage appeared to be a bad sprain and could have been better inside a week. Last night however, I learned that there is a definite break and he will be in plaster for six weeks. It appears to be piling on the trouble that has come Watson's way since he won his title in my hall, but he can rest assured that I will find him a good opponent for 1 February.

Best found Johnny Cuthbert, former British featherweight and lightweight champion. It was just two weeks since the busy Sheffield battler had hung up his gloves after losing the lightweight title to that brilliant youngster Harry Mizler at the Royal Albert Hall. In a twelve-year career, Cuthbert had put 152 fights in the book and he won 110 of them, but that defeat by Mizler convinced him it was time to pack it in and concentrate on running his pub, The Mill Inn, at Boston, Lincs, where he had moved in 1933. Then came the telephone call from Johnny Best.

Cuthbert had fought often in the Liverpool ring and was a great favourite with the knowledgeable Merseyside crowd. He agreed to help the promoter out on condition he could weigh-in at 9st 6lbs. Watson readily agreed and the fight was on, fifteen-threes for a purse of £300. Seat prices at the Liverpool Stadium ranged from 2/- to 10/6 (10p to 52½p) and there was a big crowd on hand when the men climbed through the ropes. From the first bell Watson went straight on the attack and his gloves beat a steady tattoo on Cuthbert's ribs. Then a right to the jaw dropped Johnny to one knee. The former champion recovered and fought back well through the second round and in a terrific exchange of leather caught Watson with a hard left-right to the jaw.

Seaman was building a points lead but he was cautioned for hitting low in the third. Cuthbert was relying on his right hand while Tommy hammered the body at every opportunity. There was more snap to his punches and in round four he forced the fight, dealing out heavy punishment to the body, but Cuthbert came back with a lovely left of his own to the body. Watson took the fifth as Cuthbert was more deliberate in his work and Tommy was outpunching him three-to-one. Seaman was warned for a back-hander.

In the seventh Cuthbert just missed with a vicious right swing but he did stagger the champion with a perfect right to the jaw. In the tenth he sent Watson reeling into the ropes but Tommy fought back, hammering at the ribs. Seaman's body punching was relentless and he pounded both hands as Johnny held off, looking for an opening for his right hand. Cuthbert fought back brilliantly in the thirteenth but left himself open and Watson sent him crashing to the canvas with a vicious right to the jaw.

It looked all over bar the shouting but the bell rang as the count reached eight and Watson helped carry Johnny to his corner. Cuthbert came out for round fourteen only to have his gumshield knocked out by a punch from the Geordie champion. Tommy sportingly held his fire and looked at the referee, only to be waved back into action. Cuthbert rallied strongly after his narrow escape in the thirteenth, and tried desperately hard for a decisive punch in the later stages, but, as one reporter noted, "Watson's stamina seemed to be inexhaustible." At the final bell Tommy was a worthy points winner, though the ex-champion was given a tremendous cheer as he left the ring.

"Johnny is a fine loser and a great sportsman," Watson told reporters when he reached his dressing room. "I thoroughly enjoyed the fight and rarely felt in difficulty."

Taking advantage of the fact that the venue for the Watson-McMillan fight was still not settled, Promoter Johnny Best announced that he was willing to stage a Watson-Tarleton bout at the Stadium for a £1,000 purse. "All very interesting," commented the *Newcastle Journal*, "but only to those who would like to see Tarleton champion again. It might be news to them that J J Paget offered £1,000 for Watson-McMillan at Newcastle but the champion turned it down because of the higher purse offered by Glasgow."

Mr Paget did in fact offer the use of New St James's Hall for Watson and McMillan when the promoters, still waiting for the nod from Glasgow Corporation, moved the fight date again, from 28 February to 7 March. The first breakthrough came on 16 February when it was announced that the city fathers had decided by a vote of 49-38 (11 members abstaining) to permit professional boxing in the Kelvin Hall.

This decision would be reviewed by the general finance committee who would have to approve the seating plan and set the cost of letting the hall. The committee inspected the hall a week later as John Harding of the NSC sparred in the ring while experts tested vision from all parts of the arena. Only two members of the committee were opposed to the projected seating plan and on 27 February it was announced that the Glasgow Corporation had voted 20-7 to allow the championship fight to be staged in the Kelvin Hall with seating capacity agreed at 11,000. The date would be Wednesday 21 March 1934.

However, the application from the promoters for 8,000 chairs to be hired for use in the hall, at a cost of twopence-halfpenny each, was turned down by the Parks Committee who stated they were not empowered to enter into an agreement for the letting of Corporation chairs for boxing or any other form of entertainment not within the scope of the Corporation.

With the promoters now faced with the need to make arrangements for the bringing in and removal of seats, Mr Paget once again made a bid to bring the fight to Newcastle, offering the use of New St James's Hall for the sum of £100 on any Wednesday night in March. Commenting on the report that the fight was costing £4,000 for boxers, advertising, printing, chairs, and rent of the hall, Paget said, "there was no need for such colossal expenditure for one fight."

Paget was already making plans for another fight at the Gallowgate hall involving Watson. Dick Corbett of Bethnal Green had just regained the British and Empire bantamweight titles from Johnny King at Manchester and had thrown out a challenge to Watson for a crack at his title. Paget had offered a contest made at 9st 1lb, but Corbett's manager Joe Morris stated, "If the Board will sanction a title bout, Corbett is ready to meet Watson at nine stones."

"Tommy is willing to meet Corbett any time and anywhere," was the view of Alec Lambert when he was approached about the fight. "However, the position with the boxers is peculiar. Dave Crowley beat Corbett and Tommy in turn beat Dave, so really the Bethnal Green boy should fight Crowley again before meeting my man. But we shall not let this stand in our way as long as the inducement is good enough. As to the title, that is for the Board of Control to decide. I don't mind where it is, all rings are the same to Tommy, but I should like the venue to be Newcastle and thus be able to give Watson's hometown folk a chance of seeing their champion."

Paget was intrigued with the match and with Joe Morris willing to settle for a non-title bout the match was tentatively fixed for 2 April. Watson said the fight appealed to him and Paget announced that the seat prices would be increased to 2/-, 5/-, 7/6, and 12/6 ringside.

Of course Seaman still had Mr McMillan to deal with and he was training hard at his gym behind the pub where the public were invited to watch him perform at 1.30pm daily, Sundays at 12.30pm. So many turned up to view their champion that the gym was crowded out and many had to watch through the windows. Tommy was having his usual problems, shortage of good sparring partners. He was offering as much as three shillings a round with the big gloves on for men between nine and ten stones, but there were few takers. Seaman punched too hard! Vic Foley of Leeds was there, as he often was for Tommy, and Ginger Purvis of Wallsend, and they earned their money!

Watson did get twelve good rounds under his belt on Monday 5 March when he boxed Liverpool's Billy Gannon on the annual Jewish Charities show at Leeds Town Hall. Gannon lost the decision but he found plenty for the champion to do. Seaman forced the action in round one and a beautiful left hook sent Billy down for a nine count. He survived to the bell but was under pressure from Tommy's two-handed battery of hooks and jabs and was down again in the fourth, this time for six.

Billy fared better over the second half of the fight and there were some torrid exchanges in the ninth, and again in the final round, when Gannon got home with solid rights to head and body. But the champion was usually on top and a vicious right uppercut discouraged Gannon whenever he got inside. At the final bell the referee didn't hesitate, raising Watson's glove as the winner.

Travelling home to Newcastle that night, Tommy relaxed with a cigarette. He had enjoyed the fight and it told him something he already knew. He was ready for Johnny McMillan, or anybody else for that matter!

25

"..AND STILL CHAMPION!"

Eastfield Star was just about the best team in Glasgow's junior soccer league and wee Johnny McMillan was just about the best player on the team. After every match the scouts from the big leagues would crowd the dressing room to leave their calling cards with the little dark-haired outside-left who seemed destined for soccer stardom.

However it was to be in the boxing ring and not on the playing field that young Johnny McMillan would make his name one to remember. Jerry Cassidy, Eastfield Star's enthusiastic and unpaid secretary, first spotted Johnny's promise with the gloves on. Cassidy was as daft about boxing as he was about football and most nights, when training was finished, he would put the gloves on and beg the lads on the team to go a few rounds with him. It didn't take Jerry very long to realise that young Mac was as handy with his fists as he was with his feet.

One night, Cassidy grabbed Johnny by the arm as he came off the field. "How'd you fancy a look in tonight at the Rottenrow boxing? We'll run along after we've finished here."

They hadn't been inside the arena five minutes when an official rushed up to them and said to the startled Johnny, "Right, son, get stripped. Just ten minutes till you are on."

Unknown to young McMillan, Jerry Cassidy had entered him for a novice bout at eight stones. Destiny was knocking at the door and the boy had to answer. His answer was dramatically short and sweet. Five minutes after climbing into the ring, Johnny McMillan walked back to his corner. Behind him his opponent lay unconscious on the canvas.

Now the boy was in torment, football or fighting, what was it to be? For a while he did both, dazzling them with his fists in the amateur boxing ring, and with his feet on the left wing, having signed forms with Vale of Clyde. Early in 1924 Johnny made his mind up...he would be a boxer. Soon among the top flyweights, he was selected as reserve on Scotland's team for the Olympic Games to be held in Paris that year. His pal Jim McKenzie had the flyweight berth and fought his way into the final where he was beaten by America's Fidel LaBarba.

In 1925 a severe chill knocked McMillan out of boxing and the doctors said he shouldn't fight for a year. Three months later he was back in the ring and soon afterwards took off his amateur vest to fight for money. He beat Deaf Burke at Dundee for the Scottish featherweight championship then, hungry for success and the big money, Johnny handed his title back and sailed for America. He stayed for almost two years and although he didn't crack the big time he did win 12 of his 16 fights, with two draws and just two defeats.

Growing homesick, McMillan returned to Glasgow and promptly challenged Dan McGarry who had succeeded him as Scottish featherweight champion. After twelve rounds the title looked ready to change hands, but round thirteen proved unlucky as the referee disqualified Johnny for an alleged low blow. He was devastated and long after his career ended he still claimed the punch was a fair one.

Mac kept busy, and towards the end of 1933 he was named in the eliminating series set up by the Board to find a challenger for Watson's title. Thursday 9 November saw the Scot at Liverpool Stadium to fight local hero Dick Burke, fifteen rounds or less. Of Liverpool-Irish stock, Richard Dominic Burke was hailed as the Wonder Boy of the North in a five year career that ended when he was just twenty-one. Starting as a flyweight he licked champion Bert Kirby and drew with bantam champ Dick Corbett in a fight that Norman Hurst reported, "...Burke, by his forcing and the number of clean hits scored, was entitled to the verdict."

In December 1932 Burke met Panama Al Brown at Sheffield. Brown came in overweight and had a six-inch height advantage, but it was a charity show and the Liverpool lad shrugged his shoulders and agreed to fight. He gave Brown a terrific scrap and the world champion's manager Dave Lumiansky said afterwards, "Burke had the courage of twelve men."

Dick gave a sterling performance when he handed out a beating to Italian Dominic Bernasconi who had stopped Johnny King and earned his place in the eliminators when he beat Phineas John. He was matched with Johnny McMillan and Johnny Best secured the fight for Liverpool Stadium, the winner to meet Tommy Rogers for the right to challenge Seaman Watson for the British featherweight championship. The place was packed and Referee Jack Bloomfield wasted no time getting them started.

Johnny McMillan wasted no time either! At the opening bell he shot from his corner and crashed a tremendous right to Burke's jaw. Dick was in shock and backed to the ropes where another right hand bomb took his feet from under him. Up at seven, he was sent crashing again from that dynamite right for a further count of seven. As *Boxing* reported, "..he gamely rose to fight on. He was dropped for further counts of seven, three, five, six, four, two, two, and nine. The last time he was left floundering on the boards, knocked clean out of the ring, and he looked knocked out! But it was announced the referee had stopped the fight, after 2_ minutes."

While promoters in Glasgow and Birmingham made their bids for the final eliminator between McMillan and Rogers, Johnny Best booked the Scottish sensation for the Stadium again, this time against Jimmy Walsh. The Chester man had recently beaten Dave Crowley, South African Louis Botes, and Benny Sharkey, and he survived McMillan's big punches to come out a winner. A left hook opened a bad cut on McMillan's right eye in round twelve and the doctor ordered the contest stopped. Johnny went to hospital for stitches and Walsh, calling himself the Uncrowned Featherweight Champion, issued a challenge to Seaman Watson for £500 a side for a match at nine stones. But Jimmy Walsh would have to wait his turn.

On Monday 18 December, Johnny McMillan cleared the final hurdle to his championship dream when he blitzed Tommy Rogers in two minutes at Glasgow's City Hall. This time it was the left hook that started the rot. Rogers was up without a count but Johnny caught him with the right hand and Tommy took three seconds before getting up this time. He poked out a feeble left but it was brushed aside as the Scot tore in for the finish. A barrage of leather swamped Rogers and he was down again, this time for six. A left hook dumped him for two, then another put him out for the count.

As he decorated his pub for Christmas, Tommy Watson could look forward to a busy New Year. As well as the challenge from Jimmy Walsh, Dave Crowley was anxious for a return under championship conditions, and manager Harry Levene announced that, "either Watson or McMillan can have a fight for a sidestake up to £500." Former champion Nel Tarleton also had a £500 challenge out to any featherweight in the country. First things first however. The Board of Control decreed that McMillan had earned the right to meet Watson for the championship and the fight was finally arranged for Glasgow's Kelvin Hall on Wednesday 21 March 1934.

Lieutenant Commander E W Billyard Leake of the Royal Navy, who had married Jean Laird of the Burns-Laird shipping line, was chairman of the National Sporting Club and joint promoter of the Watson-McMillan fight with Glasgow's Charles Black. Commander Leake, who had already cabled Kid Chocolate offering terms to meet McMillan should he beat Watson, placed his estate at Hollybush House, near Ayr, at McMillan's disposal for his training, an offer gratefully accepted by the boy from Glasgow. In fairness, it must be recorded that facilities of a similar nature were offered to Watson but the Geordie preferred to stay at home, training in his own gym behind the pub on Shields Road.

A week before the fight, reporters from the *Newcastle Journal* and *Evening Chronicle* visited the challenger at Hollybush. McMillan told the *Chronicle*, "A man couldn't help but get really fit here. This is a fighting man's dream so far as training surroundings are concerned. There are no distractions, nothing to take my mind off the job in hand. Some people may think that it will become boring, that the nights will be lonely. Not at all, an excellent library is at my disposal, while a powerful radio set can switch me round the world in a few seconds.

"And, of course, there will be a happy ending on March 21, for I am confident I shall win."

The *Journal* reported, "A garage on the beautiful estate of Lieut. Commander Leake has been transformed into a gymnasium for the use of Johnny McMillan as he prepares for his title challenge against Watson. Yesterday a *Journal* reporter watched the Scot in training at his new headquarters at Hollybush, Ayrshire, and the boxer said that he never tries to knock out his sparring partners as he just uses them to loosen his muscles. 'It is all nonsense,' he said, 'for a prospective champion to knock out his sparmates. They are not there for that purpose.'"

Whether Johnny would have been able to harm the hired help

had he so desired was another story, a story going the rounds in Glasgow as the big day approached. A couple of weeks before going to Hollybush, McMillan had injured his right arm in a riding accident. A regular visitor to Barrie's Riding School in Bellahouston Park, Johnny had fallen off his horse one day when going to the assistance of a young girl whose horse had bolted.

When Johnny complained of pain in the arm, manager George Aitchison took him to a doctor who advised an X-ray. This revealed a fissure fracture of the ulna bone in the forearm and the radiologist advised massage along with other treatment. For this he was taken to see Eddie McGarvey, masseur and former trainer to Celtic Football Club. Helping Eddie's magic fingers was his favourite kaolin poultice, a whole tin every day, and the fighter began to feel better.

In a press interview a few days later, Lieut. Commander Leake stated, "After McMillan's riding accident a slight swelling to the arm took place. He was able to move his fingers, and we knew by that that nothing serious had happened.

"If McMillan had thought for one minute that the injury was serious he would have told me that he wanted the fight cancelled. I was with the boxer at the weekend and he is as fit as a fiddle."

The promoters had another scare when it was announced that an attempt had been made to carry out a large scale forgery with the result that they had been compelled to cancel the printing of tickets. Police investigators advised them not to issue tickets until two days before the fight with vouchers being handed to legitimate buyers first. According to the CID, members of a London gang had offered to provide a Glasgow firm of printers with facilities to print tickets for the fight. The printer had informed the promoter however and the police were notified.

Seaman Tommy had tickets available at the Wolsington, priced from two guineas to eight shillings, but callers were advised to make it clear it was tickets for the fight they wanted since the champion was also on the lookout for sparring partners.

"Of these, he has not had a sufficient supply for so strong a fighter," observed GJO in the *Chronicle*. "Even in his training, Watson holds nothing back in the way of a punch, and he could have done with a few more boys above his weight to have helped him. A characteristic of the ex-seaman is his strength of blow for his weight. He has the power to hook to body and head with either hand with equal facility, and his right to the mid-rib section is a thing to be feared for its accuracy and viciousness.

"I saw Watson have his final try-out at his gym on Sunday and it was a real one. I have said before that there is no more conscientious trainer than Watson and he confirmed my opinion as he went through his gymnastics and dealt heavy punishment out to sparring partners Kid Foley and Ginger Purvis of Wallsend."

Later that day, with the big fight just three days away, Watson was travelling by train to Rochester to box in an exhibition bout on Monday on behalf of the Mayor of Chatham's Unemployed Relief Fund. In returning to his old stamping grounds as a sailor in the King's Navy, Tommy was fulfilling a long-standing promise, although many questioned the wisdom of his unswerving loyalty at such a crucial time.

"I understand there is some concern about my going down to Rochester for a little exhibition boxing," he said to the man from the *Chronicle*. "Do my pals think that I am foolish enough to take any risk for a fight of this importance? I know my weight to an ounce, I'll miss little or no training that I think I require, and railway travelling at the present time is as comfortable as sitting in one's own arm chair. When I enter the ring on Wednesday night I'll be all right and I think I will win."

Nevertheless, everyone was a lot happier when he returned to Newcastle safe and sound on Tuesday, and he and Kitty were comfortably on board the 4.46pm train as it steamed out of Newcastle's Central Station bound for Glasgow, and Johnny McMillan!

The London and North-Eastern Railway was running an excursion train from Newcastle to Glasgow for the fight, but for those at home there would be no radio broadcast. The *Chronicle* reported, "An account of the fight was being broadcast at 11 o'clock from the Scottish Regional transmitter, yet while Tyneside's champion is fighting for his title, Newcastle listeners have to be content with ninety minutes of Lew Stone and his Band. 'I do not know of any particular reason for the omission of the fight relay,' said a BBC official. 'The only person who could explain it is the Director, and he is away on leave. So far as I know, we have had no requests for the inclusion of tonight's broadcast from Glasgow.'"

At two o'clock on Wednesday afternoon, both men passed the scales with the champion just half-an-ounce inside the nine stones limit while McMillan settled the bar at 8st 13 lbs. That night it seemed as though the entire population of the city was trying to get into the Kelvin Hall, and long before the first contestants stepped into the ring a great crowd of almost 11,000 filled the arena with as many milling around outside in Argyle Street. Special police did their best to control them while inside the hall an army of more than 300 stewards was on duty.

In his wonderful biography of Benny Lynch, author John Burrowes described the scene. "In the first two rows there were women in evening dresses with fresh orchids pinned on them. There were men in dinner jackets and dress coats. Some were in Highland dress and others in Regimental jackets with rows of miniature medal ribbons. They had paid two guineas each for their seats. Two pounds and two shillings. More than what the dole thought was enough for a man to live on for a whole week and just a few shillings less than the average man's working wage.

"The local politicians were there, the men from the marbled splendour of the City Chambers. So were the ones who arrogantly spoke of themselves as the city's professional gentlemen, the solicitors and surveyors, architects and accountants. They had a new kick. Two men beating the hell out of each other's brains in a twenty-by-twenty foot ring that sixteen arc lights carved out of the Kelvin Hall gloom like a diamond solitaire."

Prominent in those ringside seats were such luminaries as Lord Inverclyde, the Duke of Montrose, Bailie Ritchie, chairman of the Scottish branch of the British Boxing Board of Control, and Mr James McLean, the well known bookmaker whose horse Obesity had finished second in that afternoon's Lincolnshire Handicap.

The big crowd enjoyed the preliminary contests in which Gilbert Johnstone had the measure of Johnny McGrory on points and little Benny Lynch hammered out a decision over his first continental opponent, Italian champion Carlo Cavagnoli. As the clock ticked around to nine-thirty, the atmosphere inside the Kelvin Hall was electric, last minute bets being made with Watson 6 to 4 on and 11 to 10 being offered against McMillan becoming Scotland's first British featherweight champion since George McKenzie of Leith a decade earlier.

211

"A lot of cheering greets McMillan as he enters the ring," wrote *Daily Express* Special Correspondent S Hardie Stewart. "He is in a white dressing gown. He walks with a smile to greet Seaman Watson who is in black and red, and who enters the ring almost simultaneously with him. McMillan is lithe and dark, he is smiling cheerfully. Watson, grim, determined, acknowledges the cheers with little nods. Johnny is looking particularly happy. Jackie Brown, the flyweight champion of the world, comes up to the ring and is introduced. Seconds are working in both corners, putting the mens' gloves on. The whole hall is humming. Watson allows himself to smile broadly, the first real sign of animation that he has given since he entered the ring. George Aitchison, McMillan's manager, gives him a few words of advice. Frank Blaney, the M.C., announces the fight. Jack Smith of Manchester is the referee and he makes his bow. Smith calls the two men together, they shake hands quickly...

"Round one, Watson early takes up the aggressive. Johnny has him on the ropes, he lands with the right. Johnny forces Watson to the ropes with a rush but the Seaman comes back and jolts Johnny's head back with a right. McMillan follows up a left lead with a quick rush but there is little to it. He makes Watson miss badly with a right swing.

"Johnny leads with another left but there is not too much sting behind it. McMillan hits Watson another good left but takes a right to the body in reply. He dashes in quickly with a beautiful left to the body which sends Watson to the ropes. Watson springs back and the gong goes with them both sparring in the centre of the ring.

"McMillan quickly lands with his left in the second, he is keeping Watson on the move, and misses badly with a left swing. Watson is taking up the offensive now and the Scot gets out of the way. In a spasm of infighting someone shouted 'low blow!' as Watson hit McMillan with a right hook but Johnny was not troubled. Infighting was getting more popular and Watson was scoring heavily with short rights to the body. McMillan missed badly with a left swing which would have finished the fight if it had connected. Watson was quick to jump in and punish McMillan heavily to the body. Just as the gong went Watson slipped as he retreated before McMillan's rushes. There was no damage done and Johnny helped him to his feet.

212

"Watson got in with a left to the jaw in the third but there was not much sting behind it. His left kept jabbing Johnny's face and the Seaman landed an uppercut which shook the Scot. McMillan had a lightning rush with two-handed punching which knocked the Englishman back to the ropes. He followed up with a left which jolted Watson's head. Watson was scoring at infighting and landed frequently with short heavy jabs as they were breaking away. He was making McMillan wince and caught him heavily on the jaw.Another left of Watson's shook McMillan badly and he was glad to hang on. McMillan made a blind rush but Watson, cool as a cucumber, slammed in heavy lefts and rights. McMillan seems to be too eager, he is jabbing with his left. A rush of his had the holder dazed and against the ropes but he gets himself away just in time to miss a right swing.

"The referee holds up the bout for a minute, he cautions both men for roughing. Both men are now in the centre of the ring. Watson is stolidly moving after the lithe, flashing McMillan and catching him on the ropes. One terrific rush of McMillan's gets Watson into his corner. On the gong for round five, McMillan jumped in and had Watson on the ropes. Mac leads with a good right. Watson immediately counters with a heavy left. Watson is taking his toll of the Scot at infighting then in one savage burst swings himself completely off his feet in an attempt to land an uppercut. He picks himself up and Johnny smiles at him.

"In round six Watson misses with a terrific left hook. He is trying hard to land a decisive blow but suddenly McMillan rushes him, misses, and puts his head through the ropes. Watson lands with a beautiful straight left and follows it up quickly with lefts and rights. McMillan's headlong rushes are bringing him heavy body punishment which is beginning to tell on Johnny. Watson lands a staggering left. McMillan shakes his head and spars off. Watson keeps it up relentlessly. He is making the running. He is the fresher man.

"Johnny comes out of his corner in the seventh round to be met with a left hook to the chin and a succession of left jabs. A straight left rocked McMillan to his toes and sent him along the ropes. Watson has McMillan on the ropes but he cannot find an opening for his deadly left. Watson is doing all the fighting and McMillan is glad to fall into a clinch. Johnny rushes with a succession of lefts but he only runs into a bunch of trouble from Watson's right.

213

Watson misses badly with a left swing. McMillan shoots his head back. The champion staggers for a second and McMillan rushes in. Just as the gong was going Johnny brings over a beautiful right hook which jars Watson badly.

"McMillan comes in for a fight in round eight and meets Watson with a vicious left swing. Johnny is bustling round his more stolid opponent and in a bout of infighting he lands heavily. Watson appeals for McMillan butting with his head but the men are told to box on and McMillan catches Watson with a terrific right to the body. They break away and McMillan is now in the centre of the ring with Watson bustling around him. Watson lands with heavy lefts, McMillan smashes in with his left and gets home twice on the Seaman's jaw. Johnny is much more confident now and cleverly dodges a left swing after a clinch. This is real good stuff now. Both men are fighting beautifully.

"Watson takes up the fight in round nine and shakes McMillan with a heavy right. The Scot retaliates at once and connects with a beautiful left. Watson hangs on. McMillan has another furious rush and has Watson on the ropes. McMillan catches with a left on the jaw and another. The crowd is shouting. Watson is very strong and replies with a body punch. Johnny comes back with a left to the chin. McMillan is aggressive, he is much more open and his rushes are forcing Watson to the ropes.

"Watson attacks first in the tenth but Johnny jumps in with a left and a right. He takes Watson's lead harmlessly on his head. Johnny gets him on the ropes but the champion fights his way out with a succession of jabs to the chin. Johnny is full of fight and flashes in two lefts which have no effect. Johnny tries to measure the Seaman with his left, opens up his defence and takes two rapid blows. Watson follows with a heavy blow to the jaw and Mac lands heavily with his right. They are in a clinch, Watson is punching viciously and his arms are going like pistons. Johnny rushes. They are in the centre of the ring sparring now. Watson is piling up a lead on points in this round.

"Watson rushes from his corner in the eleventh, McMillan gets in a left to the body and another left to the jaw. McMillan forces Watson on the ropes but the champion is too clever for him and fights his way out. Watson staggers McMillan but the Scot rushes him again. Watson punches his way out with heavy body blows. McMillan is bleeding from a cut above his left eye. McMillan tries to weave in again but Watson stops him with a right hook and follows up with a terrific right to the jaw. McMillan rushes him to the ropes and misses heavily with both hands. Mac has Watson on the ropes again and catches him with a terrific right. Both are trying for a knockout.

"In round twelve, Watson punches to the body and fights McMillan to the ropes. McMillan rushes again and puts Watson's head between the ropes. McMillan seems to have tired a little, Watson forces him into a corner, he attacks with both hands, he lands two good lefts to the jaw. McMillan catches Watson's head heavily and while he is staggering lands a right to the jaw. McMillan is surprised and rushes in with a beautiful left. They are fighting for all they are worth when the gong goes.

"McMillan comes up full of fight for round thirteen, rushes Watson to the ropes. Both men are plainly marked. Johnny grimaces with pain as Watson lands a heavy right. In a clinch McMillan keeps punching away as Watson falls back to the ropes. There is good two-handed punching by McMillan. Johnny rocks Watson with an uppercut and jolts him with a straight left. Watson replies with three short, telling uppercuts.

"Watson attacks in round fourteen. McMillan replies with a lightning left which shakes Watson. McMillan dashes in again with his left. He has very rarely used his right yet. Watson lands a right to the jaw. Both connect with good lefts. Watson has Mac in his own corner and is punching with both hands to the body when the gong goes.

"McMillan is going all out for a kayo in the last round. They are clinching, McMillan is staggering Watson with heavy blows. He lands five in rapid succession. Watson tries to fight him off. McMillan is relying on his left. Watson ducks from McMillan's rush and fights him off with heavy body blows. Watson pushes Mac away and chases him to the ropes. He still cannot find an opening. Johnny swings over a left, his eye is bleeding again, he is tired. They fall into a clinch and they have to be separated. Johnny rushes in two-handed, he seems to be making his last effort to finish the fight off.

"At the final gong, Watson is given the verdict on points. There is a little booing but on the whole it is a popular verdict. Johnny looks disappointed, Watson grins largely and they shake hands.

The Scot leaves the ring to a terrific cheer and is escorted to his dressing room by a large crowd. Mrs Watson rushes forward and kisses Watson as he leaves the ring."

"WATSON STILL BRITISH CHAMPION: GREAT FIGHT IN GLASGOW: MCMILLAN BEATEN ON POINTS" headlined another sports page. "Johnny McMillan followed his usual style in going all out for a KO in the early rounds and while his furious onslaught unsettled Watson, the champion soon got down to his natural fighting tactics and punished the Scot with heavy punches to head and body. Watson's left hand was a good scoring medium and in the end superior punching power and greater experience won the decision for Watson over the 15 rounds. The Scot's supporters were disappointed but recognised the ability of Watson and agreed that he was a worthy champion.

"When it was all over, Watson told reporters, 'I think that McMillan is a splendid little fighter. His rushes at first rather troubled me but after a round or two I knew I had him. He has plenty of pluck and certainly carries a nice punch.'

"The beaten challenger said, 'I just did my best for Scotland and that's all there is to it. As a matter of fact I injured my right hand during training and I could not use it very much tonight. Watson is certainly a great champion and I wish I could meet him again when my right hand is sound.'"

Among the ringside press was GJO, the *Newcastle Chronicle's* boxing man, and he recorded, "Before the fight it was said that McMillan had a poor right arm as a result of a recent accident. After the fight I saw both arms, and certainly one bicep was much smaller than the other. I merely record facts, but I must add that I never saw any reluctance on McMillan's part to use the lesser arm. The Scot never seemed to use it as though he considered it a very defective limb, either in attack or defence. Watson was often good with his straight left, his inside work was always good and at times terrifyingly powerful. It was, in my opinion, really this that undermined the Scot, who had little punch left in him in the last round."

One Glasgow paper reported, "As a championship fight it was one of the biggest flops I have ever seen but I warned my readers to some extent to look for that. Watson, without doing anything impressive during fifteen rounds of fighting, proved himself to be

216

easily the better man of the two, yet I would say that he did that and nothing more...Watson proved even more canny than the canniest of Aberdonians, He hooked with his left for the most part of the fight when McMillan was in the required position for such a delivery and then he did his stuff at close quarters. McMillan has never been and probably never will be a close quarter battler. In my opinion it was the Geordie's work inside that ultimately won him the fight. He, after all, had laid his plans and as they were successful I suppose that Tommy must be given full credit for his performance."

Two days after the fight, the *Newcastle Journal* commented, "First hand information on Wednesday's fight in Glasgow is that Watson won by so big a margin that McMillan could have had but two rounds in his favour. The Scot's rushing tactics were a trifle disconcerting at the outset but Watson had his man weighed up early on and it soon became clear that the champion knew too much for the Scot, who, in various ways showed a lack of first class experience such as possessed by Watson since he became champion. As for Watson being disappointing, onlookers with wide experience of championship fights were frankly disappointed with the class of the challenger."

Good, bad, or indifferent, whatever they thought about the fight, the Kelvin Hall promotion was a tremendous success and brought a new dimension to boxing in Scotland. The city newspapers covered every angle and devoted two and three pages to the event. "At 12.15 this morning," wrote a female reporter for the *Daily Record,* "a little figure in a blue dress, blue coat, blue hat, and blue eye veil, slipped unobtrusively through the crowd of admirers who were awaiting the return of the champion and sank into a deep chair. 'Thank heaven that's over,' sighed Mrs Tommy Watson. 'Now all that Tommy has got to do is win the belt outright. That belt,' she went on, 'I've heard so much about it, that if he does get it in the end, I'll use it for slimming.'

"'Did you enjoy the fight?' I asked, 'and were you nervous?'

"'Nervous,' she snorted. 'I should think not. After the first three rounds I saw that Tommy had him cold. Not that I ever expected him to lose, he had McMillan outclassed from the start. The Scotsman seemed over-confident, his punches looked hard, but not many of them got to Tommy. He was too clever for him.'

"Unlike some boxing wives, Mrs Watson does not like sitting at the ringside. 'I prefer a back seat,' she smiled, 'where I can see without being seen. Tommy can see me though for I wave to him.

"'Where is he now?' I asked.

"'Coming,' she said.

"'But I thought he would be resting, or being brought in on a stretcher,' I stuttered.

"She laughed heartily. 'The day Tommy comes in on a stretcher he will have been in a collision with a furniture van!'"

There was even a poet's view of the punchers, by John James Miller.

To Seaman Watson,	You won and did it fair
	The twa o'ye tried different roads,
	Twas yours that landit-there,
	So noo I say richt off the reel
	Haud oot your hand, I wish you weel.
To Johnny McMillan,	So Johnny you were beat, Brave Lad!
	Ahweel, twas nae disgrace,
	There's nane can say your show was bad,
	Or you were scaur'd to face
	A rowtin' tearin' game licht weichter,
	But a'the time a bonnie fechter!
To the crowd,	An' you ten thoosand fowk wha lukit on,
	You dinna' often see a fecht like yon!

26

"A CREDIT TO THE RING"

By the summer of 1934, after Watson had beaten Frenchman Aine Gyde and British bantamweight champion Dick Corbett in London, recognition for the champion from the north was coming gradually, if somewhat grudgingly, from the boxing pundits of the south.

A week after the Gyde fight, Ted Scales commented in his Punchbowl column in *Boxing*, "How on earth does it come about that we see so little of good men in London?...Tommy Watson last fought in London round about Christmas time, when he met Dave Crowley...I say that Watson is a worthy champion. I say that he is a great champion. I dare say that there isn't a featherweight in the world who can beat him, and that goes for Sonny Lee and Kid Chocolate and Freddie Miller and all. Watson does not demand impossible terms to fight, and we forget all about him and ask for new blood."

Commenting after the Corbett fight, Scales wrote, "To be candid, I don't understand it. Why do people say that Seaman Watson is dull to watch? I think that I would rather watch him than any of our champions. Just because he is businesslike and not spectacular, you don't care to watch him. That is the very reason that I do like to watch him. I say that boxing is work, and boxers should be workmanlike. The unworkmanlike champions are the poor champions. I don't care what you say, you must have been impressed by Watson tonight. I can't see Tarleton beating him on tonight's form. He amazed everybody by beating Corbett at his own game."

Reporting the Watson-Corbett fight, B Bennison wrote in the London *Evening Standard*, "...Not in all his days of high adventure has Corbett made acquaintance with such a complete infighter as Watson and I much doubt whether his compact body has so suffered to be rammed and stabbed and made to smart as it was by Watson...Watson was his master, the embodiment of thoroughness, and the Geordie to real life. Short of frills or flounces, a fighter to the core."

"Watson is a great fighter, as honest as daylight, and altogether a credit to the ring," observed the Editor of *Boxing*. "It is no fault of his that he does not hold a world title."

Before he left Glasgow that Thursday morning after beating Johnny McMillan, Watson met the local boxer along with Mr John E Harding of the National Sporting Club, who stated, on behalf of Lt Commander Leake, that they were prepared to stage a return fight for the championship and £200 a side, in the open air in Glasgow, just as soon as McMillan's right hand was sound. McMillan said that he had injured the hand while riding a horse during his training.

"I am feeling well today," Johnny said, "but against Watson I had to box with my left hand practically throughout. I can produce a doctor's certificate to the effect that my right hand is bad."

Watson merely said, "It was a grand fight and I cannot praise McMillan's courage too highly."

A couple of days later, GJO commented in the *Newcastle Chronicle*, "We now come to the question of Watson's next title fight. It has been said he has already promised McMillan a return contest for the championship, which is to take place in Scotland at some early date. As a matter of fact, Watson has done nothing of the kind. He has certainly promised McMillan another fight, but the Tynesider has sufficient sense to know that he has nothing to do with the arrangements to a title contest. This is obviously a matter that must be left to the British Boxing Board of Control. British championships cannot be arranged by those who are only financially interested in the game.

"Nel Tarleton, I read, has written to the Board stating that he claims a fight with Watson before McMillan. Personally, I would admit he had the greater claim, but when the Liverpool man, in a newspaper interview, talked about the present champion sidestepping him, he appears to me to be acting rather foolishly. Nel should not forget that Watson had to do a lot of searching before he caught him (Tarleton) and took his title from him, and I would also like to ask the Liverpool boxer if he is prepared to fight Watson for a similar financial consideration as did the latter."

Back home in Newcastle, Tommy was soon back in the gym

preparing for his next engagement. This would be on Monday 16 April, twelve rounds with Aine Gyde, billed as the champion of Northern France, on Alf Mancini's charity show at Lime Grove Baths in London.

Watson had already beaten the Frenchman over fifteen rounds at Kilburn in 1930, just about the time he left the Navy, and he beat him again this night at Lime Grove. A week later, *Boxing* reported, "DEVASTATING WATSON...

Seaman Tom Watson, the featherweight champion, has never been in more effective form than he was in on Monday night...Watson punched with tremendous power to the body, being especially good with short rights to the ribs and jaw and left uppercuts. The rib punches were the most hurtful and he used them to such an extent that Gyde's side was well painted before the end of the first round. At the end of the fight blood was actually flowing from the Frenchman's side...At first it looked as though the cumulative force of Watson's body blows would inevitably cause Gyde to crack up. But Gyde's toughness and gameness were amazing. He took enough punishment to put ten men on the floor, yet he showed no signs of despair at the very end, when his face and body were in the most pitiable plight."

Another titleholder who fancied his chance with Watson was Jim Cowie of Dundee, official featherweight champion of Scotland. Cowie had made his challenge to the winner of the Watson-McMillan fight and Tommy agreed to meet the Scot in Edinburgh on Monday 7 May, twelve rounds or less. But the champion was more excited by the news that Jeff Dickson was close to signing Panama Al Brown for a fight with Tommy at the Royal Albert Hall for Monday 14 May.

Before then however, Seaman had a date at Liverpool Stadium with Jimmy Walsh. Managers Dom and Tony Vairo first spotted young Walsh in an amateur club in his hometown of Chester. Just seventeen, the lanky kid had a good straight left, a cracking right hand punch, and was fast on his feet, and the Vairo brothers were convinced the boy had the makings of a champion. Convincing Jimmy's parents however was a different matter.

They were adamant they would never allow their son to become a boxer. But young Jimmy eventually got his way and headed for Vairo's gym in Liverpool. Finding Dom in the little office, he

221

yelled, "They've agreed, Mr Vairo, I'm gonna be a boxer after all."

Jimmy weighed only 8st 10lbs and they took him all over the North and Midlands, taking on pugs who weighed a stone heavier to build his strength and experience. By 1933 he was beating men like Dave Crowley, Len Wickwar, Benny Sharkey, and Johnny McMillan, and in March 1934 he jumped at the chance of meeting new British lightweight champion Harry Mizler in a non-title bout. Victor Berliner, who managed Mizler, thought his champion had an easy job as Walsh was only a featherweight and the match was made at 9st 12lbs. Mizler got the shock of his life as Walsh brushed aside his left hand with a two-handed attack that earned him an upset decision.

Now the Chester boy was going for a unique double as he faced Watson, the British featherweight champion, before Liverpool's Lord Mayor and many civic dignitaries in the crowd packing the Stadium that Thursday night in April. They were set for fifteen-threes but Jimmy nearly ended it in the opening round when he cracked Watson with a terrific right hand to the chin that rocked Tommy to his toenails! But the champion recovered and caused a sensation at the end of round two. Walsh dropped his hands as the bell rang but Watson had already launched a fierce, short left hook to the jaw that all but knocked Walsh out on his feet. The crowd booed Watson but the referee took no action.

Seaman began to work to the body from the third round and Walsh took a beating. He was floored in round six but jumped up without a count and, following a collision in the next round, Jimmy returned to his stool with a big swelling over his left eye.

Watson was forcing the action all the way and Walsh was taking a fearful beating inside as the champion hammered both hands to the body. Jimmy was banking on a straight left but Watson would not be denied and by round twelve, Walsh knew he had to do something special if he was to pull this one out of the fire. The Chester boy made a tremendous effort in the closing rounds but he was tiring from Watson's non-stop body punching, his left eye was almost shuttered tight, his nose was swollen, and the final bell was the best thing he heard all night. As Mr Tolley, the referee, pointed to Watson as the winner, the crowd rose to both men.

"It was the toughest fight I ever had in my life," Seaman

222

announced as he left the ring. Before leaving Liverpool, Alec Lambert signed contracts for Tommy to defend his title against Tarleton on Liverpool F.C.'s ground in July, on the occasion of the Mersey Tunnel opening festivities. Seaman's purse would be a staggering £800!

"Tommy, however," commented the *Chronicle* a few days later, "is not unmindful of those less fortunate than himself, and ever since he became champion has never spared himself in the cause of charity. Last year he raised £41 for the Newcastle Dispensary, and he hopes to top that this year as the result of a whist drive and dance in the Oxford Galleries, Newcastle. There is in addition to be an excellent cabaret show and Ernie Lotinga from the Empire Theatre is to present the prizes."

On Monday 7 May however, there was no charity in Tommy's fists as he faced Jim Cowie at the Marine Gardens Ballroom, Portobello. It was a third choice of venue for promoter Harold Bownas, after the Edinburgh Music Hall and then the Eldorado, Leith, became unavailable. Unfortunately it was not a case of third time lucky for the Scottish champion as Watson knocked him out with a heavy right to the body in the sixth round.

At about the same time as he was landing the knockout punch in the Scottish capital, Tommy Watson was being hit by his own hard-luck hoodoo in London. Stanley Longstaff (Straight Left) had the story in the *Sporting Life* next day, reporting, "For the second time this season an Albert Hall big fight promotion by Jeff Dickson has had to be cancelled. Mr Dickson stated yesterday that he had been forced to abandon the Al Brown-Tommy Watson bill scheduled for next Monday. The reason, he adds, is that the BBBC has refused to allow Al Brown to box and opposed the application for a labour permit for the Panama negro to enter the country.

"The following statement was forwarded to me by Mr Dickson last night. 'The Board state that they are upholding the suspension of the Mexican Boxing Commission who banned Brown for not fulfilling a contract signed by Dave Lumiansky although Brown maintained that his contract with Lumiansky had expired. I think the Board's decision unfair to both Brown and myself and I would like to point out the following facts; 1) I signed Al Brown to box on my promotion several months ago before any action was taken in Mexico. 2) Dave Lumiansky had his licence taken away by the Board over a year ago and that action was upheld recently in the law courts. Yet Brown and I are being penalised for something that Lumiansky signed a few months ago. 3) Al Brown has been debarred by the Board without any justification as I have put all data and documents in their hands to prove that he had no knowledge of this Mexican engagement.'

"It is true that Brown was suspended for failing to appear against Baby Casanova, the Mexican bantamweight champion, but there is little doubt that the action taken by the Board of Control was partly prompted by the unfortunate business of the NSC's Olympia promotion when Brown failed to appear against Watson.

"Brown, whether or not it was his own fault, ruined the Club's Olympia show and contributed to their fade-out as big fight promoters in London this season. Brown owed everything to the NSC for his successes in England. When attempts were made to prevent him entering the country to box Johnny Cuthbert and Teddy Baldock, the Club's influence was a deciding factor which enabled the bouts to be staged...Watson will surely go down to posterity as the unluckiest boxer who ever won the British crown."

That sentiment was echoed by the Editor of *Boxing*, who wrote, "More than two months ago, in dealing with the many disappointments met with during his ring career, I suggested that there must be a hoodoo on Seaman Tommy Watson, our featherweight champion. If there was any doubt about it then, there cannot be much room for doubt now...Watson must be the unluckiest boxer of recent years. It was a bitter disappointment when Brown failed to carry out his contract with the NSC because Watson was then keyed up with the idea of making a name for himself in London by upsetting the odds against the negro. Whether Watson would have succeeded or not is problematical, but the fact remains that bad luck robbed him of his chance. Once again he is doomed to disappointment, and one wonders how much longer he is to be dogged by ill luck."

Facing the loss of a sum estimated at £500, Watson shrugged his sturdy shoulders as he said, "I am almost getting used to these disappointments now. There is a clause in the contract that I made for a small forfeit, but what is this compared with my purse, and, above all, an opportunity of beating this physical freak who has played such a big part in the boxing world during the past few years. I have no definite plans at the moment, but I am sure to have another fight before I meet Nel Tarleton in defence of my championship."

Tommy actually managed to engage in two more fights before beginning serious training for Tarleton. On Monday 18 June, he stepped out for twelve rounds with old rival Francois Machtens, the Belgian he had already beaten in three fights. This time they boxed at Belle Vue, Manchester, where the top-of-the-bill contest saw local hero Jackie Brown hang on to his world flyweight title with a draw against Valentin Angelmann. The crowd of some twelve thousand sitting in the open air booed long and loud as the Frenchman looked a good winner from where they sat.

As in their previous fights, Machtens gave Watson a tough argument before conceding defeat via a points decision. It was a splendid contest with Tommy's superior left hand work giving him the edge. Watson's punches to the body were tremendously heavy and a less strongly built man than the Belgian champion would have been taking an early shower. Twice Machtens claimed a foul for low punches and a heavy body blow dropped him for an eight count in the fifth round. He was still plugging away at the final bell as Watson made it four out of four.

While he trained for the Machtens fight, Watson's name was in the news. He was to meet British bantamweight champion Dick Corbett over twelve-threes in a match made at 9st 2lbs at Wandsworth Stadium, London, on Wednesday 27 June. It was also announced that he would defend his title against Nel Tarleton at Anfield football ground, Liverpool, on Thursday 26 July, which came as a blow to his many Tyneside supporters, many of whom would have made the trip had the fight been on a Saturday. Should Watson beat Tarleton and make the Lonsdale Belt his own, he would move up to the lightweight division and go after Harry Mizler's British crown. This would leave the way open for Watson's stablemate, Scot Johnny McGrory, to grab a spot in the eliminators to find a successor to Seaman.

Dick Corbett and his older brother Harry were sent along to the local boys' club in Bethnal Green by their father in order to learn how to look after themselves in the tough streets of the East End. The kids were naturals in the boxing ring and they would practise for hours, jabbing, ducking, bobbing and weaving. They were doing well in the amateurs when Harry decided he wanted to fight for money. Unfortunately, Dad wasn't at all keen on the idea. So the boys dropped the family name of Coleman and adopted the ring name of their hero, Gentleman Jim Corbett, the former heavyweight champion of the world.

The old champ would have been proud of the boys from Bethnal Green. Harry became British featherweight champion while Dick won the British Empire bantamweight title and had two reigns as British champion. Dick had just regained the British title from Johnny King when he went after Watson who agreed to meet him in a non-title bout. Dick went into training at the Star and Garter at Windsor where he was ably assisted by Sam Haines, Harry Daly, and Nipper Fred Morris.

Writing of the match in that week's *Boxing*, veteran Charlie Rose predicted, "The Tommy Watson-Dick Corbett disturbance at the Wandsworth Stadium tonight should be a humdinger. Fights between men with styles so dissimilar usually furnish interesting scraps, and I am looking forward to seeing how Tom, dour, determined fighter all the time, will act against Sorrel-Topped Dicky's 'spoiling' left hand glove."

And elsewhere in the same issue..."There is no unanimity among the prophets with regard to the Watson-Corbett contest. It is generally held that Watson will have to win inside the distance if he is to win at all, but it must be remembered that he is at his very best when at about two pounds over the featherweight limit.

"It seems likely that he will be so forceful and strong in attack that Corbett's admirable left will not be sufficient to keep him away. Watson will obviously do his utmost to be inside all the while to score with his double-handed body attack. Corbett will do his best to score with his left and his right hook to the jaw and use his footwork to keep himself out of trouble. Our final choice, if one were called on for a tip, would be for Watson."

It was a wet night at Wandsworth yet a crowd reckoned at between fifteen and twenty thousand turned out. They saw a good fight between two champions at two different weights and two vastly different styles, Watson the heavier puncher and unceremonious fighter, and Corbett the clever boxer and exponent of the straight left. Corbett was the first to attack, two fine lefts snaking into Watson's face, and he took the round as Watson swung his left and missed. Tommy was more aggressive and accurate in

226

the second and Corbett was glad to box on the retreat. Dick managed to get in one or two lefts but Watson took the round.

Watson's physical advantages began to tell in the third round as he warmed to his job and he piled up the points with two-handed attacks, Corbett's efforts to stem the tide coming to nought as Watson scored well to the body. In round four Corbett was caught with a beautiful left hook to the body which sent him crashing to the canvas and it looked all over.

Boxing reported, "Corbett made as though he had been hit low, but the punch had been perfectly directed and it was in no way questionable. Actually it could be seen that Corbett's pants were high on his body. Even so, the blow landed above the top of the pants. Watson did drop his right once, in the sixth round, and he duly received a caution from the referee. He never repeated the offence."

"Corbett pulled through a bad time cleverly," reported the *Daily Express*, "and surprised everybody by winning the sixth and seventh rounds. The next round aroused the crowd to a high pitch of excitement. Corbett was not doing badly when he ran into a right to the mark, enabling Watson to get on top again. Corbett's body must be iron-ribbed for he gallantly withstood Watson's terrific body blows and wilted but seldom...

"Watson went all out for a knockout as the eighth round started but ran into a well-timed right uppercut which steadied his pace. Making the most of the opportunity and with regained confidence, Corbett scored many times with lefts to the face until he in turn was steadied with a right to the mark. The remainder of the bout was fought on furious lines with Watson generally having the better of the exchanges and the verdict in his favour was well received."

However, James Butler reported in the *Daily Herald*, "I was astonished when Mr C H Douglas held up Watson's right glove as the winner to hear a few members of the crowd hoot. Watson won definitely beyond argument, but it was a great fight although one-sided. Watson's policy was evident, he depended entirely upon solid hitting. Corbett, as is customary with him, was content to score with straight left leads and the different styles of the two champions made the exchanges very interesting...It was more exciting when Corbett stood toe to toe with Watson but Watson was too strong, too clever, and was a good winner."

Bennison, the *Evening Standard's* man at the ringside, commented, "It is an old and familiar story I have to tell, a good little'un can not beat a good big'un. That was precisely what happened and what I expected. The contest was at 9st 2lbs so that there was nothing at stake save the professional pride with which I will credit both men.

"That is a rare circumstance in this pardonably sceptical fighting age and to me it was a fight far removed from a fight for the mere sake of fighting. There was in Corbett, fiery-headed and innocent looking, all the inherent brazenness of the true Cockney, and in Watson, tense, unsmiling, provocative-nosed, big-hearted, willing-fisted, the intolerance of everything, man or things, down South, of polish little, of guile positively none, but a hammer in either hand.

"Corbett gambled on his fighting brain as opposed to downrightness, he was taught that discretion is the better part of valour by ribs that were made pink and sore, yet I admire his courage, he stood up to his job like a hero though upon reflection I am sure he will confess that to employ the vernacular of his immediate circle he bit off more than he could chew...The sailor did not seek to be clever, he fought as became a sailor who on shore leave chances upon a rough-house. To look on was to know why Kid Chocolate would not meet him a second time and why Al Brown also scuttled.

"The wonder was that Corbett took a pile-driver to the solar plexus and scarcely did more than take a breather, or that he weathered other punches and built up a defence which would have been invulnerable against a less persistent opponent. Corbett ducked and dodged with expert cleverness but not often did he have it in him to give a Roland for an Oliver. Perforce he played the role of receiver-general. Baby-faced Corbett fought in the true tradition of Bethnal Green, not once did he quake or flinch but he had shouldered more than he could carry and in the end he had lost by more points than he will perhaps allow."

A delighted Alec Lambert told reporters, "And now we're just waiting for the all-important moment when we enter the ring at Liverpool to find Nel Tarleton in the opposite corner."

27

TARLETON'S REVENGE

The bottom fell out of Nel Tarleton's world that November night in 1932 when Seaman Watson took his beloved British featherweight title away from him in the big Stadium ring at Liverpool. The trip to America for a crack at the world championship was cancelled and he was not on board the s.s. Berengaria when it sailed out of Southampton for New York. The Yanks wanted a British champion complete with Lord Lonsdale Belt, and Nel Tarleton no longer fitted that description.

It was two months before he climbed through the ropes again but when he did there was a new Nel Tarleton on view. The Merseyside ringmaster had often been criticised for playing to the gallery as he dazzled opponents with his boxing artistry. No more! That defeat at the hands of Seaman Watson changed Tarleton from an exhibitionist into a more direct ruthless fighter.

Leon Mestre was stopped inside six rounds at the Stadium, and a few weeks later Dan McGarry faced Nel in the same ring. The record book tells us that the Scottish champion lost on points over fifteen rounds, the reality was that McGarry was just five seconds from being a knockout victim of the new Tarleton. The Scot was hammered from pillar to post and coming up for the final round looked a sorry sight. Nella dropped his man with a right cross to the jaw. Up at eight, McGarry was dumped again, this time for nine. A vicious left hook sent him crashing again and the referee had counted five when the bell ended his torment.

Tarleton had issued a £500 challenge to anyone in the country up to 9st 10lbs, but when there were no takers he decided to accept an offer for a series of fights in Australia. After forcing Alec Law to retire in two rounds and thrashing the tough Frenchman Auguste Gyde, Tarleton set sail for the Antipodes along with Ernie Roderick, the younger brother of his best pal, and Johnny Peters of London.

In Sydney he was billed as Nelson Tarleton and his first engagement pitted him against lightweight champion Jimmy Kelso, already booked for a five-fight tour of America. Kelso was tough but he hadn't met anyone with Tarleton's skill and Nel boxed Jimmy's ears off for eight rounds before the frustrated Aussie lost his temper and floored him with a low punch. The referee was about to disqualify Kelso when Tarleton got to his feet and begged him to let the fight go on. At the end of fifteen rounds Tarleton was awarded the decision but he was booed from the ring.

"Referee Joe Wallis certainly crowned Tarleton when he was on the floor," wrote sportswriter Jim Mathers. "Tarleton was hooted by the crowd, but his sportsmanship in refusing to be presented with the decision was one of the finest gestures imaginable inside or outside the ring."

It was in Sydney that Tarleton met American lightweight Tod Morgan, the man he would call, "by far the hardest puncher I ever met. He made me wish I wasn't a fighter!" Morgan, a former Junior lightweight champion, hammered Nel all over the ring for seven rounds, putting him on the canvas several times. But the American couldn't keep him on the canvas and as Morgan tired from his efforts, Tarleton staged a brilliant recovery to earn a draw after fifteen rounds in what one critic called, "..the best scrap ever fought on Australian shores."

Nella outclassed Young Llew Edwards over fifteen rounds in Melbourne where the decision for Edwards triggered off a riot. Tarleton challenged the Aussie to a return contest but Young Llew had had enough and Nel sailed for home in disgust.

In February 1934, Tarleton's fans turned out in force to welcome him back to the Liverpool Stadium ring where he stopped Nick Bensa in eleven rounds, dumping the tough little Frenchman twice in the process, something only Kid Chocolate had been able to do. A few days later he was at Belle Vue, Manchester, to meet Norman Dale of Newcastle on the Johnny King-Dick Corbett British bantamweight title bill. A fine boxer, Dale had recently given Harry Mizler a good hiding at The Ring in London. But Mizler had already been selected to meet Johnny Cuthbert for the British lightweight championship and he came out with the decision.

Harry went on to take the title from Cuthbert and his manager, Victor Berliner, said that if Dale beat Tarleton at Manchester he could have a crack at Mizler's crown. The Newcastle boxer put up a tremendous fight against Tarleton and dropped Nel for a count of eight in the second round, but the Liverpool stylist weathered the storm and finished up a narrow points winner.

Johnny Best was staging a big Jewish charity show at the Stadium and Nel agreed to meet George Covacci, billed as the Rumanian lightweight champion. The week of the fight Tarleton was knocked out by the 'flu bug and a few hours before he was due in the ring he was in bed with a raging temperature. But he insisted on going through with the match and for seven rounds he boxed Covacci's head off, holding the centre of the ring and poking his left out every time the continental came near him. He was feeling the pace however, and before going out for the eighth he told his seconds, "This is the last round. I can't take any more. I retire after this round."

The bell brought them out for round eight and Tarleton was hammering away at the body when Covacci's second, Nick Cavalli, suddenly entered the ring, grabbed his man around the waist, and dragged him back to his corner, kicking and struggling all the while. The referee accepted the Rumanian's retirement and Tarleton was given the fight. Upon reaching his dressing room Nella collapsed with a temperature of 101 and was ordered to bed by the doctor. It would be just over two months before he was fit enough to fight again.

His recovery was helped enormously that night in April when he went along to the Stadium to see Seaman Watson fight Jimmy Walsh. After the champion had beaten the Chester man, a call over the Stadium's loudspeakers summoned Tarleton to Johnny Best's office where he was asked to sign a contract to box Watson for the British featherweight title and Lonsdale Belt at Anfield, the home of Liverpool FC, on Thursday 26 July.

Nel boxed twice before meeting Watson again. At the Blackfriars Ring in London he took a points decision over Harry Brooks and a week later lost the verdict to Sonny Lee in the Liverpool ring.

Both Watson and Tarleton trained away from home for their big fight, with the champion again setting up camp at Hexham in the Northumberland countryside where he had prepared for the ill-fated fight with Tommy Rogers. The *Chronicle's* boxing columnist watched Tommy's final workout at the gym behind his pub before he left for Hexham, and, with the fight seventeen days ahead, noted that Seaman was eight pounds over the featherweight limit.

Next day he would write, "On the long car journey upon which I accompanied Watson to Manchester (for the Francois Machtens fight) the boxer kept gargling his throat with aerated water but he swallowed none. He was looking forward to the weigh-in the following day at 2.00pm after which he could have a drink...Whether Watson will remain in the feather division after this is doubtful. Certainly some of his best supporters would like to see him go up into the lightweight division, where he could do the weight in absolute comfort."

When the same reporter visited Watson at his camp at Hexham a few days later however, he recorded that Tommy, "was down to about 9st 5lbs, so should easily do the specified 9st by the 26th. I have never seen him in better humour or better trim. He fought some hard rounds with Jim Hurst of Blaydon, Jim Bird of Gateshead, and Jim Campbell, an Australian now living at South Shields, and did all the gym stuff with a will and sincerity that could not be excelled."

Yet even in those last two weeks of intensive training for the defence of his championship, Tommy would find time to arrange a boxing competition for the Poor Childrens' Holiday Association, to take place at Gosforth Park, Newcastle, two days after the Tarleton fight. There would be a cup valued at fifteen guineas for the winner, donated by the champion.

As in his previous stay in Hexham, Tommy levied a small charge on those who came to watch his workouts and on his final day, the sum of seven pounds, six shillings was handed over to local charities. "Watson has to me, a remarkable personality," observed one sportswriter. "He has a strange mixture of kindness and pugnaciousness. He can be so gentle, and he can be so hard."

"I think Tommy has been working too hard," commented manager Alec Lambert when he arrived from London, "but we will put that all right. The Seaman is as fit as a fiddle and I am most confident that he will win." His opinion was shared by most of the national boxing press.

In the *Daily Herald*, James Butler wrote, "Unless my judgement is altogether wrong I feel confident that that straight forward and

232

up-and-at-'em boxer Seaman Tom Watson will retain his featherweight title when he has finished with Nel Tarleton on the Liverpool FC ground at Anfield...Tarleton is greatly fancied in Lancashire to beat Watson. I'm afraid I cannot agree with this prophecy. Tarleton is a boxer of the copy-book class, fast and accurate but a negative puncher...Watson is a typical sailor, he does not stand upon ceremony inside or outside the ring, bluff and hearty with his conversation as he is with his punches.

"I am sure that Tarleton has not achieved any outstanding victory to make me fancy him to beat Watson. Sonny Lee of Leeds defeated Tarleton recently. Lee however is one of those curious fighters who can lick champions without ever winning a title themselves. Watson's hard body punching, straight left leading, and all round ability are so pronounced that it will be an astonishing result to me if Watson is beaten...I do not believe there is a featherweight in the world who is good enough to beat Tom Watson of Tyneside."

The headline on Stanley Longstaff's preview in the *Sporting Life* ran, "TARLETON MUST STAGE FIGHT OF LIFETIME TO BEAT WATSON" and Longstaff noted, "..in two years we have witnessed a steady improvement in the ringcraft and tactics of Watson. There will be broadly contended on behalf of the champion that what he was able to accomplish two years ago he can repeat. To add weight to this argument facts prove that Tarleton has declined...for the winner I pin my faith on the man who is approaching his best form rather than leaving it behind, who knows the value of correct body punching, and who savours of the workman rather than the artist."

For *Boxing*, the trade paper, Ted Scales spent three days on Merseyside and wrote, "I went on Tuesday night to see Nel Tarleton give his public workout at the Stadium. Liverpool is so Tarleton-conscious that I suppose there were well over a couple of thousand men who paid to come in. Can you imagine that happening in London? I'll tell you about my state of mind. I imagined that Tarleton had no chance against Watson. I could not see him keeping him out. I could not see him giving Watson more trouble than Dick Corbett. I could not see him standing up to Watson's body punishment.

"But Liverpool wouldn't hear of it. If you went into a teashop you would hear everyone discussing Nella, and what he would do after he had won back the title. I gathered that he had not been over-impressive in his last few fights at home, but nobody set much store by that. Then came the public workout. I watched it pretty carefully, and at the end of it I strengthened my opinion that Tarleton had not an outside chance. Nel sparred a round each with four sparring partners, Tommy Bailey, Tony Butcher, Peter Clarke, and Young Nat Williams. Each one showed him up to my mind. He seemed to have no valid defence to a right to the body, and his judgement of distance seemed deplorable.

"What, however, was most noticeable, was the fact that Nella was in the most brilliant physical condition. I decided that Arthur Goodwin had trained Tarleton perfectly from a muscular point of view. But I thought, beyond that, Nel had reached a stage where no trainer on God's earth could help him. I thought he was finished because his muscles, beautifully trained and loose and strong though they were, could no longer do what the brain ordered them to do."

A few days before the fight, a local correspondent who visited Tarleton at his training quarters at Aughton, just outside the city, reported, "His speech was very thick owing to the hay fever which has been hanging over him for a week now, but there was no doubt that he looked in great shape. He was bright of eye and beautifully muscled. His sparring partners all say that he is hitting like a sledgehammer and that his defence is brilliant.

"He has eight sparring partners. 'I want variety of tactics while I am in training,' he explained, 'and I'm pretty confident that between the eight of them these boys can show me a bit of everything that Watson knows. As for this hay fever, well, forget about it. I'm trying to, and though it's keeping me a bit sleepy just at present the boys will have me working so hard tomorrow that I'll never know I had it. I'm going through those ropes with the idea of boxing my best, and I hope that will be sufficient to bring the title back to Merseyside.'"

Watson was equally confident as he finished his training. "Apart from my fights with LaBarba and Kid Chocolate in America I look upon this as the most serious one I have had during my boxing career," he told the *Sunday Sun.* "How could I do otherwise? I took the title from Tarleton and if I beat Nel again the Belt, valued at £300, will be my own property.

"And with the Belt, there is associated a pension of £1 a week. I hope I never need claim that pension, but one never knows what will happen, and I have a wife and three bairns to think about...Of course I think I'll win. How can I think otherwise? I was never better in my life than I am at present, and I can do the nine stones that I will have to scale at Liverpool next Thursday quite easily.

"When I put up my fists to Tarleton I will do so with confidence, and I will not forget for whom and what I am fighting. I am glad to learn that I will have a lot of Tyneside support. It really does buck you up a bit if the fight is not going quite your way. To hear, 'Gan on Tommy!' is as refreshing as the flaps of the seconds' towels. Whatever happens, however, I am out to win, not only for myself, but for the great sporting public of the North who have been with me in all my efforts."

There was a big crowd at Newcastle's Central Station on that Wednesday afternoon to see Tommy off to Liverpool for the fight. Just before he boarded the train, along with his wife Kitty, manager Alec Lambert, and second Jim Falcus, Watson held up the Lonsdale Belt for the crowd to see. Then, as the big clock showed ten minutes to one, the train eased out of the station and the crowd gave the Seaman a rousing cheer that sent the pigeons fluttering from their perch in the rafters high above the gleaming rails.

On the eve of the fight, GJO wrote in the *Evening Chronicle*, "I am glad to learn that, apart from Alec Lambert, his manager, Watson will have Jim Falcus in his corner at Liverpool. I could not imagine a better second. He must, however, as must Alec, allow Watson to fight his own fight."

As in the first Tarleton fight, Tommy's stay-at-home supporters were again denied the chance of listening to the radio broadcast.

Commented the *Chronicle*, "The BBC have failed to consider Newcastle listeners this evening over a sporting event of paramount importance to the North-East. The Featherweight Boxing Championship fight, in which Seaman Watson, of Newcastle, defends his title against Nel Tarleton, takes place at Liverpool tonight. An eye-witness account is to be given in the North Regional programme, while Newcastle Station relays the short mid-week service from National. The explanation is that the Newcastle authorities were only informed of the boxing commentary at a late hour last night.

"There seems to be a distinct lack of understanding between Manchester and Newcastle over the matter, and it is high time that these arrangements for outside commentaries were made known to our local station earlier, in order that listeners, to whom the broadcast of such a feature is of importance, may be assured of a local relay."

"And now Thursday, Thursday the great day," Ted Scales reported in *Boxing*, "the day that is to bring back a championship to Merseyside. I need not describe that dawn, because it was wet and nasty, and I stayed in bed for it. But it was a great dawn for Liverpool and the weather thought the better of it...There was the weigh-in. Both men inside. Tarleton was half-a-pound inside. Watson was exactly nine stone. Some said he had difficulty in making the weight. I don't know anything about that. I do know that my opinion is that if your match is for nine stone you should come in at nine stone. I think Alec Lambert agrees with me."

Jim Falcus was not there when Seaman stepped on the scales. Along with several members of the Tyneside party, Jim was being escorted to the weigh-in by a Liverpool friend who was under the impression that the ceremony was to take place at Anfield, where the fight was to be held that evening.

When they arrived at the big football ground, some three miles out of the city centre, Falcus was surprised there was not a crowd there to see the boxers. "Where is the weigh-in?" a casual worker was asked. "Oh, just to the left, and the second door," was the reply. So while Falcus and the others found their way in, to the ground, they did not see the weigh-in, much to their disappointment.

The bills posted up outside the ground advertised...15 3-MINUTE ROUNDS AT 9ST FEATHERWEIGHT CHAMPIONSHIP OF GREAT BRITAIN AND PURSE OF £1000.. TOMMY WATSON (NEWCASTLE) V NEL TARLETON (LIVERPOOL)...RINGSIDE 25/- STANDS 12/6 7/6 5/- PADDOCK AND STANDS (UNRESERVED) 3/6 SPION KOP 2/6.

That Thursday night, 26 July 1934, a crowd of some fifteen thousand gathered around the brightly lit ring on the pitch at Anfield to see if their beloved Nella could win his championship back. The referee appointed by the Board was Mr C B Thomas of Wales, and just before the contest began, a bowler-hatted Lord Lonsdale addressed the crowd from the ring, saying, "I do wish these two competitors every happiness in life. May the better man be successful tonight."

Tarleton set the crowd going from the opening bell as he came straight out and staggered Watson with a tremendous left to the body. Watson fought back with a furious two-fisted attack and they swapped punches along the ropes. Tarleton got home a stinging blow to the body and a right to the jaw as Watson tried hard to get inside. Nella boxed well throughout the round but the champion seemed unworried, content to bide his time.

"Watson's time came in the second round," reported *Boxing*, "when he did get to close quarters. Tarleton danced in with the left and tried to score with rights to the head, but Watson got stuck into the body."

Round three, and a magnificent right hand punch, flush on the jaw, made Tarleton glad to hang on. Watson was fighting furiously now and twice had Nella on the ropes. "Watson went fiercely for the body," observed Ted Scales in *Boxing*, "and his work was sound, effective, and worthy of a champion. The fourth was perhaps Watson's best round of all. He scored with considerable fluency, but Tarleton was clever in his anticipation and was always going away as the blows landed. About the only effective blow landed by the challenger during the round was a smart left hook to the jaw."

Tarleton sent the Seaman into the ropes with a splendid right hand punch in the fifth, only for Watson to come back with two-handed onslaughts to the body that forced Nel to call upon all of his ringcraft to survive to the bell.

"Watson did well again in the sixth," reported *Boxing*. "Tarleton's tactics became tiresome in this round. He persisted in his hitting and holding. He was quick with his left leads, but they were not weighty. He improved as the round ended but did not do enough to draw level on the round."

Covering the fight for the *Daily Herald*, James Butler wrote, "Watson began to warm up during the seventh round, he mixed clever boxing with heavy hitting, yet Tarleton kept retaliating with a verve and spirit that kept us enthralled."

In the eighth, Tarleton forced Tommy to the ropes and his left hand work was excellent. Watson missed badly with a vicious swing, but he did get home with a smashing right to the jaw that brought a roar from the crowd. Nel came back in the ninth to score to the head and body with both hands and a moment later sent Watson into the ropes with a left to the body. Tommy fought back to land a left to the chin.

It was in the ninth round that a moment of light relief broke the tension of the grim struggle taking place inside the ropes. Ted Scales reported in *Boxing*, "There was a distressing moment when a bucket flew heavily down on to a press table and soaked an unfortunate telephonist. The uproar was such that Tarleton failed to hear the bell and landed a left after the round had ended."

However, according to James Butler's report in the *Daily Herald*, "A big laugh went up during the ninth round when in a fierce mix-up in Watson's corner, the pail of sawdust was sent flying out of the ring!" Water, or sawdust? For the sake of the unfortunate telephonist, let's hope it was sawdust!

Round ten saw Watson touch down briefly from a swinging left but he was not hurt and he jumped up quickly to catch Tarleton with a right to the head. The Liverpool man fought back to the body and his left hand work kept Tommy busy defending till the bell. Tarleton attacked furiously as the eleventh began but was steadied by two thudding rights from Watson. Nella's left was darting out at every opportunity and with Watson always coming back for more there was still little between them at this stage.

The *Evening News* recorded, "There was an abundance of thrills in the twelfth session which was characterised by a rally from the champion. Tarleton was unbalanced by a left hook to the temple and Watson followed up with workmanlike hitting to the body. It was evident that Watson was the stronger and Tarleton did wisely in keeping the exchanges as long as he could at a distance."

"Watson was at his best throughout the twelfth round," wrote James Butler in the *Daily Herald*. "when he kept close to Tarleton and scored successfully with a barrage of body blows.

"Tarleton never lost his head, he fought back with brainy endeavour, straight lefts to the face, left hooks to the body, and Watson was not only worried but unable to deliver a solid punch."

"There was precious little in it in the next two rounds and Watson held a slight lead at the end of the thirteenth," wrote Ted Scales in *Boxing*. "The real thrills of the contest came in the fourteenth.

Watson did well in the early moments of the round, and suddenly Tarleton came in close with his head down and smashed away at Watson's jaw with lefts and rights. It was not possible to see actually what did the trouble, but suddenly Watson dropped by the ropes and took a long count. It may have been the hooks to the jaw that dropped him, but it certainly seemed as though Tarleton must have unintentionally caught Watson with his head.

"Watson came up bleeding over the left eye and apparently quite stunned. He had not the slightest idea where he was. He stood unable to defend himself by the ropes. He covered himself up by instinct alone and swayed as though he were about to fall again. But somehow, more by luck than judgement, he contrived not only to keep his feet to the end, but also to avoid further punishment during the round. He came back to his corner glassy-eyed and was obviously still not himself when he left it for the last round."

An anonymous reporter for the *Evening News* recorded, "The incident in the fourteenth in my mind settled it. Tarleton accidentally caught Watson with his head sending him to the boards, the first time I have ever seen Tommy taking a serious count. At eight he got to his feet and how he withstood the onslaughts of the Liverpool boy will always be a mystery to me. He did though, and fought well in the last round, showing all his old time grit."

The bell for the fifteenth round bringing champion and challenger to the centre of the ring for that final three minutes also brought a tremendous roar from fifteen thousand throats that threatened to split the night sky over Anfield. Come on, Nella, you can do it, you can be champion again!

Ted Scales in *Boxing*. "Watson pawed vaguely with his left occasionally but did no effective work. Tarleton could do what he wanted. But he could not manage to put Watson down again. After about forty seconds of the round one could suddenly see Watson come to himself. He must have immediately realised the situation and went in for a final fight. But it was too late. Tarleton had done just enough work in that round and a bit to wipe out Watson's lead and put himself just ahead. There was a harrowing pause after both men had gone to their corners. C B Thomas walked into another corner and added up his points in an unbelievable silence after the storm of the last few rounds. Then he walked to his left and the roar swelled again as he took the hand of Tarleton and raised it. Nella was champion again...And then the excitement began. I don't know how many people there were there. But they all went mad at once. I have rarely seen such excitement."

In the *Evening Express*, "The Pilot" reported, "Never shall I forget the silence which fell as the referee turned to a neutral corner to reckon his scorecard. Never shall I forget the mighty cheer which went up when he walked across and raised Tarleton's hand in victory."

"Liverpool fight fans were wildly enthusiastic over their favourite's success," wrote James Butler in the *Daily Herald*. "They shouted themselves hoarse when Lord Lonsdale stepped into the ring and placed the handsome belt bearing his name around the winner's waist...a contest such as we saw last night is the best testimonial British boxing can have for its future."

"I made Tarleton win by exactly one point," wrote the *Daily Express* reporter. "I gave him six rounds, Watson six rounds, and I made three level. But when twelve rounds had gone I would not have taken ten pounds to a penny for the Liverpool boxer's chance of bringing the title he lost to Watson two years ago back to Liverpool.

Somewhere in that big, crazy, heaving crowd still pressing around the ring long after the fight had ended, were two young women, one happy, one sad. Miss Barbara Day, Nel Tarleton's fiancee, had watched the fight from ringside along with her mother and her sister. She had been engaged to Nel almost a year now, but shared his dream of a world title before a wedding.

Kitty Watson just wanted to get through the throng so that she could console her husband. She had fought every second of the fight with Tommy, right down to the final bell, and she knew how desperately disappointed he must have been to see his beloved belt being fastened around the slim waist of Nel Tarleton by Lord Lonsdale.

In the dressing room, Seaman refused to speak to reporters, just asked for the doctor to have his eye attended to. Eventually he had a few words with a correspondent for the *Newcastle Journal*, telling him, "Tarleton fought splendidly. He is a great little fighter."

Kitty smiled ruefully as she added, "It was a good fight and Tarleton boxed finely. I only wish Tommy could have made the belt his own."

28

EX-SEAMAN...EX-CHAMPION

The headline in the Newcastle *Evening Chronicle* clarioned WATSON SHOULD STILL BE CHAMPION! with GJO writing, "It is my opinion, definitely, that the Novocastrian should have been announced as the winner. For me, at the end of the thirteenth round, Tarleton could not possibly beat him on points, and my opinion was evidently shared by most ringsiders at that time, for offers of three-to-one received no answer from the Liverpool man's supporters.

"I would not try to ignore the fact that the last two rounds were tragic, and, as it turned out, disastrous to the Seaman, but even when I concede to Tarleton ten points to two in the two final bouts I still make Watson out to be a winner by five points. Here is my scorecard for the contest, round by round, with Watson's score given first...4-5,5-4,5-3,

5-2,5-2,5-5,5-5,5-3,5-4,5-4,5-4,5-5,5-5,1-5,1-5 Total 66-61.

"I have reviewed and revisualised the contest and couldn't change my view that Watson had won, and this in spite of the fact that I have seen him fight better fights, especially in his left leading. This was slower and weaker than it used to be, but his body punching was as heavy, if not heavier, than it has ever been since he came from America. I'll make this concession, that the referee may have conceded more points to Tarleton for the remarkable way he stood abnormal body punishment than I have. That may bring Referee Thomas and myself nearer together in judgement, but not to the extent of the Lonsdale Belt changing hands."

A few days later, in his weekly boxing column for the *Chronicle*, GJO commented, "Not in nearly forty years experience of boxing have I known the result of a fight so much regretted among people of the North-East as that between Watson and Tarleton last Thursday night. It has been the chief topic in sporting circles over the weekend and a hundred times during the past few days I have been asked how it happened...

"For the greater part of the fight Watson simply hammered his man at will to the body, and too much credit can not be given to Tarleton for the way he took it. Tarleton's body must have been sore on Friday morning, but his stomach muscles must have been prepared for the hard onslaughts of the Tynesider. Then came the fateful last two rounds. I thought that it could not have been the right punch to the jaw received by Watson that could have kept the champion wobbling about the ring like a drunken man, for he was on his knee at once and only rested for about six seconds. The explanation came the following day, the real trouble was an accidental clash between the brow and the temple after Watson had risen from the floor...There has been a lot of talk of Watson losing by weakening himself to get down to nine stone. This is wrong and should not be made an excuse for the defeat.

"Now that the Belt has gone I am able to state that Watson will not contest for it again. He is going right into the lightweight division. Up to 9st 9lbs I think Watson will be the heaviest puncher and best boxer in the country. He's after Mizler's title and I think he will get it."

The news of Watson's defeat by Tarleton surprised many fight traders in America. Reporting that Freddie Miller had been offered ten thousand dollars to defend his world title, as recognised by the National Boxing Association, against Tarleton at Liverpool, *Boxing's* New York correspondent Peter Varley quoted Pete Reilly, the champ's manager, as saying he 'thought quite a piece of Seaman Watson when the Newcastle navigator clashed with Fidel LaBarba and Kid Chocolate, but although Tarleton showed class in plenty when he made a trip to these parts several years ago, it doesn't seem logic he can be any more a formidable proposition, he's more'n likely even less a fistic force. Weight troubles are reckoned the Seaman's troubles this side, but we may be wrong.'"

Although Tommy refused to claim weight-making as an alibi for losing his belt to Tarleton, he set his sights firmly on the lightweight title and had more than a passing interest in the contest for the Northern Area lightweight championship at New St James's Hall that Monday night in September 1934. His old pal and former victim in three fights, Douglas Parker, was defending his title against Norman Dale of Newcastle. The Sunderland Scot had seen better days and Dale had him in trouble in the twelfth round, but Duggie rallied and his strong finish earned him the decision as he retained his title.

"I'm keeping my eye on them," Tommy told a reporter. "There is plenty of time for me, though. I just started training this morning as Mr Lambert has arranged two fights for me next month."

The day of the Parker-Dale fight, the front page of every newspaper carried the terrible news of a big mining disaster in Wales. A massive explosion had rocked the Gresford Colliery, some three miles from Wrexham, and when the pit was eventually sealed up with concrete, the death total stood at 264. The Lord Mayor of London organised the Gresford Colliery Disaster Fund and money poured in from all over the country.

America's NBA champion Freddie Miller, who had retained his title against Tarleton at Liverpool, announced that he was willing to fight anyone on a promotion being staged in Cardiff, and donate his entire purse. Tommy Watson, ever ready to heed the call of charity, offered to meet Miller anywhere with all proceeds going to the fund, the only stipulation being that the contest be made at 9st 4lbs. Miller did not appear too keen on fighting Watson however, much to Tommy's disgust, so the Geordie set about organising a carnival dance at the Oxford Galleries in Newcastle in aid of the bereaved families.

A friend of Watson's since his early days, the *Chronicle's* boxing man was just as pleased to note that the fight with Miller had fallen through. "Far be it from me to put a damper in Watson's naturally generous nature," he wrote, "but I do think it is too big a sacrifice for one man to make, no matter how deserving the cause. There is another aspect of this proposed fight, for which Watson would be entitled to a purse of several hundred pounds. Considering what he has done in the game, he has made less out of it than those who have struck a lucky patch and made their thousands. What are these big-moneyed fellows doing for the disaster fund? What about Petersen, who has made his thousands out of Welsh crowds? Charity is one of the three great virtues, but where sacrifice is called for I think it should be more equitably distributed."

Those who had seen Miller beat off Tarleton's challenge for his title, were of the opinion that had the American faced Watson the

Newcastle man may well have beaten him. The Editor of *Boxing* commented, "I have an idea that Seaman Watson would beat Miller if they were to meet in a contest at 9st 4lbs or 9st 6lbs, but if Watson allows himself to be dragged into a match at 9st it will be the height of folly on his part. Watson is restarting as a lightweight on Friday when he begins a series of engagements that are intended to work him up to a fight for the lightweight title. I use the word restarting because it is a fact that Watson used to box as a light-weight before he realised that he could train down to nine stones. I think that he will be all the better for fighting at a weight more suited to his natural physique."

Rested after a short holiday, Watson was soon back in the gym. Alec Lambert had arranged two contests for him within the space of four days, the first one against Con Flynn of Islington at West Hartlepool, on Friday 19 October 1934. The fight, over 12 two-minute rounds at 9st 10lbs, was the star feature at the brand new Festival Hall, built in the grounds of the Pools Club in Clarence Road. A capacity crowd of some 2,000 spectators was on hand for what would be Watson's first, and only, appearance in West Hartlepool, and they saw him gain a comfortable points win over the Londoner. Out of serious ring action for almost three months, Tommy was off in his timing and his showing against Flynn disappointed even if he was a good winner. The only thrill came towards the end of the first round when Seaman put his man down for a count of eight with a solid right to the jaw. As always, Watson's body punching was impressive. and the young Londoner's knees sagged several times in the bout when he made the mistake of mixing it with the former champion.

That fight was just what Tommy needed and was ideal preparation for what promised to be a tougher job three days later, against Camden Town's George Odwell on a show for the Booth Street Relief Institution at the Stadium Club, Holborn. The twenty-three-year-old London boy had put together a terrific record in just over four years as a professional fighter, with almost 90 bouts under his belt, 50 won inside the distance, proof indeed of the power in his fists. Among George's victims were such men as Alby Kestrell, Harry Brooks, Len Wickwar, twice knocked out by Odwell, South African Louis Botes, and the Belgian Jules Steyaert. From May 1932 to March 1934 Odwell was unbeaten in 42 contests, and significantly, the man who snapped that winning run was Norman Dale of Newcastle who took a decision off the Londoner at the Blackfriars Ring. Now Odwell was to face another Novocastrian, the redoubtable Seaman Tommy Watson, former featherweight champion of Great Britain.

Training at Bill Klein's gym in Fitzroy Street, Odwell told reporters, "This is my first important contest and I mean to make the most of it." Watson was equally determined, stating on his arrival in London, "I never barred a featherweight in the world, and that goes for the lightweights. I am after Mizler's title."

Watson opened cautiously in the first round and Odwell got through with a good right hook to the head before the bell. The punch was too high to do any damage and Watson took charge of the fight in rounds two and three, using an accurate straight left and pounding the body with both hands. Coming out for the fourth, Seaman banged in a fierce left hook to the body that shook Odwell. More body shots brought his guard down and a perfect right hook to the jaw dropped George in a heap. His brain tried to send a message to his legs but the lines were down and he was counted out.

The knockout of George Odwell set Watson firmly on the road to lightweight honours and made a favourable impression on the national boxing press. A few weeks later however, Charlie Rose would write in *Boxing*, "George Odwell wants another shot at Tommy Watson or any other lightweight aspirant to Kid Berg's crown. Dr Cook of Cavendish Square has informed me over the phone that he treated Odwell for ten days prior to the Watson disturbance, and on the morning of the contest, for a badly strained chest. I have satisfied myself that the alibi is cast-iron, but I must apportion blame to the promoters (if they knew) and also Odwell and his manager for going on with the contest."

Alec Lambert was keeping Tommy busy and a week after beating Odwell Seaman was back in London to fight Camille Desmet of Belgium at Nine Elms Baths. Like most of the continental boys popular in British rings at the time, Desmet was as fit as a fiddle and as hard as nails, and he gave Watson a stubborn argument for ten rounds. Tommy was soon attacking the body but the Belgian soaked it up and was dangerous with hooks to the head. Seaman was the better boxer however and his accuracy and heavier hitting, especially inside, gave him a comfortable lead at the final bell for his third win in eleven days.

That same Monday night, 29 October 1934, Jackie Kid Berg hammered the British lightweight crown loose from the sleek head of Harry Mizler in their fight at the Royal Albert Hall. Berg was a tremendous all-action fighter who had beaten such stars as Kid Chocolate, Tony Canzoneri, and Billy Petrolle in an extensive American campaign. Since coming home however he had been stopped inside three rounds by Jimmy Stewart and his best days looked behind him. But manager Harry Levene talked the Kid out of retiring by promising him a title shot at Mizler.

Levene had no trouble selling the fight to Jeff Dickson for one of his Albert Hall shows and the American-born promoter seized on the rivalry of the two Jewish favourites from the East End to sell the fight to the public. A big crowd was on hand when the bout got under way and the Mizler fans were happy as their boy boxed his man off for the first two rounds. But the champion was in trouble, both of his hands had gone by the third round and he could no longer hold off the fierce onslaughts of Berg. Mizler was swept aside by the man they called the Whitechapel Whirlwind and his seconds threw in the towel at the end of the tenth round. Jackie Kid Berg was the new lightweight champion of Great Britain and Tommy Watson had a new target.

It was almost a year since Tommy had appeared in the Newcastle ring, in a fight he would rather forget, the unfortunate disqualification against Sonny Lee. Monday 12 November 1934 saw the annual show for the Jewish Charities at New St James's Hall, backed by Mr Lionel Jacobson and Dr Coller, and Seaman agreed to meet Harry Brooks of St Georges in the main attraction over 12 rounds. Chief supporting bouts featured Benny Sharkey against Liverpool's Billy Gannon, who had just beaten world champ Freddie Miller, albeit on a foul, and the fiery Scottish flyweight champion Benny Lynch in a return with Peter Miller.

Watson had beaten Brooks in one of his last fights before leaving the Navy and he beat him again, taking a well-earned decision from Mr C H Douglas, but Harry made him step along in an excellent contest that saw Tommy rely more on orthodox boxing rather than the heavy punching that had marked his recent fights. Both men received a big hand from the capacity crowd which cheered Sharkey to a points win over Gannon. There was no joy for Miller however as Lynch again knocked out the Gateshead lad.

Impatient for a crack at the lightweight title, Watson lodged a cheque for £100 with The *Sporting Life* to accompany a challenge to any British boxer for a match at 9st 9lbs. He was still keen to fight Freddie Miller at catchweights, but the American had taken himself off to Spain for a fight with Jose Girones in Barcelona. Alec Lambert had also received a very tempting offer for a series of fights in South Africa, but before then Tommy had dates with Norman Snow and Sonny Lee that figured to keep him busy up to Christmas.

Charlie Rose commented in *Boxing*, "What a fight that will be between Tommy Watson and Norman Snow, the hard-hitting Northants lightweight. Both are terrific hitters. It is true that dour Tom from Newcastle has had much experience and can give and take a wallop with here or there one, but so can Snow. Anyhow, it is a natural match and may save the Board many headaches in that it will eliminate one of the lightweights presently questing for Kid Berg's crown, even though the weight is one pound over the 9st 9lbs limit."

Starting his professional life as a featherweight, Norman Snow stopped Billy Carter for the Midlands Area title in 1931 and beat men like Billy Quinlan, Arnold Kid Sheppard, Pat Butler, Nobby Baker, and Ginger Jones, before Harry Mizler knocked him out at Olympia in a final eliminator for the British lightweight title. He bounced back with a string of knockouts, one of them over Peter Price for the vacant Southern Area title, and although he was a stablemate of the champion, Kid Berg, Norman was after the British crown and knew he had to beat Seaman Watson to stay in contention. The week before he was to face Watson, the Northampton youngster was in sparkling form as he hammered Fred Carpenter to defeat inside two rounds at Whitechapel.

That Tuesday night in November 1934 the Stadium Club at Holborn was a complete sellout for the Lion Hospital Aid Society show and a collection realised over £250. The generosity of the fans was rewarded with a terrific fight between Watson and Snow that had the boxing writers reaching for superlatives as they scribbled their reports.

"There have been few better fights at the Stadium Club than that in which Watson outpointed Snow," said the *Evening News*. Ted Scales wrote in *Boxing*, "Tommy Watson did his devastating stuff against Norman Snow. Snow is certainly game. What he took from Watson would, in the eyes of Monsieur Louis Trigger

(*Boxing's* French correspondent) justify the immediate arrest of Watson. It was a gem of a fight, and it backs up what we all said about Watson after his defeat of George Odwell. Watson as a lightweight is going to take a hell of a lot of beating!"

From the first bell Watson was the better craftsman and he surprised Snow with his speed of punching, particularly at close range. Tommy was in good form and his left hand leading was much quicker than that of Snow, who fought very strongly, but experience was on the side of Watson. The boy from Northampton found many of his efforts reduced to nothing by the quick body movements of Watson and he was hurt by heavy countering blows. In the third round, Snow dropped to one knee after taking a left to the body and indicated to Referee Moss Deyong that he had been hit low, but the official waved him back into action.

The fourth brought the crowd to its feet as both men sent in heavy body blows. Snow went halfway through the ropes as Watson evaded one of his rushes and Tommy sportingly waited for him to recover his balance. Watson was allowing Snow to lead, making him miss, and stepping in with hard punches to make the youngster break ground.

Seaman was well on top in round six as he landed repeatedly with hard rights to the jaw but the lad from Northampton fought back in the seventh to get his own right on target. Watson was relentless in his attack however and he sent Snow crashing to the canvas in the eighth from a vicious left hook to the jaw. Mr Deyong counted six before Snow was on his feet and Watson moved in to shake his man several times before the bell. Snow was down again in the ninth round, this time for nine, and the crowd roared as Watson tried to finish it. But Snow made a tremendous effort to survive and the final three rounds were fought at a terrific pace with the former champion maintaining his lead to have his glove raised in triumph.

"Watson was quite irresistible," wrote one observer, "and Snow could not by any stretch of the imagination be said to have won more than two of the twelve rounds, some people would not have given him one. The fact was that Watson knew too much for the game young Southern Area champion. He was the better boxer and he never gave Snow a chance to bring one of his devastating hooks into action. His defence was at all times excellent...

Watson showed that he was not only a murderous infighter, but also highly skilled at long range. It was one of his finest performances."

The *Evening News* columnist reported, "John Mortimer rang up this morning from London to tell me about the Watson-Snow fight last night. He said that Watson, who won on points, fought like a champion. 'I always said he would. He proved himself once again to be a great boxer-fighter and credit must be given to his less experienced younger opponent. It was a very clean and great fight between two lads who were demons. Tommy, however, showed how cool he was when he called the attention of Referee Moss Deyong to an irregularity committed by one of the seconds of his opponent, who interfered as his man was taking a count.

"'Watson received an accidental cut over his left eye early on, which made him use his boxing sense. Otherwise I think he would have put Snow out. As it was, Snow took three counts during the fight. He is a plucky youngster and will certainly be heard of again. Watson left early this morning for Newcastle where he resumes training for his important weight contest with Sonny Lee at Portsmouth next Wednesday.'"

James Butler wrote in the *Daily Herald*, "'He's the greatest fighter I've watched since Owen Moran's days,' declared one of the veterans of the National Sporting Club yesterday when we said au revoir to ex-Seaman Tom Watson. The Newcastle publican and former featherweight champion was leaving London by road so that he could reach Walkergate on Tyneside to continue his training. Watson is meeting Sonny Lee, the Leeds surpriser of champions, at Portsmouth on Wednesday, and he said, 'I know that Lee is clever and not easy to beat so I must be fit and well if I am to beat him.' Watson was none the worse for his smashing fight with Norman Snow, in fact if I had not known him, I should not have thought Watson had been in a scrap overnight.

"Watson is 26-years-old but has the mature mind of a man twice that age. Snow is a boy, just twenty, but a wonderfully game battler. Said Tom, 'I was taken to Snow's dressing room by Mr John Mortimer and I could not do other than compliment him on the magnificent fight he gave me.' Watson naturally considers that he should meet Jack Kid Berg for the lightweight title without any of the palaver which is associated with present-day championship matchmaking. I agree with him. Furthermore, it is my contention that Watson was badly passed over when Berg was chosen to meet Mizler for the title. Still, Watson does not worry, he's a real north country type, dour and phlegmatic."

Snow's supporters had greatly underestimated Watson and lost a great deal of money betting on their man. They were anxious for a return fight and the *Sporting Life* reported, "There is backing of £50 to £100 for Norman Snow of Northampton for a rematch with Watson. The pair fought a terrific battle at the Stadium Club, Holborn, on Tuesday night when Watson gained a well-merited verdict on points in a match over 12 rounds at 9st 10lbs. The suggestion is that the return contest should be at the lightweight limit of 9st 9lbs over 15 3-minute rounds so that it could be regarded as a title eliminator for a match with Kid Berg."

A week after the Watson-Snow fight, the Editor of *Boxing* commented, "Kid Berg is the lightweight champion because he holds the title but it would be drawing very strongly on the imagination to describe him as the best lightweight in Great Britain. He defeated Harry Mizler because that boxer was a poor champion. Prior to this, as all the world knows, Mizler was beaten by Jimmy Walsh of Chester and Berg was very decisively beaten by Jimmy Stewart of Liverpool. Both Walsh and Stewart were very unfairly treated by having Berg foisted above them. Since it has been plain to nearly everybody interested in boxing, with the exception of the Board of Control, that Stewart and Walsh have indisputable claims to be recognised as challengers for the lightweight title, Seaman Watson has established himself in the lightweight division.

"Most people thought it a very sound scheme when Johnny Best suggested that he would match Jimmy Stewart and Seaman Watson in a contest at nine-nine. He did the right thing in applying to the Board for permission to bill the match as a championship eliminator, and he must have had a shock when he received the Board's reply stating that the match could not be sanctioned because there are several other claimants under consideration.

"If instead of 'several' the Board's communication had read 'another', that other being Jimmy Walsh, it would have been merely stating the obvious. Walsh is sensible enough to realise the position and he must know that his chance will eventually come. The Watson-Stewart match is one that should be decided without delay, and if Johnny Best is wise he will carry on with the promotion. Here is a match that does not require a label. It is almost certain to attract a full house at Liverpool, and if the Board of Control ignores the result the sporting public will not."

Posters all over Portsmouth heralded the fight Tommy Watson wanted more than any other, the return with Sonny Lee who had defeated Seaman on a disqualification at Newcastle just a year ago. The fight had been signed by John Mortimer for the Connaught Drill Hall on Wednesday 5 December, 10 x 3-minute rounds at 9st 9lbs under forfeit of £20. The boxers would weigh-in at the Connaught Drill Hall at 2.00pm on the day of the contest with the public cordially invited to view the proceedings. Admission charges were 1/2, 2/6, 3/6, 5/6. with boys under fourteen years admitted half-price. The posters also stated that the Board of Control had agreed to take into consideration the winner of this fight when they make their final selection of championship contenders.

The twenty-two-year-old Leeds boy had been busy since the Watson fight in Newcastle, and among his victories was a fifteen rounds points decision over Nel Tarleton in his own Liverpool backyard a couple of months before Nella regained the featherweight title from Watson. A few days before he was due in Portsmouth, Lee whipped Bert Ison at the Brunswick Stadium in Leeds, and his manager, Professor Louis Marks, announced that his 'Sonny boy' was ready for Watson, or anybody else!

Seaman Tommy Watson however, was not ready for him. On the morning of the fight the *News Chronicle* reported, "Tommy Watson has unfortunately broken down in training and this prevents him appearing tonight at the Connaught Drill Hall, Portsmouth. Watson was to have met Sonny Lee of Leeds and in his absence a very good substitute has been found in Norman Snow, who belongs to the same stable as Dave Crowley."

Writing in the *Newcastle Chronicle*, GJO commented, "Seaman Tom Watson will not, after all, be seen in the ring again for at least a month. He is resting on very definite advice from his medical adviser, who considers that he has rather overdone things in the fight game during the past month or two, and is completely run down. Watson admitted to me the other night that he had felt 'queer' for some weeks, and had decided to follow the medical instruction. Watson also told me that his fight with Norman Snow was probably the hardest of his career."

The *Sporting Life* reported, "Tommy Watson's lightweight title

251

aspirations have received a check from a totally unexpected quarter...ill health. Doctors have discovered that he has sub-normal blood pressure with consequent 'loss of tone.' Actually the ex-Seaman has been working too hard. Since he lost his title to Tarleton, his one ambition has been to capture the nine-stone-nine title. Watson embarked on a strenuous campaign in the lightweight division, and apart from his serious work, the calls of charity have never found him unwilling to respond. Now he is paying the penalty of overdoing it and the opinion of his medical advisers is that unless he takes it easy, his health could be seriously affected. Watson has decided to take the warning and he will not be seen in action again for several weeks."

29

LIGHTWEIGHT CONTENDER

Although no longer holding the British featherweight title, Tommy Watson was still charity's champion, and on a cold December night there was still the warm-hearted gesture. Tom and Kitty were enjoying a night out at Newcastle's Empire Theatre when bandleader Jack Hylton walked on stage to conduct an auction on behalf of the Chronicle's Sunshine Fund. A picture of the Duchess of Kent caught Kitty's eye and Tommy's winning bid cost him nine pounds and ten shillings, a tidy sum in those days.

For some weeks there had been speculation that Seaman would accept an offer of a fight in South Africa against their lightweight titleholder Laurie Stevens, but that fell through when John Mortimer received word from the Secretary of the Transvaal Sporting Association that the former Olympic champion had been taken to hospital and was likely to remain there for at least two months.

As he looked forward to Christmas with the children (Kath was now six, Tom was four, and Joan three) Tommy was already feeling better. The seedy feeling that had hung on him since that hard fight with Norman Snow was gone and the cut eye he received had proved a blessing in disguise as it had caused postponement of the fight with Sonny Lee at Portsmouth at a time when he wasn't in condition to fight anyone. When John Mortimer asked Lee if he would accept Norman Snow as a substitute for Seaman, the Leeds boy replied, "I don't mind, but I want Watson."

Sonny got his wish, sooner than expected. The morning edition of *The Sporting Life* for 20 December 1934 reported, "BOARD SOLVE LIGHTWEIGHT PROBLEM...Jack Kid Berg will not be called upon to defend his British lightweight title until the end of April and it is considered unlikely that he will jeopardise it before that date. With the lightweight division one of the strongest in the country, the Board have decided to organise a series of eliminators as follows...Jimmy Stewart (Liverpool) v Jimmy Walsh (Chester), Norman Snow (Northampton) v Harry Mizler (St Georges), Tommy Watson (Newcastle) v Sonny Lee (Leeds), Boyo Rees (Aberdare) v George Daly (Blackfriars), Tommy Spiers (Clackmannan) v Harry Brooks (St Georges), with Liverpool's Frankie Brown as reserve. Promoters and managers have been given until 10 January to arrange for the staging of the fights."

When the local press gave Tommy the news he said that in spite of the holiday season he would begin training straight away. That disqualification defeat against Lee still rankled with him and now he had the added incentive of the return bout being labelled an official eliminator. However, in saying that he hoped the fight would come to Newcastle, Watson added that as keen as he was to cross gloves with Berg for his title, he would retire from boxing should he lose in any of the eliminators.

It was the first public admission that the former British champion was possibly beginning to feel the strain of the hardest game of all. Although not yet twenty-seven, Tommy had been fighting as a professional for just over nine years through 113 fights against the best in the business, in championship class for the last three years. It was a tough way to make a living but it was what Seaman Tommy Watson did best, and in January 1935 he knew that his best was still too good for fellows like Sonny Lee!

Professor Louis Marks, Lee's manager, made it known to promoters as well as the Board of Control, that he was willing to let the fight go to purse offers with the winner (his boy Sonny!) receiving 60% and the loser 40%. Newcastle promoter John Paget put in a substantial bid on behalf of New St James's Hall, but 'Uncle John' Mortimer talked the right numbers with Marks and the fight was signed for Wednesday 27 February at the Connaught Drill Hall in Portsmouth.

Kitty accompanied Tommy on the long journey south, she still had family living in the area and it was a good opportunity to visit with them, and of course she wanted to be there for Tommy's important fight. Seaman finished off his training at Southsea and at Portsmouth Football Ground and was raring to go. Sonny Lee had trained at home in Leeds and arrived in town the day before the fight. When they stepped on the scales at the Drill Hall at two o'clock the following afternoon, both were just over 9st 7lbs, well within the class limit.

The fight was scheduled for twelve rounds and the Board had appointed Mr Moss Deyong of London as referee in charge of the action. A horribly wet night failed to dampen the enthusiasm of the local fans as they packed the Connaught Drill Hall, with many naval uniforms in the crowd as the boys of the Senior Service turned up to cheer one of their own.

They gave Seaman a big hand when he came down to the ring and Kitty gave him a kiss for luck just before he climbed through the ropes. As they answered the bell for round one it was seen that Watson enjoyed height and reach advantages over the stocky Yorkshire lad. They both went in close and the action was fast with heavy swings to the body and short arm jabs. When the fight opened out Watson made Sonny miss and scored with solid lefts to the face. A vicious left hook shook Lee just before the round ended.

Watson had taken the first round but Lee fought on even terms through the second, a round that saw both men attack the body with relish although Tommy was ever mindful of the errant punch that had cost him their first fight back home in Newcastle. No mistakes this time! Round three and Watson landed a solid right uppercut, forcing the pace but finding Lee an elusive target. They swapped leather in a fierce exchange and if the round was Watson's it was by the merest margin.

The action was even again through the fourth as Tommy forced his man into a corner, only for Sonny to escape and put him under pressure with two-handed punching. The hardest shot in the fight so far came from Lee, a heavy right that tested Tommy's chin. He survived and was blocking body punches when the bell sent them back to their corners.

Watson stepped up a gear in round five, slipped a left lead and countered with a thudding left hook. Sonny surged back but was again steadied by those hammering Geordie fists and in the final minute a beautiful left and right to the jaw sat the Yorkshire lad on his backside. He beat the count but it was a good round for the former champion. Tommy became careless in the sixth as he tried to cash in on the knockdown and Lee fought back with a fierce determination that won him the round in the view of many ringsiders.

Round seven and one reporter noted, "Lee stopped one of

Watson's uppercuts in a place where he did not like it and was checked for holding." The Leeds boy was still full of fight but when he opened up Watson caught him with a smashing left hook and a following heavy right that rattled his ribs. Although Sonny fought on even terms through the eighth round he was beginning to feel the pace and Watson's experience was showing the way home. The ninth was quiet with Lee bringing applause from the crowd when he stepped back as Tommy slipped. Watson recovered and banged in a solid left as the bell rang.

Seaman sailed through the tenth, covering well when Lee attacked and picking up more points with that accurate stabbing left hand, yet the Tyke was able to summon up enough aggression to shade the eleventh as Tommy boxed on the retreat. Twelfth and final round and Watson back in top gear, he had more left in the tank than his younger opponent. Lee was rocked by a smashing left hook to the jaw, then a thudding right turned his legs to rubber. He reeled across the ring with Watson in pursuit but managed to stay on his feet till the final bell ended hostilities. Sonny looked hopefully at Mr Deyong but it was a forlorn hope as the third man's arithmetic added up to a clear-cut victory for Seaman Watson.

Geoffrey Simpson, who had been covering big-time boxing for the *Daily Mail* since 1920, wrote, "For about the first time in his career, Seaman Watson abandoned body punching in his fight at the Connaught Drill Hall last night and he spent twelve rounds slashing out a straight left in the best Driscoll style. He revealed himself such a splendid exponent of this old English punch that he outpointed Sonny Lee of Leeds by such a wide margin that there was not a dissenting voice when the referee raised his gloved hand aloft.

"Watson...set about beating a big-chested swinging puncher by twinkling footwork, sound generalship, and a straight from the shoulder left. The way he jumped in and out to ram that left into Lee's grimly set face was artistic. He timed his leads brilliantly and it was rare that he was caught by a countering punch."

"Watson was always just on top," noted another observer, "but according to his sensible custom he did not try to win by a mile when he could save his energy and win by a hundred yards...the majority of the crowd, many of them naval ratings, seemed to have an excellent knowledge of the game so that they were able to realise the solid excellence of the work of both men. There were no

256

fireworks, there was some fine boxing, which is something far better. A couple of mugs could have produced fireworks, it took two good men to produce this fight."

Ted Scales wrote in his Punchbowl column in *Boxing*, "I enjoyed it utterly. It was a beautiful battle of wits with Watson boxing as carefully as he did against Dick Corbett. Some people seemed surprised to see that Watson could box. They forget that he showed a better left last year than the man who is supposed to have the best left hand in England, the ginger-haired gentleman from Bethnal Green."

"Although it had been a keen contest," commented another ringside critic, "general opinion was that it was not the old Watson who carried all before him as a featherweight. His punches were not so damaging and he was apt to be slow following up after shaking his man. However he showed all his old defensive skills, a big feature being his blocking, slipping, and drawing back, and it was agreed he would win through to a title shot at Berg and be too good for the champion with his better defence and punching power at close quarters."

Watson's victory over Lee was the second of the official eliminators to take place, Jimmy Walsh having defied Jimmy Stewart's attempts to knock him out at Liverpool a couple of weeks previously, winning a 15-rounds decision. At Mountain Ash on 11 March, George Daly outboxed Boyo Rees from Aberdare to join Walsh and Watson in the frame, and three days later Frankie Brown stepped in against Norman Snow when Harry Mizler withdrew, still suffering from the hand injury that had kept him idle since losing the championship to Kid Berg in October. Fighting in his own backyard at Liverpool Stadium, Brown grabbed his big chance with both hands, forcing Snow to retire after twelve rounds. Another to enjoy home advantage was Scot Tommy Spiers who accounted for Harry Brooks of St Georges over 15 rounds at Leith.

The next stage of the elimination series pitted Daly against Jimmy Walsh and Watson against Spiers, but Tommy was once again under the doctor. Daly was anxious for a fight with any of the other contenders and offered a sidestake, while Walsh wanted to fight Watson again with the winner going in with Berg for the title.

"Just let them carry on," Tommy told the *Chronicle*. "There is plenty of time for me, and I have decided to have a month's rest before I go into the ring again. This is not an unreasonable period between contests leading to a British title and a Lonsdale Belt."

There was a strange item in *Boxing's* Punchbowl column of 27 March, with Ted Scales writing, "It is always unpleasant when the spectators at a boxing match begin to scream vile comments in order to annoy one of the fighters. The trick was tried on on Sunday at the Whitechapel Pavilion when some gentleman with an advanced sense of humour called out to George Odwell, 'Where's Seaman Watson?'

"Odwell (in round six of a contest with Jackie Flynn) became so annoyed that he dropped his hands and walked to his corner and retired. It was but natural that the referee should feel that Odwell had retired without due cause, and he was correct in disqualifying Odwell. But I wonder how the great humorists feel about it. I feel that Odwell must have been unduly sensitive, if that is the true reason for his retirement. I was told that by Syd Burns, the second in his corner, and also by Sam Russell, who spoke to Odwell and asked the reason for his retirement. But the net result was that Odwell was deprived of a victory which he deserved by one or two vile creatures whose desire to attract attention was greater than their good taste. For the sake of these pests a fine little boxer has to suffer and the public in general has to be deprived of the remains of an interesting fight."

If the inference was that the mere mention of Seaman Watson's name was enough to strike fear into the hearts of other fighters, then those poor mortals could have drawn strength from the news out of Newcastle that the former British featherweight champion had again been forced to break training due to ill health.

It was well into April before Tommy was able to resume training for the Spiers fight, but the good news was that John Paget had secured the contest for New St James's Hall, beating off fierce competition from Scottish promoters. The announcement was welcomed in North East boxing circles, and when Tommy attended the Monday night show at the Gallowgate hall on 29 April, he was called up into the ring to take a bow. "I cannot recall Watson being accorded a warmer welcome," wrote GJO in the *Chronicle*, "and I know that the Tyneside title bidder appreciated the pleasure which the crowd expressed."

Watson's sparring partners for the Spiers fight were George

Willis, his regular man Billy Sheldon, and a young Gateshead boxer named Billy Charlton. Billy was only nineteen then. He is in his eighty-first year now but he still remembers that first meeting with Seaman Watson in his gym behind the pub in Shields Road.

"It was the Wednesday before Tommy's fight," Billy told me, "and I boxed Harry Edwards of Birmingham at New St James's Hall, winning on points. When I went into the office for my money, Mr Paget said, 'Billy, Tommy Watson wants you to go down to his Walkergate gym to be his chief sparring partner.' Well, it seemed to me that I was the best sparring partner in the North East, first of all it was Norman Dale who wanted me, next it was George Willis, and now it was Seaman Tommy Watson. Mind you, being wanted by Watson seemed an honour, but there again it was an honour to be wanted by Willis and Dale.

"Well, it was to the Walkergate gym that my father and I arrived that following afternoon. It was about ten-to-three when we got there and Tommy was getting himself ready for his afternoon session of training. Anyone who knew Tommy Watson will know how outspoken he was and the Tyneside language he used. Well, as we went into the gym Tommy said, 'What do they call you son?' 'Billy Charlton of Gateshead,' I replied. 'Mr Paget said you wanted me as a sparring partner.' 'Aye, that's right,' said Tommy. 'Now get ready and we'll have a round or two of sparring to see how you are.' 'Right,' said I and began to undress, listening to Tommy's chatter. 'You'll be all right here son, so don't worry, just do your best and try to stick me on the floor because I'll stick you on the floor if I can.' At that I began to put my trousers on again and Tommy said, 'What are you doing, man?' 'I'm getting ready and going home,' I said.

"'What for?' said Tommy, and I replied, 'I didn't come down here to try and knock anyone's block off, nor to get my block knocked off. I came down for sparring.' 'Take no notice,' said Tommy, 'I'm only kidding man, but don't be afraid to get stuck in and do your best to beat me.' 'I won't, don't worry,' I replied.

"Well, to tell the truth I entered the ring that afternoon full of fire and grim determination to show Tommy Watson what I could do, which of course suited Tommy, except for one thing. I was no fighter, but by heavens I could box, and I went in that afternoon to show Watson just how fast I was. But I also found out very soon what a good box-fighter Tommy was. My job was to pop my left hand upon Tommy's nose and jump smartly back and then step to one side. It was all right the first round and I thought I was going to be all right with the speed that I had, but in the second round it was different, because when I jumped back and moved smartly to my right, Tommy just stepped smartly over to his left and there I was right in front of him.

"Naturally I jumped back smartly again but most times I was near to the ropes and then that was when Tommy went to work. He would push me on the shoulder so that I fell back on the ropes, then in he would come under my lead, right up to my body and punch away underneath. All I could do was grab him and hold on like hell until we broke. As Tommy was boxing on the Monday I don't think he worried much about me running away from him and after all it was my first day there. Tommy had his manager coming up for the training so it was natural that he wanted to look good, so on the Friday after we had finished our three or four rounds of boxing and were going for a shower, Tommy said to me, 'You will never be any good just boxing, son, because you will never be able to draw the crowds in.

"'That's what the promoters want, a crowd pleaser.' 'I've never been shown anything about fighting,' I said, and Tommy replied, 'Well, I'll teach you all I can, the rest is up to you.' So from then on we had a wee lesson or two when the gym was quiet. Believe me when I say that if anyone tried to be a box-fighter it was I. I took in everything that Tommy Watson said, I practised at home for hours, and I felt that with luck I would eventually get to the top like Tommy did.

"He showed me how to get the fullest power from my punches, punching from the toe right up through the lateral and dorsal muscles, how it was necessary to turn your knuckles on top using those four knuckles to sink into the rib cage, how to move a fellow just enough to find the dial. There was such a lot he tried to teach me and I was learning slowly but surely. It all takes time, Tommy would say, but one day it will all come to you and you'll just think you are outside watching what you are doing in the ring."

The following Monday night, 20 May 1935, young Billy Charlton was outside watching what Seaman Watson was doing inside the ring at New St James's Hall against Tommy Spiers. The fight was set for fifteen rounds at the lightweight limit and that afternoon Watson weighed in at 9st 8lbs to 9st 6½lbs for the Scot.

With prices at six bob ringside, four shillings outer ring, three shillings balcony, and two bob in the gallery, there wasn't an empty seat in the Gallowgate hall when Referee Jim Kenrick called the men to the centre of the ring. It had been thirty-two years since Mr Kenrick was last in a boxing ring in Newcastle and on that occasion he defeated Charlie Exall at Ginnett's Circus for the 7st 8lbs championship of England. He would later fight Johnny Coulon in America for the world title, recalling, "It took the champion 19 rounds to lick me, and during the last ten rounds I fought with a smashed hand!"

Tommy Spiers had knocked out Jim Hunter to win the Scottish lightweight title in May 1933 and a few weeks later had given British champion Johnny Cuthbert a helluva fight in a non-title bout at Liverpool when a storm of booing greeted the decision for Cuthbert. But Spiers himself came a cropper in November 1933 when he was knocked out by Douglas Parker in the Newcastle ring, although it was later revealed that he had been in a motor-cycle accident just three days prior to the contest. He had done well since and was a good winner over Harry Brooks last time out to earn his place in the eliminator with Watson.

Watson took charge of the ring from the first bell, scoring solid lefts to the face, then a fast exchange of punches inside had the Scot rolling on the canvas. He was up without a count but was shaken by a heavy left to the head just before the bell. Round two and the local favourite was again first to score, but in his efforts to land a finisher Tommy was missing most of his big shots and Spiers took advantage to ram home a right to the jaw. Watson absorbed the leather and at the bell was handing it back to the lad from over the border.

In the third Watson missed with a terrific right aimed at the jaw but was then bang on target with two vicious lefts to the face. The former champion's experience and expertise was already marking his ringwork in a different class to that of the other Tommy. Seaman was out for work early in the fourth, missed with a right, then smashed the same hand to the jaw and followed with a cracking left uppercut. Spiers fought back with punches to the body but Watson danced away and came back with his own devastating body attack to consolidate his lead. Round five and Seaman again made the body his prime target, but the Scot had done his gym work and he fought back with a right that just fell short.

Spiers hammered in two solid hooks that pulled Watson up in his tracks but the Geordie was soon back on the attack and several times Spiers was forced to hold to stay in the fight. In the sixth Watson piled on the pressure and a vicious right to the ribs sent Spiers crashing to the canvas for a short count. He survived to the bell when Watson's follow-up was wild of the mark. The seventh saw the Scot taking a savage belting to the body but he was still game for a fight and he managed to get home with a couple of solid lefts to the face.

Eighth round and the trend of the bout was reflected in the odds being offered at ringside with Watson a ten-to-one on choice. Stepping up a gear, Seaman hammered a heavy right to the jaw to send Spiers reeling across the ring. Seaman closed in for the kill but the Scot avoided the finisher and even banged Watson on the chin with a good right of his own that gave the local pause for thought. In fact Tommy thought he had better get this thing over with and he was relentless in the ninth, with Spiers taking tremendous punishment. The bell was sweet music to his battered ears and so was the storm of applause from an appreciative crowd as he went back to his stool.

Rounds ten, eleven, and twelve, were three-minute nightmares for the game Scottish boy as his dream drifted away in the smoke haze swirling around the hot ring lights. Occasionally he would land a punch on Watson but he was firing blanks now, his shells bouncing off Watson's armour-plated hide.

The best round of the fight was possibly the thirteenth. Seaman fired a broadside at the jaw, but Spiers surprised him with a right of his own that stirred Watson to fierce retaliation. Punches rained home and Spiers was in serious trouble, only courage and will power keeping him on his feet and at the bell he was hanging on grimly.

The boy from Bonnie Scotland was determined to go out on his shield and he brought a roar from the crowd in the fourteenth when he launched a two-fisted attack that reminded Watson he was still in a fight. Seaman only just avoided a terrific right swing to the head and the impetus almost carried Spiers through the ropes. Coming out for the final round Watson fenced his man off cleverly as the Scot made a dying effort to snatch victory from the jaws of defeat. But he would not be a winner this night in Newcastle and at the bell Mr Kenrick's decision was for Seaman Tommy Watson.

Another hurdle had been cleared on the road to Kid Berg!

A few days later, *The Sporting Life* reported, "Seaman Watson is not a showman in the ring but his ability as boxer and fighter and his dour spirit have won for him a big following. It is only seven or eight months ago that he decided to throw in his lot with the lightweights. He has had seven contests since then and is now being freely discussed as the best nine-stone-nine man in the country. Naturally Jack Kid Berg as British champion disputes this claim and Harry Levene declared yesterday that Berg was ready at any time to put his crown at stake against the Northerner. So far as he was concerned it was only a matter of a promoter offering satisfactory terms.

"When I acquainted John Mortimer of Portsmouth, who is interested in Watson's career, of this statement from the Berg camp, he was not at all flattered. 'It is all very well,' he said, 'for them to make this offer now when they know Tommy has a full list of engagements. They seem to forget that several months ago I had £100 lying at the *The Sporting Life* offices for many weeks with a challenge from Seaman Watson to Jack Kid Berg or any other lightweight. After Tommy has fulfilled all the contracts he has signed, a contest with Berg will fill a long felt want.'"

Mortimer was right, Watson did indeed have a full list of engagements. On Sunday 26 May, just six days after beating Spiers, he was to meet Belgian Jules Steyaert at Temple Mills, Stratford. On Wednesday 29 May he was matched with Carlo Orlandi, the deaf and dumb Italian holder of the European championship, at the Stanley Track at Liverpool, and on 10 June he had a date with Nobby Baker at Carmarthen.

Reporting the Steyaert contest in *Boxing*, Ted Scales wrote, "Jules proved himself a smashing runner against Tommy Watson on Sunday at Temple Mills Stadium. I suppose he must have thought Tommy needed roadwork for his contest with Carlo Orlandi. Or perhaps it was something left over in the atmosphere from the whippet racing at the stadium earlier in the day. Anyway, Jules ran. The grim Watson unbent. He mimicked Steyaert and ran backwards himself. He begged him to 'Eh, look here,' and 'Give us a chance.' But Steyaert wasn't having any. At least not until quite late in the fight when he suddenly remembered that he wasn't a whippet after all. He began to use both his hands. And that just gave Watson the chance he had been longing for, so he went in and had a nice little fight."

263

"I'd back Steyaert against all comers as a long distance runner," said boxer Harry Brooks as he made his way out of the stadium. "When I fought him, I dropped from sheer exhaustion!"

"There was very little of the grim business of fighting in Seaman Watson's 12 rounds contest with the Belgian lightweight," reported another newspaper. "It was more like a ballet dance than a prizefight with the puzzled Tommy following the fleet-footed Belgian round and round the ring...in the fifth round, the Belgian's second protested that Tommy was holding, and there was a roar of laughter from ringsiders when Watson replied, 'I don't get the chance!'"

As so often happens in untidy contests of this nature however, Watson received a cut eye that forced him to pull out of his fight with Orlandi at Liverpool. Jimmy Walsh grabbed the chance to stand in for Watson and came through with a fine victory over the Italian. Tommy was there that night, but only as a second to his new protege, Billy Charlton.

"When I first went down to be Watson's sparring partner," Billy told me, "I was to get thirty shillings a week, but after the first week he asked me if, instead of paying me would I rather he got me a job on his bills. I jumped at the chance, since I hadn't expected to get paid for sparring anyway. My first job was in Liverpool, Tommy wasn't on the bill but I'm sure he was supposed to be. Well, I don't know what was wrong with me because I had never been troubled with nerves before.

"I don't know but I must have boxed terribly because Tommy gave me a right coating when I came back to my corner at the end of the first round. I was on the deck two or three times and I don't know why, I didn't feel any punches on my chin, I didn't feel hurt in any way, not fuzzy nor dizzy. At the start of the second round I am put down again and the referee stops it and sends me to my corner. I was disgusted with myself and wondered if Tommy would bother with me after that, but not to worry, Tommy said nothing and put it down to nerves.

"Tommy's next bout was at Carmarthen in Wales and he had me on also. We travelled down in Tommy's car, it was great, and Tommy boxed well to beat Nobby Baker on points. I put Tommy in a good mood by beating Cliff Peregrine inside the distance. Tommy's next bout didn't have me on the bill. He was to box that great featherweight champion of the world from the Unites States, Freddie Miller."

30

SOUTHPAW NEMESIS

In 1933, the *New York Sun* held a National Boxing Consensus to determine the best fighters in the game, pound-for-pound. The results saw Freddie Miller in third place after Barney Ross and Max Baer. One leading sportswriter called Miller, "..a quick thinker with lightning reflexes, his footwork the envy of any great dancer, his work was magnetic, he was a pint-sized giant of technique."

Freddie Miller was undoubtedly one of the greatest and certainly one of the most popular American fighters ever to campaign in Britain. "There was never an inch wasted when Miller was in the ring," wrote Norman Hurst. "Every move, every gesture, had its uses. A sway of the body and he was in or out of distance...the lithe looseness of every move of Miller's, the easy play of the powerful muscles as they slid up and down his back as he swung his arms to loosen up, told the story of a fit man all ready to go!"

Yet when he came to Britain in 1934, Miller surprised the boxing writers by seemingly spending more time on the golf course than in the gym. As manager Pete Reilly explained however, "Freddie is a good-living lad, he does not need what your athletes call special training. Golf is ideal, after all it is merely roadwork."

"Golf helps me get in condition, and relaxes my mind," explained Freddie. "In the gym, or in the ring with a crowd looking on, what's the difference?"

Miller always maintained that the best training was actual ring fights and he carried out his belief during his first visit to Britain. In just ten months the American crammed in 35 fights, losing only two while boxing one draw and one No Decision bout. He appeared in rings all over Britain, Ireland, Spain, France, Belgium, and Majorca. Freddie proved a boon to the small promoter and would box for as little as £50 a fight! When he fought Liverpool's Billy Gannon at Belle Vue, Manchester, the American was disqualified for an accidental low blow. It was a charity show and Miller, who had refused to take any purse, was fined a fiver for hitting low!

Freddie Miller was raised in Cincinnati, Ohio, where he was born of German-American parents. He was a baby-faced, half-pint of a kid when he started boxing in a local amateur club and only sixteen when he became a professional fighter. Freddie won his first fight wearing a pair of red woollen shorts and, believing them to be lucky, wore them every time he went in the ring. When manager Danny Davis bought him a new pair of red silk trunks, Freddie wore them reluctantly. Davis scoffed at the kid's superstition when he won the city championship, but Freddie had the last laugh, he had worn his old 'lucky' shorts under the new pair!

At nineteen, young Miller was fighting his way up the ladder when he signed for the best match of his life, he married his sweetheart Louise Somhorst. Louise became not only Mrs Freddie Miller, she became his financial adviser, banker, accountant, and investment broker. Her original engagement ring contained only one tiny diamond chip, but as the size of Freddie's purses increased, so did the size of her ring. "I must have had fourteen or fifteen engagement rings before he bought me this one," she would recall in later years.

Just before they were married, Freddie was knocked out in a severe bout of pneumonia, and was so ill doctors thought he would never box again. Rumours swept the city that he had died and the hospital switchboard was swamped with a thousand calls. But the little fighter won through and was back in the ring after six months!

He was only twenty when landing a shot at world featherweight champion Battling Battalino, in an open-air fight in Cincinnati. The kid was in over his head and the veteran won easily, dumping Freddie twice in the eighth round on the way to the decision. Young Miller won something that night, the admiration of Battalino's manager Pete Reilly, and when the champ left town next morning, Reilly had Freddie Miller's signature on a contract.

Many years later, Battalino would reveal to author Peter Heller, "Pete Reilly, my manager, wanted me to buy Miller's contract. I bought his contract for thirty-five hundred dollars, so it would be Reilly and me, be business managers of Freddie Miller. I was supposed to throw the title to him but I was disqualified. I wasn't even throwing no punches. I'd get hit and I'd be all covered up, just as if I was afraid. I laid down, stretched out. The referee says for me to get up. I told him to count. He says no contest. They suspended me for a month and that's all there is to that!"

That second fight came in January, 1932, by which time Battalino was having trouble making the featherweight limit. Reilly figured he may as well keep things in the family and matched his fading champ with the new kid on the block, but the Connecticut Boxing Commission refused to sanction the fight between the two stablemates even though Battalino was a Hartford man. So Reilly took them to Miller's hometown. The old champ came in three pounds overweight and tried to throw the fight to Miller, but Referee Lou Bauman wouldn't buy it and declared a No Contest in the third round. Reilly promptly claimed the title for Miller but within twenty-four hours both the National Boxing Association and the New York State Athletic Commission had suspended Battalino and declared the title vacant.

The NBA, which then governed boxing in some thirty states, staged an elimination tournament to find a new champion and, to everyone's surprise, Miller was beaten in his first bout by Frankie Wallace. When Tommy Paul of Buffalo emerged as the NBA's champion, Pete Reilly went after him for a title shot for Miller. They had already split a pair of decisions and the rubber match was scheduled for the Chicago Stadium in January, 1933.

It was Friday the thirteenth, but Freddie Miller was no longer superstitious and in front of 6,000 fans he hammered his way to the championship over ten rounds. Paul opened well, drilling in rights to head and body and one sizzling right late in the third round sent Miller reeling into the ropes. But Freddie fought back in the fourth and with some beautiful boxing began to take charge of the contest. Tommy rallied in the seventh but Miller was back in the driving seat in round eight and crossed the line a good winner. Pete Reilly was a happy man that night as he embraced his third featherweight champion. He had managed Frenchman Andre Routis who took the title from Tony Canzoneri before losing it to Battalino!

In the American fight game, Pete Reilly was known as the Silver Fox, the Sage of Bay Ridge, Brooklyn. "He is a credit to boxing," Maurie Waxman wrote in the *1937 Everlast Boxing Record.* "I have seen him walk over to a youngster suffering from ring injuries, press a bank note in his palm, and walk off just as casually as though nothing had happened...Reilly has managed and handled some of the greatest money makers in boxing in the past twelve years or more, including Jack Delaney, Andre Routis, Bat Battalino, Freddie Miller, Wesley Ramey, Sammy Vogel, and Mike Belloise. At one time he had more than just a little to do with Max Schmeling. His fighters were all big money getters and all of them, so far as I know, wound up with enough to carry them along in comfort and leisure for the rest of their days on this earth. He is pleasant and genial and has a sunny disposition. He asks only one thing of his legion of friends, 'Do for me only what I would do for you.'"

In September 1934, Reilly brought Freddie Miller to Liverpool to defend his title against British champion Nel Tarleton for a reported purse of £2,500. "I like this title," Miller told reporters when he arrived on Merseyside. "It keeps me warm in winter. I aim to keep it for my old age."

He kept it that night at Anfield in a brilliant contest and there was no dissent from the 31,000 Tarleton fans when Freddie had his glove raised at the final bell. Showing footwork rarely seen in a British ring, he danced in and out of Nel's guard, hitting at every opportunity. It looked all over in the sixth when Tarleton was dumped on the canvas, but he got up and fought back and in round nine it was the American who wobbled from one of the hardest right hooks Tarleton ever threw. Nel's nose was bleeding heavily and Miller turned on the pressure through the final rounds to clinch the verdict.

Freddie had left his pretty young wife Louise and their baby Pat back home in Cincinnati, expecting to be away just a few weeks. He was away eleven months! "Every time we thought he'd sail for home," recalled Louise, "someone, somewhere, wanted a return bout. We couldn't plan to join him because his plans were constantly changing."

Freddie had nine fights in Liverpool and Johnny Best Jnr, son of the famous promoter, later wrote, "Miller was undoubtedly the most popular American boxer ever to visit Merseyside. He and his manager, that grand person Pete Reilly, made a host of friends in Liverpool. I remember when Reilly was returning to America how he went into the Stadium, where the 'chars' were cleaning up, and gave them each a note. No wonder they called him the manager with a million friends!

"Miller feared no fighter. There was the occasion when there was a big charity show being staged at Liverpool Stadium. The main attraction was a bout between Jackie Brown, world's flyweight champion, and an Italian, Cavagnoli. Just before the contest Brown had to cry off owing to illness. It was decided to put on a new top of the bill, Miller versus Jimmy Stewart. Miller and his manager were on the Continent, but Mr Best got in touch with them and told Pete Reilly the situation. 'Okay,' he replied, 'we're catching the next plane.' No question about weight or purse, and this despite the fact that Stewart was one of the hardest punching lightweights in the country. Although considerably outweighed, Miller registered a points win."

In December 1934, the American fought European champion Jose Girones in Barcelona and won on a foul in the fifth round. The Spaniard had done well up to the unfortunate ending and demanded a return with the world championship at stake.

Reilly agreed, but his terms were somewhat unusual. If Miller lost, he was to be paid three times the agreed purse! Pete wasn't taking any chances. Neither did Freddie. Before 40,000 excited fans in the Bull Ring he knocked out Girones with one punch!

The handsome little personality puncher and his silver-haired, silver-tongued manager barnstormed around Britain and the Continent winning fights and friends wherever they went...Manchester, London, Newcastle, Glasgow, Barcelona, Liverpool, Paris, Madrid, Brussels and Belfast. Between fighting and travelling, Miller didn't have time to train. He had to buy another suitcase just to stick the destination labels on!

Ernie Jarvis, the great little flyweight from Milwall who gave the ill-fated Johnny Hill two stiff arguments for the British and European titles and took Hill's place against Frankie Genaro for the world championship in 1929, later became a boxing columnist for *The People*. Recording the untimely death of Freddie Miller in May 1962, Jarvis wrote of, "the man who was perhaps the best southpaw the ring produced. Miller was a colourful, aggressive fighter, a great puncher, and equally a great drawing card. His willingness to fight anybody made him popular with boxing promoters in the hungry 'thirties. He was also a great enthusiast for the dog tracks, Harringay, White City, and Wembley waited eagerly for him after each fight. With my old pal, his manager

Pete Reilly, he would bet high, wide, and handsome. He lost a lot of money at these places, but it was fun while it lasted."

Since losing to Miller at Anfield, Nel Tarleton had begged Johnny Best for a rematch and it was agreed they meet again in Liverpool, this time at the Stanley Dog Track, 12 June 1935. The American did a bit more training for this one, telling reporters, "This guy Tarleton is pretty good!"

Tarleton took comfort from three things as he prepared for the big one; nobody had ever beaten him twice, the fight was in Liverpool so he would be able to go for his customary early morning walk in Newsham Park, and he would be wearing his old boxing boots. "If I don't wear my old boots, I don't win," he said.

"It didn't look as though his boots were going to help him in the opening round, unless he was going to kick Miller!" one observer wrote of the fight. "The Yank stormed into his man with a ferocity that shook everyone, including Nella, and down he went for a seven count. But as always he got up and in round six surprised Miller by turning fighter and punching away with the southpaw. After twelve rounds Freddie's title was up for grabs and Tarleton was reaching for it. The turning point came in unlucky round thirteen as Miller rushed Nel through the ropes, out of the ring and on to the floor, and tumbled out on top of him! That took the wind out of Nel and from then Miller was on top, taking Jack Smith's decision at the final bell, a signal for the fans to show their opinion as they threw all sorts into the ring, from rolled-up programmes to beer bottles and even sods pulled from the pitch. 'I enjoyed every minute of it,' said Miller afterwards. 'It will live forever in my memory. It was a pity such a great fighter as Nel Tarleton had to lose.'"

In the 19 June issue of *Boxing*, the Editor wrote, "At Liverpool on Thursday Johnny Best has assuredly backed a winner in bringing together Freddie Miller and Seaman Watson. This is a match that will go as near as anything can do towards setting the Mersey on fire. The American has so far proved invincible...If Miller is to be beaten on this side of the Atlantic, Watson appears the only man likely to accomplish the feat."

Pete Reilly had returned to America by this time, leaving Freddie in the capable hands of Johnny Best, the Liverpool promoter. When the match with Watson was made, Reilly cabled Best to say that should Watson beat Miller he would be able to offer him a shot at world lightweight champion Tony Canzoneri in the States.

When the offer was relayed to Watson at his gym in Walkergate, he refused to comment on it, merely saying, "I'm okay, I'll do my best." His best still looked pretty good to the *Chronicle* man when he paid a visit a few days before the fight. "Watson was especially pleasing in his inside work," he wrote, "and he has trained down to 9st 9lbs, the stipulated weight for the fight. Tommy has had two southpaw sparring partners working with him and one of them told me, 'If Watson reproduces his present punching power next Thursday then Miller will know he has been in a fight.'"

Pete Reilly had seen Watson in his American fights with LaBarba and Kid Chocolate and he cabled Miller instructions on how to box the man from Newcastle. That night at Anfield, 12,000 fans sat in a torrential downpour and not one of them left his seat till the final bell ended a memorable encounter. Miller won all right but the decision was not a popular one and the crowd booed when Referee Jack Smith of Manchester held up Miller's glove.

The taller of the two, Watson boxed cleverly in the early rounds, scoring with heavy short punches inside to the American's jaw. A roar went up from the fans in the second round when Seaman smashed a right to the head and the American went down. He was back on his feet at three and the bell stopped Watson doing any more damage. Tommy tried desperately to follow up his advantage in the third but Miller twice sent him to the boards for short counts with right hooks to the jaw.

In round four Miller again floored Watson with a tremendous left swing to the head and Tommy took nine before getting back into the fight. The southpaw American was hitting with more power now and in the fifth Watson could do little bar land a few lefts to the face. Miller's footwork was a revelation and Watson was having difficulty pinning him down. He himself was pinned down on the canvas again in the sixth when a whistling right swing found his chin and Mr Smith counted eight before he got up.

The Geordie rallied in the seventh round and his body punching was particularly effective as the crowd got behind him. Both men were big favourites with the Liverpool fans and this was a helluva fight! Watson fought well in the last two rounds, crowding his man and hammering the body, but Miller was boxing like the champion he was and his fancy footwork kept him out of harm's

271

way as they fought down to the wire. Despite the crowd's reaction to the verdict for the American, most reporters considered it a fair one. John Mortimer was not satisfied however, and he issued a challenge to Miller for a return bout with a sidestake of £500. The American, who was finally talking of returning home, said he would have the fight and back himself. Pete Reilly cabled acceptance and Johnny Best signed the fight for Thursday 25 July 1935 at the Liverpool F.C. ground.

Before then however, Watson had another date in Liverpool, fifteen rounds with Frankie Brown. The drawn-out elimination series to find a challenger for Kid Berg's British lightweight title was finally reaching the end of the road, with the winner of Watson and Brown to face George Daly of Blackfriars who had just beaten Jimmy Walsh on points. The Board of Control appointed Mr Ben Hardwicke of Wales as third man in the ring when Seaman climbed through the ropes at the Stanley Track to meet Brown, the reserve who had replaced Harry Mizler.

For ten rounds the reserve fully justified his selection as he gave a sterling display, and the former featherweight champion, who at times boxed below his best form, was fully extended. But whenever Brown landed a decent punch, Watson was stung to retaliation and his blows were by far the harder. In round fourteen the Seaman stepped up a gear and Brown was sent crashing to the canvas from thudding rights to the jaw. With seven seconds left in the round Mr Hardwicke decided Frankie Brown had taken enough for one night and called a halt. Seaman Watson was now just one fight away from a crack at the lightweight championship of Great Britain.

However, as Billy Charlton recalled for me, "It was becoming clear to me that Tommy's heart wasn't in the game like it had previously been, the training and such was beginning to be a bit of a drag for Tommy, but we still had some right barneys in the gym. I was forever trying to give him stick and he used to go all out with me, but of course he wasn't the Tommy Watson of some four or five years previously. But he was still boxing regularly and once again he fixed me up with a bout on his next bill. He was boxing a return with Freddie Miller and there was quite a crowd of us set off from Newcastle for Liverpool.

"I well remember going down in the train and one of the company asking Tommy if he was going to win this time. Tommy's only comment was, 'If this fellow hits me in the solar plexus like he did in the last bout then I am stopping on the floor.' I was to follow Tommy's bout and naturally I wanted to see him box the world champion, so I pleaded with Tommy to let me go down and watch it. 'All right,' he said, 'but get well wrapped up and ready to go straight in after me.' They found me a seat right down at the ringside and I settled down to watch the big fight, my own contest with Les Carter pushed right to the back of my mind!"

Another ringsider with more than a passing interest in the fight was American manager Al Lippe who had just arrived in Liverpool with a couple of fighters, Phil Zwick and Vernon Cormier. One night Al was sitting in the hotel lounge when he overheard two racing men discussing the coming fight. One of the men wanted to lay odds that Miller couldn't knock Watson out. Lippe asked him what odds he would lay and when he replied, "five-to-one" Al put his money down and the bet was struck. When Freddie Miller heard about the bet however, he found himself in a bit of a quandary. Pete Reilly had already cabled his instructions from America, "Do not risk a KO. Win on points." If Freddie carried out Pete's orders, his friend Al Lippe would lose his money! The American fighter was staying with promoter Johnny Best and the night before the fight he told Best that he was going to disobey Reilly's wishes. "I will try a punch on Watson," he said, "and if it lands he will go out like a light. He won't see where it came from."

One man who saw every punch was Norman Hurst, chief boxing reporter for the Kemsley Press, and he recalled them graphically many years later in his book *Big Fight Thrills*. Referring to Watson as, "One of the toughest fighters this country has ever produced," Hurst wrote, "There was a solid ruggedness about Watson, which to those who had seen him in his last fight with Miller, was a good enough sign to start betting on. Mr 'Pickles' Douglas, son of a family of referees, handled the contest. Just a short lecture to the boys and he waved a hand to the timekeeper to let him know that all was ready to start. Miller walked coolly from his corner, his right glove, as was his wont, pawing tentatively towards his man's face... The seaman was bent upon getting into action. He was in there for battle rather than any finesse and with real sailor-like bluntness he carried the fight to his man.

"He charged in and smashed a right that landed high up on Miller's cheekbone! There was a cheer which was repeated as the gallant tar followed up the punch with a hard right drive to the body as Miller coolly broke ground before Watson's determined

273

attack. Miller timed his man's rush and banged home a left to Watson's body. Tommy gasped as the blow registered, but fought back fiercely while those in his corner urged him on. Angered by the very thought that he was being outfought, and forced on the defensive before such a big crowd in the city where he had made himself a favourite, Miller for once lost the iron control he usually kept over himself in a fight. He forgot finesse, the value of footwork. His eyes blazing with fury, Miller drove in to trade blows with the ready and willing Watson. The gong sounded with the two boys pounding away at each other while from the ringside to the back of the big Anfield stands, yells of applause greeted their epic battle. What a round, and Watson took the honours.

"Advice was ladled out freely in the precious minute's interval between the rounds. 'Keep on top,' I heard Watson's second whisper to the flushed and confident Tyneside battler. In the other corner Miller was receiving a quiet dressing-down for losing his head, for forgetting his boxing, and mixing it with his rough-and-ready opponent. With a few seconds to go, Miller stood up, flexed his muscles, and stood looking to Watson's corner as if impatient for the round to start. Bets were being made round the ringside, both men having plenty of supporters who were willing to back their fancy with hard cash. If Miller had any idea of taking the initiative in the second round, his chance went in the first second, for setting himself as if ready for the old naval order of 'Boarders away!' Watson left his corner with a rush and was on top of the American and flailing away with both hands before Freddie realised what was happening!

"The crowd went mad. Here was an old favourite pounding his way to victory over a world champion, a man who had beaten the world's best and taken 'em as they came. The storm of Watson's attack drove Miller back. He tried hard to set himself and make a stand, but the punching, forceful tactics of Watson gave him little breathing space or time for thinking out any plan. Fighting desperately, Miller moved slowly backwards across, and then round the outer edges of the ring. All the time Watson was tossing in punches so fast it seemed as though the power that provided the expenditure of such energy was provided by some dynamo rather than the heart, lungs, and guts of a human being.

"Flick! Flick! would go that pawing, irritating right of Miller's in a vain effort to try and halt the pressure of his opponent. Bang! Crash! would go the right and left gloves of the sailor to the reddened ribs of the American. With every rib-scorching blow, Watson was becoming more confident. With every second that went, Miller was becoming more wary. He knew, better by far than most of those around the ring, that there must come a lull in the storm.

"Fit, game and confident as was Watson, he was only human, and he must ease up for a breather. When that moment came Freddie Miller had made up his mind that with the breath he had been saving, he would step in, make one big effort and try to swing the fight in his favour. But I make so bold to say that even · Miller himself never dreamed that there could be such a reversal of positions as was soon to be brought about. Flushed with success, and with the knowledge that he could and had made the redoubtable American back away from him, Watson started to become careless. The guard that he had kept well up, and which had provided a sound defence to the left swings that Miller had made for the jaw, began to drop.

"Miller was watching. He saw that his chance was coming. Watson staged still another rush. He scored with both gloves hard to the body. Miller never flinched. Watson, pleased as punch at what he had done, danced away, and, under the impression that he was out of distance, and safe, dropped his hands. Miller had, however, not stood still. He also had moved, ever so slightly it is true, but he had moved, and had slithered forward on flat feet as Watson danced back, and when Tommy dropped his arms Miller acted like a striking rattlesnake! His pawing right flicked out towards Watson's face, and almost simultaneously, his left glove started from away below his knee on its 'rock' em to sleep' message!

"Ringsiders saw it, we in the Press seats saw it, someone yelled, 'Watch it, Tommy.' Too late Watson made a surprised and bewildered attempt to guard this surprise punch that was being hurled at him from nowhere. He was too late, the bandaged fist inside Miller's glove was as tightly shut and as hard as any knobkerrie. The glove zoomed upwards, and landed on Watson's jaw with a smash that made a noise like a mallet landing on a fence stake! Watson's arms flew high in the air! His whole body started to spin backwards and over as if he were trying to turn a back somersault, and his feet were still high in the air when the back of his head hit the floor of the ring with a bang that could be heard five rows back in the ringside seats!

"As the timekeeper called 'Two,' Referee Douglas was across the ring, and standing over the prone form of the punch-drugged fighter, took up the count. At 'Five' some inner consciousness that is in all game fighters rung the bell in Watson's brain that he was DOWN and MUST get up. His head moved. At 'Seven' he was trying to force his head higher and feebly feeling for a pushing off place for his hands so that he could push himself erect.

"Nine came with the gallant sailor making a heroic bid to beat the count, while Miller waited like a stalking tiger, and front row ringsiders held their breath, wondering would the game warrior make it! At last 'Out' said Referee Douglas and with a whoop of glee Freddie Miller leaped a couple of feet in the air, happy at having pulled a fight out of the fire in as spectacular a manner as the most case-hardened fight followers would wish to see in a decade of ring battles."

"I can see it to this day," recalls Billy Charlton. "The first round was keenly fought and Miller was his usual lethargic self, letting the other fellow do the leading and attacking was Miller's idea, while he would work for the opening to counter with that terrific left hook. Tommy was going forward to try and slide underneath to the body while Miller was always looking for that counter. The first round was pretty even and if anybody got it it would have been Watson, moving forward all the time.

"The second round began like the first but now Miller was attacking occasionally. About halfway through the round, as Miller was coming in to Tommy, Tommy went back into the ropes and suddenly in he goes, but Miller didn't do what Tommy expected. Tommy went at Miller with his hands held low to cover his solar but Miller swung that vicious left hook for Tommy's unprotected chin. Down goes Tommy but in fairness to him I would say that his head hit the canvas with a terrific bang which would have floored an ox! At the count of four Tommy made as if to struggle up but as he raised his head from the canvas, suddenly flopped back again and that was that.

"As Tommy was ready to come out of the ring, I was ready to go in, and as he passed he said, 'Don't worry about what happened to me, just go in there and lick this fellow for me.' Which I did, inside two rounds."

31

THE FINAL ROUND

For the rest of that summer in 1935 following the traumatic knockout at the fists of world featherweight champion Freddie Miller, Tommy Watson took time out from the gym to take stock of his career. At twenty-seven he was hardly ready for the pipe and slippers, but he had been fighting for ten years with 120 professional fights against the best in the business. Only six men had lowered his colours, but you can't walk in the rain without getting wet and there had been many tough nights out there on that canvas battlefield, and none tougher than that last fight with Miller when the American left him unconscious in the Liverpool ring.

In one of his early fights, while he was still in the Navy, Tommy had suffered a temporary loss of memory after taking a blow to the side of the head. "Matter of fact, I was scared then," he would recall. "I'd seen enough of injuries to other blokes to warn me off."

Following the second defeat by Miller, speculation was rife that Watson was about to hang up his gloves. A Glasgow promoter made it known that he had received a letter from the Newcastle fighter stating that he was soon to retire. However, when a *Chronicle* reporter asked Tommy about it, he said that the letter had been a reply to the promoter saying that the purse offered for a Glasgow fight with Jake Kilrain was unacceptable. To the retirement rumour, Tommy added that he had as yet made no decision.

He was of course still in the frame for a challenge to Kid Berg for his British lightweight title, with only George Daly standing between him and the champion. The Board had asked for purse offers by 30 July and Mr John Paget had tendered on behalf of New St James's Hall in Newcastle. At the end of August came the good news/bad news announcements.

Mr Paget received confirmation from the Board that his purse

277

bid for the Watson-Daly final eliminating contest had been accepted, but no sooner had he set the date for 30 September, with seat prices at 7/6 ringside, 6/- outer ring, 4/- balcony, and 2/- gallery, than both Watson and Daly said they were not willing to box for the purse on offer. It was £175 and it was not enough!

"That total purse of £175 is a sum I would want for myself," Watson told the *Chronicle*, "and in view of the fact that I have received more for fights of much less importance, I think I am entitled to it. Sooner than agree to the sharing of such a purse, I would hang up my gloves."

At the same time, a telegram arrived from manager Ted Broadribb in London, stating, "Purse offer no good. Daly refuses."

"It can be pointed out," reported the *Chronicle*, "that Watson and Daly received double this purse figure in their eliminating contests with Frankie Brown and Jimmy Walsh respectively."

Low as it was, the winning purse bid by Paget was one of only two submitted within the Board's time limit, yet when both fighters refused to accept the purse and talk of a money match between them hit the sports pages, no fewer than four promoters came up with offers up to £250 with London, Plymouth, Portsmouth, and Swansea interested. The Board of Control gave the boxers until 17 September to confirm their acceptance of the Newcastle bid, and when this was not forthcoming, the Board issued the following statement; "Seaman Tommy Watson (Newcastle) and George Daly (London) having withdrawn from the final eliminating contest for the lightweight championship of Great Britain by refusing to accept the highest purse offered, received, and approved by the Board, the Stewards have decided to call upon Jack Kid Berg, holder of the title, to defend same against Jim Walsh (Chester)."

In a lengthy interview with the *Chronicle*, Watson explained his reasons for turning down the Newcastle purse offer. For such an important fight, he pointed out his training expenses alone would be £70, and with other necessary expenses he reckoned he would lose even if he collected the winner's share which would be £105.

"When you go into big boxing," he said, "you have to do big spending. Three featherweight championship fights, with Kid Chocolate for the world title, and with Nel Tarleton and Johnny McMillan for the British title, brought me in roughly £2,500. But let me tell you that if the fight with Chocolate meant £1,000 to me, the expenses were so heavy that I came back to Southampton with a dime in my pocket and in debt to the extent of a few hundred pounds as the result of the trip. I cannot now expect to remain in the game for a long spell and what contests I undertake have to be paying propositions."

In this respect, the offer of a fight with Daly for £100 a side and a purse of £500 made by Jeff Dickson, the Paris-based American then putting on shows at the Royal Albert Hall in London, found Seaman Watson a willing listener. John Mortimer agreed to the sidestake and the contest was on, scheduled for Wednesday 2 October 1935, twelve rounds at the lightweight limit of 9st 9lbs.

George Daly was born in Lambeth, London, in 1914, just a month or two after his father was killed in the retreat from Mons. A baby-faced kid, George got into boxing through his elder brother Tom. "Tommy became a pro boxer appearing often at Blackfriars Ring," he told Ron Olver of *Boxing News*, "so I became a programme seller so I could watch him box. He trained at Duffett's Gym in Camberwell so I followed him and had a couple of bouts with Lynn ABC. I was a southpaw and Tommy spent hours trying to change me to orthodox. He eventually succeeded. One day I met Bill Klein who ran a gym at Fitzroy Square and he asked if I would like to turn pro at Kingston Baths, a quid for six rounds. So after paying my fares I would be left with fifteen bob! I beat Jackie Jordan and that was how it started.

"After a few more contests Billy O'Doherty told me that I had attracted the attention of Jeff Dickson and his agent Ted Broadribb, so I went up to their office and Ted became my manager. I became Dickson's office boy. Some thought this was a job in name only but I worked hard, typing, collecting and delivering letters." One of young Daly's chores was to fetch a packet of twenty cigarettes for Dickson each morning. He was always told to keep the change out of the pound note, and when Dickson asked him one day what he did with the money, George replied, "I give it to my mother, sir." Dickson promptly gave him another fiver!

A gentleman in and out of the ring, George Daly was never known to swear, and he had one rule about his professional boxing career, nothing would prevent him attending Mass each Sunday. He was a brilliant boxer who could punch a bit when he had to, stopping men like Norman Snow and George Odwell. One night, at Manor Place Baths in London, George boxed a young lad to a standstill and the kid hasn't hit George yet! After receiving the decision, Daly stepped down from the ring to be confronted by the boy's mother. She swung her handbag at George who instinctively pulled back his head, remarking, "You're just like the lad, Ma, you're always just out of distance!"

With men such as Sonny Lee, Len Wickwar, Pat Butler, Tommy Hyams, Snow, and Odwell among his victims, Daly was included in the eliminators set up by the Board to find a challenger for Kid Berg. In his first contest George travelled to Mountain Ash to fight Boyo Rees in his own backyard, winning the decision in what one reporter called, "one of the finest bouts seen in Wales for a decade." That fight was in March 1935 and a week later Daly was ruled out for an alleged low blow against Jimmy Walsh which many observers considered a fair punch. That unfortunate defeat snapped Daly's unbeaten run of 54 fights over three years!

A few months later George met Walsh in an eliminator, on Jimmy's door-step in Liverpool, dazzling the Chester man with his speed and putting him down in rounds ten and twelve on his way to the decision. Between those two fights with Jimmy Walsh, Daly met the Italian champion Carlo Orlandi at the Royal Albert Hall. A friend had told George that Orlandi was deaf, so he dropped his gloves during one round and half turned to his corner as though the bell had rung. Carlo was not kidded! "His right hook nearly tore my head off," smiled George later.

When the final eliminator threw Daly and Watson together, Jeff Dickson could see a major London attraction looming with the Blackfriars boxer against Kid Berg for the British title, a sure box office winner for the capital. All George had to do was beat Seaman Watson! Dickson and Broadribb agreed that the youngster, still seven weeks shy of his twenty-first birthday, would stand a much better chance in London than in Newcastle, and Dickson was prepared to pay good money to see that he had that chance. So Broadribb sent the telegram to John Paget, "Purse offer no good. Daly refuses." Since it was already known that Watson himself was unhappy with the purse, which would be split £105 to the winner and £70 for the loser, Dickson found Watson, John Mortimer, and Alec Lambert easy to do business with and the fight was set for the Albert Hall, 2 October 1935.

"Tommy Watson never confided in me," recalled Billy Charlton, "maybe I was just a boy and too young for Tommy to tell a confidence to, but I do know from all I heard in the gym that the purse tendered by Mr Paget was ridiculously low and the boxers weren't going to accept it. I thought Tommy was a fool because he would have been at home for all his training, no change of water, and no strange beds nor strange environment."

"Tonight," ran one newspaper story, "Watson and Daly meet under Jeff Dickson's promotion and despite the action of the Board the general opinion is that the winner will be the right person to challenge Berg. Instead of being over fifteen rounds, tonight's fight is over twelve rounds at the class limit for £100 a side. Daly is years younger than Watson and regarded as better versed in the finer points, but Watson is still one of the best fighters in the country at short range and this plus his experience in major fights is expected to win him the fight."

Daly had suffered from a bad cold and postponement was considered at one point, but he rallied and looked fit enough at the weigh-in when he scaled 9st 8½lbs, with Watson just four ounces heavier. When the two contenders climbed through the ropes later that night however, whatever they did their fight was never going to match the sensational contest that had just ended, leaving the Albert Hall crowd limp with excitement.

For seven rounds, Harry Mizler, the former British lightweight champion, had been punched all over the ring and floored six times by Gustave Humery, the French Tiger. Coming out for the eighth round however, Mizler had stunned Humery with a sizzling right to the jaw. Seizing his chance, the Londoner savaged the Tiger with a barrage of punches that had him reeling drunkenly all over the ring. Humery finally escaped by turning to his corner, holding his left glove up in the air, the signal for manager Louis De Pnthieu to throw in the towel. That desperate, magnificent right hand punch had broken Humery's jaw and Mizler's final blows had broken his spirit.

"The scenes after this sensational ending," wrote Gilbert Odd in his book *Ring Battles of the Century*, "were the most extraordinary I have ever witnessed. The air literally vibrated with the storm of cheering that followed the M.C.'s announcement that the Britisher had won. The ringside patrons, as with those in the far away tiers, rose to their feet as a man; hats and programmes were thrown into the air, arms were waved, and the officials had the utmost difficulty in preventing the ring from being stormed by the over-excited spectators. Mizler, who in this great hour of victory, was finding it hard to smile and forget his bruised and battered body, was lifted high on the shoulders of his seconds and marched round the ring to further add to the excitement."

Despite the former champion having stolen their thunder, Seaman Watson and young George Daly answered the bell that night each determined to prove that he was the rightful challenger to Kid Berg, the man who had beaten Mizler for the title some twelve months previously.

The *Newcastle Journal* reported next morning, "George Daly set his feet firmly on the championship ladder last night when he beat Watson who was handicapped by a cut left eye which happened in the opening seconds of round one! Daly played on the cut and blood streamed down Watson's face all through the contest. Watson fought bravely until the eighth round was almost over before having to retire.

"I sat under Watson's corner and I thought he started well against a boxer who used to be promoter Dickson's office boy. In went Watson, both hands working, Daly clinched, and it appeared more by accident than design that Watson broke away with his eye deeply cut. The injury was patched frequently afterwards but re-opened and in the end Watson was practically boxing blind. Sometimes he boxed well, but Daly was cool and carried on steadily, preferring long range exchanges.

"Whenever Watson got close he punched to good advantage and Daly was on the ropes more than once. I thought he kept his head rather low when he decided to swap punches. Twice Watson slipped and he had nothing like the snap in his work that made him a champion. Watson, in my view, might have been too strong for Daly but for the cut eye. 'He can scarcely see,' his manager told me as the fight went on. I hesitate to judge him as a title challenger in the circumstances. Perhaps the wonderful fight that preceded this one spoiled the interest. Daly was perhaps as lucky as Mizler for he did not have the better of the exchanges until the cut eye told its inevitable tale."

"NOT HIS LUCKY NIGHT," headlined the *Evening Chronicle* story. "Tommy Watson, the Newcastle lightweight boxer, had a hectic bout so long as it lasted with George Daly of London at the

Royal Albert Hall last night and his opponent by what may be described as a somewhat lucky win is now to be considered a probable opponent to Kid Berg for the title. It was an unfortunate affair for Watson who had a cut opened above his left eye in the opening clash, and from this handicap onwards he was always waging a losing battle. It was therefore no surprise when in the eighth round he retired. Daly had administered severe punishment in close quarter work, but Watson had 'lammed' him very severely in several rounds, particularly in the third. In the next Daly was booed for the manner in which he used his glove to start the bleeding from Watson's eye afresh, but Watson fought on well under a big handicap until in the seventh he appeared to weaken."

With the eye injury still giving Tommy concern, a proposed fight with Joe Connelly at Glasgow had to be cancelled, and when a reporter asked him if he had come to a decision regarding his boxing future, Tommy just shrugged his shoulders, saying, "It just depends."

The decision was not long in coming however. On Tuesday 15 October 1935, the *Chronicle* reported "Watson's Farewell…With the announcement by Tommy Watson, the Newcastle lightweight, that he has bid goodbye to the ring, there goes the man who more than anyone else in recent years brought the North-East into the boxing limelight. Our only Lonsdale Belt winner, his was a national name in the game and the big regret in his own area is that his admirers did not have the opportunity of witnessing him gaining his biggest distinctions in Newcastle's rings. Still, they saw him a sufficient number of times in Newcastle to realise that the object of their admiration was a credit to the game.

"In the ring he was a gentleman: outside he was one of those fellows who had little to say. Never boastful, he would tell me before a contest, 'I'll do my best,' and afterwards, 'I did my best.' Tommy Watson's exit has been occasioned by a damaged eye. This particular optic has troubled him for some time, and there being possibilities of great danger he makes his decision thinking more of the future than the present."

"Tommy got beaten that night at the Albert Hall," recalled Billy Charlton, "but anyone who knew Tommy Watson would have realised that it wasn't the same Watson that night in London compared to a few years back."

The day before Watson's retirement was announced in the *Chronicle*, the Board of Control held a meeting in London attended by Kid Berg, Jimmy Walsh, Norman Snow, and Harry Mizler. The claims of the former champion were pushed after his amazing victory over Humery, but Harry told the Stewards that he could not guarantee to be fit for championship boxing by any specified date, and Walsh was named to meet Berg for his title.

My old pal Joe Shepherd was a boxer, second, promoter, and manager before becoming matchmaker at New St James's Hall. Whenever we talked of Seaman Watson, Joe would say, "In my opinion, John Mortimer committed a grave managerial error in pulling Tommy out of that final eliminator with Daly in Newcastle. As things turned out, Jimmy Walsh went on to stop Berg in nine rounds to become British lightweight champion. When they had fought at Liverpool, which was like his own backyard to Walsh, Watson had thrashed Jimmy. So sorely punished was Walsh that he tried to leave the ring before the fight was ended and had to be restrained by manager Tony Vairo. For my money, Tommy Watson would have been ten-to-one on to beat Kid Berg and win his second British championship."

32

PRIVATE LIVES IN PUBLIC HOUSES

"George Daly, that was his last fight," remembered Frances. "He always said that Jimmy Falcus let him down, 'cause he left his corner. He was away from the corner, Jimmy Falcus had been with him through thick and thin but Jimmy liked his beer, he was there at the fight but he wasn't there when he was needed so they threw the towel in. He had two terrific cut eyes, they were just like fishes' mouths! They were opened up and that was when they threw the towel in. And he was a nobody, George Daly, he was a nobody compared to our Tom, and that was his last fight."

"I think that Daly and I were justified in taking the stand we did and refusing to fight for such a purse," said Tommy. "We received consolation in the £500 purse offered by Mr Jeff Dickson. My end, as the loser, was £210 and of this sum I cleared about £140...had we fought in Newcastle for the £175 purse one of us would have been on the losing side financially."

"When he came home," said Frances, "I used to have a meal ready for them when they came home from the fights, and our Kitty said it is either his eyesight or his career, and he has chosen his eyesight. They all knew where his weak spots were at the end, and I suppose it is the way they go on, if they have a weak spot, the opposite party will go for it. Our Kitty was behind him to pack it all in and that was it."

The Newcastle *Sunday Sun*, the paper young Tommy Watson sold on the streets of Byker, carried the exclusive announcement of his retirement from boxing in its issue dated 13 October 1935. In the first of a series of articles entitled Inside Secrets of the Ring, Tommy wrote, "I have decided to hang up the gloves for good!...My decision is quite final. There will not be any attempt at a comeback and my boxing career has definitely come to an end. Why? The deciding factor has been my eyes. During the past two years I have sustained a number of severe cuts on the eyes and I am not going to risk the possibility of blindness."

Within a few hours of the paper hitting the street, Tommy would record later, "I was approached by a group of Newcastle sportsmen who were ready to put up a sidestake of £1,000 for me to fight Kid Berg, whether it be for the championship or not. Two of these enthusiastic sportsmen were personal friends of mine, Mr P Wears and Mr E Wears, who, perhaps, were surprised when I straightaway refused the offer, and once again gave my decision that I had hung up my gloves for good!

"To those who think that I am a spent force as far as boxing is concerned, I will say that I am just as fit as I was a year ago and could take on the best lightweights in the country, including Kid Berg. Still, I had a grand run in boxing, I enjoyed myself, and had I got Chocolate over here I'm sure I could have taken the world title."

"George Daly was Watson's last bout," Billy Charlton remembers, "but not the last time he appeared in the ring because I can claim to be Tommy Watson's last opponent. Tommy never turned down an offer for charity and he had promised that he and I would box an exhibition bout in aid of a benefit show that was arranged for Douglas Parker, and that we did."

Within a year of hanging up his gloves however, Seaman Watson made an application to the Board of Control to get back in the ring, this time as a referee. "There was an awful lot of controversy with the Boxing Board," recalled Frances, "because of these articles he was supposed to have written in newspapers, but it wasn't what Tommy said, it was what was added to it that put him on a bad level with the Board people. Tommy was mad when the stories appeared under his name in the *Sunday Sun* following his retirement, and would cry out, 'That's not what I told them!' That was why he had no time for reporters after that and would literally chase them from his bar. Anyhow, in the end he got his licence."

On Tuesday night 23 March 1937, Seaman Tommy Watson was back in the ring at New St James's Hall in Newcastle, as referee on the Benny Sharkey benefit promotion, and he was given a big hand by the small crowd. A few months later, Joe Shepherd penned a note to the Editor of *Boxing* that read, "Ex-Seaman Tom Watson, who now holds a referee's licence, was given two contests to handle on the Jim Rice promotion last Wednesday at Belfast and Tom did his job like an old general, which looks as though the old featherweight champion will attain the same honours with the book and pencil as he did with the gloves."

When Ernie Roderick stopped Jack Powell at Liverpool Stadium in January 1938, there was a warm reception for Referee Mr T Watson when the crowd recognised the man who licked Tarleton in that same ring.

The National Sporting Club moved into new premises in March 1938, the Empress Hall at Earls Court, and celebrated with a dinner to which leading sporting personalities were invited, among them Seaman Tommy Watson. Tom worked for his dinner that night for he was in the ring afterwards handling the contest between Con Flynn, an old opponent of his, and Angus McGregor, the Scot finishing strongly to take the decision.

"London appreciated Watson as a boxer," noted the *Chronicle*, "and now he is appreciated as third man in the ring."

Joe Shepherd always told me as how he was instrumental in getting Tommy the job as resident referee at the NSC. "Watson had held his licence for a while without working a fight when I spoke to him at The Red Lion, a pub he was running in North Shields. I took him down to London where I had a couple of fighters on the bill at the National Sporting Club. Mr John E Harding, fight boss at the club, agreed to give Tommy a job as referee, and he did in fact become one of the resident third men there."

In November 1938, the *Chronicle* asked, "What About Watson? When are the claims of Seaman Tommy Watson to be recognised as a boxing referee? The British Boxing Board of Control appear to be leaving Watson high and dry with a 'B' certificate, which amounts to nothing when you consider there are three higher classes. All very discouraging, especially in view of the fact that Watson has now had considerable experience as a third man and has had numerous engagements at the NSC in London."

Maybe someone at the Board took notice, anyhow Tommy was soon handling top-of-the-bill contests. When he worked the Billy Charlton-Frank Kenny fight at Newcastle, the *Chronicle's* 'Corner Man' observed, "I though Tommy Watson did a fine job of refereeing. There was nothing ornamental in his ruling but we always knew he was there.

"That is just as refereeing should be. Boxers go into the ring to fight and Watson sees that they don't forget. He is on top of the fighters all the time and, well, let us see a bit more of this real third man business. Watson is good."

On another occasion, the *Journal* reported, "We want to see more of Tom Watson's refereeing in the Newcastle ring. He is as imperturbable as he was as a fighter and knows all the answers. What is more, the boxers know he knows them."

Of course, like every other referee, Tommy had his bad nights, and Frances told me, "I had people come over to me and say, 'How did your lad give that decision?' after some fight at St James's Hall. I used to say to him, 'Our Tommy, you're getting yourself talked about, you know!' But he would just say, 'Frances, don't let them worry you like that, because I see more inside the ring than they can see watching from outside. I hope I never give a bad decision.' He did get a bit of a name for giving bad decisions, but he never accepted it. It never worried him."

"My father ran pubs for thirty-odd years," remembers Tom Watson Jnr. "Starting at The New Hawk Inn on Byker Bank, then The Wolsington on Shields Road, and when he finished boxing in 1935 he was at The Blagdon Arms in Blyth. After a short spell at The Red Lion in North Shields, he took over The Gun on Scotswood Road in Newcastle and he was there about twenty-odd years. He was one of the first to get a music licence in the city and when he took over The Blackie Boy in the Bigg Market he transferred the licence there. He always had the place spotless, the music upstairs, no trouble, nothing. But there was this big, cheeky policeman, Inspector Scott, he had it in for my father and he would come into the pub on a regular basis and he used to give him hassle.

"There was this little bookmaker used to come in the pub every day for a drink and a chat with my mother. He took the bets in The White Horse, a pub up the street where all the police used to drink, but he never took any bets in my Dad's place. Well, he came in one day and the police followed him and made him turn out his pockets and of course he had all these betting slips. He was fined and my father was fined and he lost the licence for the pub and I went to see this Detective Latimer and he agreed it had been a set-up. It had been through Inspector Scott and that's when I went looking for him, didn't I, I was going to flatten him!"

"He was such a proud lad," recalls Frances. "I remember being in The Blackie Boy with him one Monday morning, we were behind the bar and these two detectives came through. 'Morning, Watson,' they said. 'Mr Watson from you!' snapped Tommy. When they had gone, I said, 'Our Tommy, what do you want to be like that for?' He said, 'Frances, they are out to get me, and they will.' And they did, with the betting slips. I said to him, 'Well, you prophesied all this, you asked for it, didn't you?'"

"My father was all for charities," says Tom Jnr, "boxing for the kids in Byker and having big Christmas parties for them. Poppy Days, anybody that came in the bar and didn't have a poppy, they were forced to buy one. He collected a lot of money for the Ear, Nose, and Throat Hospital, and the Newcastle Dispensary, he did them all proud. He would do it for anybody, anybody came to my father, no problem, he would do it. Sarah, who was our maid, used to collect all the money together, count it, then distribute it all around, and we would have piles of receipts lying all over the place. He was a true Geordie, a terrific Newcastle United fan, used to go all over to their matches, used to take all the bar people, have busloads, go and get all the tickets, even for the cup-ties.

"To me, he was a good father, a great little guy, and I don't think he got the breaks he deserved with the ability he had to fight, because he could really fight. Being the small man that he was, his fitness was beyond belief, he used to run around the Town Moor ten, twelve times a day. When he took over the pubs, great big fellows used to come in, three and four of them, and he would put one hand on the bar counter and vault straight over the top, bang! bang! bang! one after the other, out! But out of that he had very successful pubs because he kept law and order. He had a fantastic pub, crowds coming in, men could bring their wives in, in the tough areas like Scotswood Road, all the nice people used to come in there because they knew there was no trouble, no fights, no swearing, my father was very strict, any trouble, out!"

"My mother worked hard in the bars all her married life," remembers Seaman's oldest daughter Kath, "but she loved it. All her friends used to come in to see her. Dad knew a lot of the music hall stars through the charity work he did and I remember Sandy Powell was a very good friend. We always lived upstairs above a bar, except when he had the pubs at Blyth and North Shields where there was no living accommodation and we had a house in Woodhead Road, Walkergate. I remember when he had The Red Lion at North Shields because he wanted me to learn the piano and this man used to come and give me lessons. Well, I didn't want to play the piano so I used to hide until I heard the man's motorbike go away and then I knew it was safe to go back in the bar."

Seaman had been landlord of The Gun on Scotswood Road for about twelve months when World War II beckoned him back into uniform. He served as a Petty Officer Physical Training Instructor in the Royal Navy, based at Tor Point most of the time.

"When Tommy was called up," recalls Frances, "Kitty kept The Gun going for him, it was a good pub because it was right opposite Vickers ammunition factory, it was a little goldmine. Kitty made a lot of money for him, which he spent freely."

Kath remembers those days. "We were evacuated from The Gun during the war, I was just eleven, Tom was nine, and our Joan was eight, and we all went together on the train with our gasmasks and a tag around our necks, to Crosby, near Maryport in Cumberland, for three years, the worst three years of my life. It was a good life in a way because you were away from the air raids on Newcastle and you got plenty of fresh air, but I was glad to get home, even if I didn't like going back to school. We'd had to go because Dad was away in the Royal Navy, our maid Sarah had joined the ATS, and my mother was running the pub just across the road from the Vickers factory. It is amazing when you think it was never bombed, and I think my mother was quite brave to stay there all by herself.

"I was the only one who ever worked in his bars, our Joan would never work in a bar and our Tommy was never into it. I was working in the bars long before I should have been, you had to be twenty-one and I was in long before I was twenty-one, maybe eighteen. Mam and Dad used to have one day off a week, a Thursday, they would go to the Crown Hotel along Clayton Street for a drink, then to the Odeon Restaurant for a meal. That was their big day out! My Dad was always so immaculate when he dressed to go out, and he walked so quickly he almost ran. My mother was always miles behind him!

"We moved so many times and so many things happened when you were a child, I don't remember his boxing at all. To me he was just away working, or something like that. Even then, we were so young we probably wouldn't have been interested anyway.

"We saw more of him after the war because he was back from

290

the Navy and in the bars, and when he started refereeing again me and our Joan used to go to St James's Hall to watch him. If anybody called him over a decision I used to be up in arms."

As a regular patron of New St James's Hall myself from 1947 I saw Seaman many times in the role of third man and I was there that Monday night in April 1966 when he worked his last fight. British lightweight champion Maurice Cullen was in the ring with Roger Younsi of France, set for ten rounds or less, and less is what the fans got as Watson suddenly stopped the contest halfway through the second round. Confusion reigned throughout the Gallowgate hall as neither the fighters nor the fans had any idea what had happened. Then Tommy held Cullen's hand up as the winner and it was announced that the fight had been stopped because the Frenchman "was completely outclassed."

The crowd booed long and loud and threw programmes into the ring. Shouts of "money back!" were heard and in Younsi's corner, agent Bobby Diamond said, "I will certainly report this to the Boxing Board. There was no justification for what could have been a fine fight being stopped."

Younsi was a fourth-choice substitute opponent for Cullen and the North-East favourite had dominated what action there was with his trip-hammer left jab. But as Watson explained to the press while the hall still buzzed, "I stopped it for the simple reason that Younsi got thirty punches in his face in four minutes and threw only four in return. I was even thinking of stopping it in the first! Younsi looked a canny young lad. He was a substitute and from my own experience I knew it is hardly likely that he would be fighting fit. In any case, my duty is to the boxers, not to keep the crowd happy, or cover up for a bad match."

A couple of days later, Tommy Watson made another decision. He sat down at his pub, The Eden Arms in Bishop Auckland, and wrote a letter to the Board of Control in London, tendering his resignation as a referee.

"I have had a wonderful life out of boxing," he told a *Journal* reporter, "and it's a pity it should end in this way. I don't intend to even watch a fight again."

"We used to trail the kids through there, to Bishop Auckland, every weekend," remembered Kath, "and I would work in the bar. The pub belonged to the picture hall next door, The Eden, and whenever you went through my Dad would always be in there watching a film. He loved his films. It was there that he started to change, his mind, he was doing little funny things, and he had to come through to Newcastle to have this operation on his legs, he had thrombosis, and the operation seemed to do something to his mind because when he was in the operation he was pulling the tubes out and all he could talk about was when he was young, he could only talk to his sisters, they were the only ones who knew what he was talking about. Mam had to give up the pub because she couldn't cope so she came back and lived with me in Amelia Street, in Newcastle."

"He had this operation," Tom Jnr told me, "from smoking, his veins were all furred up and I saw this specialist and he said they were going to have to clean out his veins. It was not an easy operation and when I went in to see him, sometimes he wouldn't recognise me. He never got over it. He had a few blood clots, and fighting in those days he would take punches to the head and I think that did affect him badly."

Frances recalled the final days of the brother she loved. "He was in the St Nicholas Hospital and my husband and I used to go and have our tea with him on a Wednesday.

"This Wednesday I set the table, we had brought some ice cream and cakes and stuff, and I said to one of the nurses, 'Will you bring Tommy for us, pet.' He just looked across and said, 'Oh, do you not know?' I asked, 'What am I supposed to know?' Well, Tommy had taken a brain haemorrhage. I went hysterical when I knew he was gone, but as my husband said, 'Frances, how many times have you said you wished the Lord would take him?' And now, he had."

EPILOGUE

Evening Chronicle...Deaths; Watson, (Newcastle) 52 Maytree House, Hawthorn Terrace, in hospital 27 January 1971, aged 62 years, Thomas Samuel (Seaman Tommy Watson) ex-featherweight champion of Great Britain, beloved husband of Kathleen (nee Vines) dear father of Kathleen, Tommy, and Joan, and grandad of all the grandchildren. Cremation at West Road, Newcastle, on Monday 3.30pm, leaving daughter's residence at 1 Cookson Close at 3.10pm. Friends please meet at Crematorium.

"Scores of ex-boxers, managers, and North-East fight fans turned out in Newcastle yesterday for the cremation of one of Tyneside's greatest boxers, Seaman Tommy Watson," recorded the *Chronicle*. "The chapel in the West Road Crematorium was crowded with old timers who had fought at St James's Hall during the golden era of the 1930s.

"Among the mourners were Billy Farrell, Joe Thompson, Mickey McGuire, Billy Charlton, Charel Baert, Joe Corbett, Harry Craster, Joe Shepherd, Bob Graham, Billy Sheldon, Bombardier McLeod, Paul McGuire, and Ginger Roberts.

"Mr E J Waltham, General Secretary of the British Boxing Board of Control, said, 'Watson was a very courageous fighter who always gave of his best, whether he was the underdog or not. He displayed the same qualities as a referee.'

I spent many hours in the company of Joe Shepherd when he was matchmaker at New St James's Hall, talking about the old days, and he always called Seaman Watson, "the finest boxer to ever come out of the North-East, without a doubt!"

"You know," Kath remembers, "he never used to push his scrapbook at anyone, but once he took ill and he changed, he wanted people to see it, anybody could see it then. Before that, it was always put away and only taken out if someone asked specifically to see it. But when he became ill he just wanted people to look at it and read it. Even now, people from that era still talk about him, to be remembered after all these years, as a boxer, I think is fantastic."

293

"I mix with people today," says Frances, eighty-two years young, "and they remember our Tommy, and I am so proud to talk about him because he was a lovely, wonderful brother."

Tom Watson Jnr, who retired in 1995 as general manager for NEI Clarke Chapman's Gateshead works, now lives at Warwick on Eden, near Carlisle. "I am extremely proud of my father's achievements," he told me, "he was in his day the King of Tyneside, the one and only true Geordie Champion!"

PROFESSIONAL BOXING RECORD OF SEAMAN TOMMY WATSON

1925

Sep 28	Tom Pinkney (Annfield Plain)	wpts 6	Newcastle
Oct 5	Alf Paolozzi (North Shields)	wret 4	Newcastle (6)
1926	Inactive..Serving in Royal Navy		

1927

Mar	Jim Pemberton	wrsf 5	Plymouth (6)
Mar	Seaman Cartlidge (RN)	wpts 6	Devonport
	(Final of Port lightweight championship)		
Apr 11	Billy Jones (Torquay)	wpts 6	Torquay
Apr 25	Tom Pinkney (Annfield Plain)	wpts 6	Newcastle
May 2	Billy Graham (Walker)	wpts 10	Newcastle
Oct 24	Ted Power (Lewisham)	wko 1	Catford (10)
Oct 28	L/Cpl Davis (RM)	wko 2	Chatham (6)
	(Final ISBA lightweight championship)		
Nov 28	George Swinbourne (Maidstone)	wpts 10	Rochester
Dec 27	Tom Slattery (Hoxton)	wpts 10	Hoxton

1928

Jan 2	Billy Graham (Walker)	wret 6	Newcastle (10)
Jan 9	Tommy Hall (Lambeth)	wpts 12	Rochester
Jan 10	Signalman Morris	wpts 3	Chatham
	(RN v Royal Corps of Signals)		
Jan 16	Fred Fox (Sheffield)	wpts 8	NSC, London
Jan 23	Jim McCarthy (Poplar)	wko 8	Rochester (10)
Feb 6	Tommy Hall (Lambeth)	wpts 12	Rochester
Feb 13	Johnny Gordon (Aldgate)	wpts 12	Southampton
Feb 27	Ernie Beresford (Chesterfield)	wpts 8	NSC, London
Mar 5	Don Jeal (Plumstead)	wrsf 2	Blackfriars (8)
Mar 7	Leading Stoker Clarke	wpts 3	Chatham
	(Port lightweight championship)		
Mar 19	Joe Batten (Notting Hill)	wpts 12	Rochester
Mar 29	Billy Handley (Hackney)	wpts 15	Blackfriars
Mar 30	Piper Connor (Guards)	wpts 3	Chatham
Apr 18	L/S Ellesmore (RM) semi-final	wrsf 2	Chatham (3)
Apr 20	AB Pledger (RN) final	wpts 3	Chatham
	(RN & RM lightweight championship)		

May 10	Billy Brown (Barnsley)	wrsf 4	Blackfriars (15)
May 14	George Rumsey (Stepney)	wpts 12	Rochester
Jun 10	George Rose (Bristol)	lpts 15	Blackfriars
Aug 4	Harry Pitt (Hazlerigg)	wpts 15	Newcastle
Sep 3	Billy Jones (Barnsley)	wpts 15	Newcastle
Sep 22	Harry Best (Sunderland)	wpts 15	Newcastle
Sep 24	Johnny Gordon (Aldgate)	wpts 12	Gillingham

1929

Oct 12	Horace Barber (Leicester)	wpts 15	Sunderland
Oct 14	Harry White (Scunthorpe)	wpts 8	NSC, London
Nov 6	Charlie Chew (Aberdare)	wpts 15	Paddington
Nov 17	Charlie Chew (Aberdare)	wpts 12	Kilburn
Nov 20	Tommy Little (Notting Hill)	wpts 15	Paddington
Dec 2	Billy Reynolds (Ealing)	wpts 12	Rochester
Dec 11	Stoker Little (RN)	wpts 6	Chatham
Dec 18	Frank Warne (Plymouth)	wpts 15	Paddington

1930

Jan 7	Joe Cadman (Sheffield)	drew 15	Shepherds Bush
Jan 20	Johnny Quill (Stepney)	wpts 15	Fulham
Jan 22	L/Cpl Grainger (RN v Army)	wpts 4	Chatham
Feb 2	Jack Wright (Paddington)	wpts 15	Kilburn
Feb 11	Slosh Saunders (Marylebone)	wret 4	Gillingham (12)
Feb 17	Teddy Byrne (Mile End)	wret 4	Rochester (12)
Feb 20	George Swinbourne (Maidstone)	wpts 10	Chatham
Feb 24	Johnny Quill (Stepney)	wpts 15	Fulham
Mar 10	Trevor Gregory (Treherbert)	wpts 12	NSC, London
Mar 16	Horace Barber (Leicester)	wpts 15	Kilburn
Mar 20	A/B Castle (RN)	wpts 3	Chatham
	(Final RN & RM lightweight championship)		
Mar 27	Jim Hocking (Canning Town)	wpts 15	Blackfriars
Mar 31	George Rose (Bristol)	lpts 12	Rochester
Apr 20	Nipper Pat Daly (Marylebone)	wrsf 11	Kilburn (15)
Apr 28	Sid Raiteri (Stratford)	wpts 12	Rochester
May 30	Billy Streets (Portsmouth)	wpts 15	Portsmouth
Jul 2	Harry Brooks (St Georges)	wpts 15	Gillingham
Sep 11	Aine Gyde (France)	wpts 15	Kilburn
Oct 5	Roy Berresford (Burslem)	wpts 15	Kilburn
Oct 14	Jack Garland (Belfast)	wpts 15	Paddington
Oct 29	Joe Cadman (Sheffield)	wpts 15	Shepherds Bush
Nov 23	Jim Briley (Peckham)	wpts 15	Shepherds Bush
Dec 7	Jack Garland (Belfast)	wrsf 7	Shoreditch (15)

Dec 13	Nash Shakespeare (Wakefield)	wko 3	Newcastle (15)
Dec 28	Francois Machtens (Belgium)	wpts 15	Shoreditch
Dec 29	Jim Travis (Oldham)	wko 12	Newcastle (15)

1931

Jan 4	Jim Hocking (Canning Town)	wpts 15	Blackfriars
Jan 18	Douglas Parker (Sunderland)	wpts 15	Kilburn
Jan 28	Nobby Baker (Trealaw)	wpts 12	Portsmouth
Feb 9	Jim Travis (Oldham)	wret 8	Rochester (10)
Feb 15	Victor Cohen (Egypt)	wret 5	Blackfriars (15)
Mar 13	Teddy Brown (Forest Hall)	wpts 15	Newcastle
Mar 23	Bert Swaddle (Gateshead)	wret 10	Rochester (15)
Mar 30	Douglas Parker (Sunderland)	wpts 15	Newcastle
Apr 22	Dom Volante (Liverpool)	lret 6	Albert Hall (10)
Jun 10	Julian Verbist (France)	wpts 12	Oxford
Jun 23	Benny Sharkey (Newcastle)	wpts 15	Newcastle
Aug 17	Benny Sharkey (Newcastle)	wpts 15	Newcastle
Oct 5	Douglas Parker (Sunderland)	wret 12	Newcastle (15)
Oct 28	Francois Machtens (Belgium)	wpts 12	Paddington
Dec 14	Ernie Bicknell (Doncaster)	wpts 12	Rochester
Dec 21	Peter Cuthbertson (Dunfermline)	wpts 15	Newcastle

1932

Jan 18	Battling Sandjack (Egypt)	wpts 15	Blackfriars
Feb 2	Boyo Rees (Aberdare)	wpts 15	Shepherds Bush
May 2	Ginger Jones (Ammanford)	wret 10	Newcastle (15)
May 20	Selwyn Davies (Caerau)	wpts 12	Oxford
Sep 19	Francois Machtens (Belgium)	wpts 12	Newcastle
Oct 10	Phineas John (Pentre)	wpts 12	Newcastle
Nov 10	Nel Tarleton (Liverpool)	wpts 15	Liverpool
	(Won British featherweight championship)		
Dec 5	Luigi Quadrini (Italy)	wdis 3	Newcastle (12)
Dec 18	Billy Wiper (Newcastle)	wko 6	Middlesbrough 12

1933

Jan 27	Fidel LaBarba (USA)	wpts 12	New York City
Mar 31	Auguste Gyde (France)	wpts 10	Portsmouth
May 19	Kid Chocolate (Cuba)	lpts 15	New York City
	(World featherweight championship)		
May 26	Bobby Lawrence (Canada)	wpts 10	Toronto
Jul 31	Benny Sharkey (Newcastle)	wpts 12	Newcastle
Nov 29	Sonny Lee (Leeds)	ldis 2	Newcastle (12)
Dec 19	Dave Crowley (Clerkenwell)	wko 10	London (15)

1934

Feb 1	Johnny Cuthbert (Sheffield)	wpts 15	Liverpool
Mar 5	Billy Gannon (Liverpool)	wpts 12	Leeds
Mar 21	Johnny McMillan (Glasgow)	wpts 15	Glasgow
	(Retained British featherweight championship)		
Apr 16	Aine Gyde (France)	wpts 12	Shepherds Bush
Apr 25	Jimmy Walsh (Chester)	wpts 15	Liverpool
May 7	Jim Cowie (Dundee)	wko 6	Edinburgh (12)
Jun 18	Francois Machtens (Belgium)	wpts 12	Manchester
Jun 27	Dick Corbett (Bethnal Green)	wpts 12	Wandsworth
Jul 26	Nel Tarleton (Liverpool)	lpts 15	Liverpool
	(Lost British featherweight championship)		
Oct 19	Con Flynn (Islington)	wpts 12	Hartlepool
Oct 22	George Odwell (Camden Town)	wko 4	Holborn (12)
Oct 29	Camille Desmet (Belgium)	wpts 10	Nine Elms
Nov 12	Harry Brooks (St Georges)	wpts 12	Newcastle
Nov 27	Norman Snow (Northampton)	wpts 12	Holborn

1935

Feb 27	Sonny Lee (Leeds)	wpts 12	Portsmouth
	(British lightweight championship eliminator)		
May 20	Tommy Spiers (Clackmannan)	wpts 15	Newcastle
	(British lightweight championship eliminator)		
May 26	Jules Steyaert (Belgium)	wpts 12	Temple Mills
Jun 10	Nobby Baker (Trealaw)	wpts 12	Carmarthen
Jun 27	Freddie Miller (USA)	lpts 10	Liverpool
Jul 15	Frankie Brown (Liverpool)	wrsf 14	Liverpool (15)
	(British lightweight championship eliminator)		
Jul 25	Freddie Miller (USA)	lko 2	Liverpool (10)
Oct 2	George Daly (Blackfriars)	lret 8	Albert Hall (12)

Career summary..121 contests; won 111, drew 1, lost 9

Boxing record compiled by Vic Hardwicke

BIBLIOGRAPHY

Newspapers:

    Newcastle Evening Chronicle
    Newcastle Journal
    Sunderland Echo
    Sunday Sun

Magazines:

    Boxing
    Boxing News
    The Ring
    Boxing Illustrated
    True Boxing Yearbook

Books:

    THE RING RECORD BOOK Edited by Nat Fleischer
    BRITISH BOXING YEARBOOK Edited by Barry J Hugman
    BOXING NEWS ANNUAL Edited by Gilbert Odd
    BLACK DYNAMITE VOL V by Nat Fleischer (1947)
    FIGHTING IS MY LIFE by Ted Broadribb (1951)
    PRIVATE LIVES OF FAMOUS FIGHTERS by Arthur
    Helliwell (1949)
    WORLD ENCYCLOPEDIA OF ORGANISED CRIME by
    Jay Robert Nash (1992)
    THE ENGLISH GODFATHER by Graham Nown (1987)
    TED KID LEWIS, HIS LIFE & TIMES by Morton Lewis
    (1990)
    BENNY by John Burrowes (1982)
    IN THIS CORNER By Peter Heller (1973)
    BIG FIGHT THRILLS by Norman Hurst (1948)
    THE WEARSIDE CHAMPIONS By Archie Potts (1993)
    FAREWELL TO SPORT by Paul Gallico (1936)
    WEEKLY SPORTING REVIEW ANNUAL Edited by Isidore
    Green (1950)

INDEX

303

311